Words Made Flesh

THE HISTORY OF DISABILITY
A series edited by Paul K. Longmore and Lauri Umansky

The New Disability History:
American Perspectives
Edited by Paul K. Longmore and Lauri Umansky

Reflections:
The Life and Writings of a Young Blind Woman
in Post-Revolutionary France
Edited and translated by Catherine J. Kudlick and Zina Weygand

Signs of Resistance:
American Deaf Cultural History, 1900 to World War II
Susan Burch

The Radical Lives of Helen Keller
Kim E. Nielsen

Mental Retardation in America: A Historical Reader
Edited by Steven Noll and James W. Trent, Jr.

Helen Keller: Selected Writings
Edited by Kim E. Nielsen

The Ugly Laws: Disability in Public
Susan M. Schweik

Words Made Flesh: Nineteenth-Century Deaf Education
and the Growth of Deaf Culture
R. A. R. Edwards

Words Made Flesh

*Nineteenth-Century Deaf Education
and the Growth of Deaf Culture*

R. A. R. Edwards

NEW YORK UNIVERSITY PRESS
New York and London

NEW YORK UNIVERSITY PRESS
New York and London
www.nyupress.org

References to Internet Websites (URLs) were accurate at the time of writing.
Neither the author nor New York University Press is responsible for URLs
that may have expired or changed since the manuscript was prepared.

Library of Congress Cataloging-in-Publication Data
Edwards, R. A. R.
Words made flesh : nineteenth-century deaf education and the growth of deaf culture /
R.A.R. Edwards.
p. cm. — (The history of disability)
Includes bibliographical references and index.
ISBN 978-0-8147-2243-5 (cl : alk. paper) —
ISBN 978-0-8147-2402-6 (ebook) —
ISBN 978-0-8147-2403-3 (ebook)
1. Deaf—Education—United States—History—19th century.
2. Deaf culture—United States—History—19th century.
3. Deaf—United States—Social conditions—19th century. I. Title.
HV2530.E39   2012
371.91'20973—dc23   2011041545

New York University Press books are printed on acid-free paper,
and their binding materials are chosen for strength and durability.
We strive to use environmentally responsible suppliers and materials
to the greatest extent possible in publishing our books.

Manufactured in the United States of America
10 9 8 7 6 5 4 3 2 1

Contents

Acknowledgments

This project had many incarnations, and I owe thanks to the many people who helped shape it along the way.

My thanks first to Ross W. Beales Jr. and Rev. Joseph Bruce, S.J., who were there at the beginning. Thanks as well to Robert Westbrook, Daniel Borus, Ted Supalla, and Deidre Schlehofer for their support at the University of Rochester. Thanks to Douglas C. Baynton. My thanks to everyone at NYU Press. I was greatly aided by the support of the series' editors Paul Longmore and Lauri Umansky. I, like so many other scholars, owe Paul Longmore a special debt. He encouraged me to attend the NEH Summer Institute on Disability Studies in 2000, and the intellectual impact of that event can be seen in these pages.

Much of the research was conducted at the American School for the Deaf, in West Hartford, Connecticut. My sincerest appreciation goes to Gary Wait, their archivist, whose aid was invaluable.

Finally, my thanks to my husband, David, and my daughter, Victoria, for everything.

Introduction

Deaf and hearing people share a common past. How could it be otherwise? Most deaf people are born into hearing families. Their lives and histories are radically intertwined. Nevertheless, Deaf culture is not familiar territory for most hearing people. In fact, deafness is still largely understood by hearing people as a medical condition in need of a cure. For hearing people, the term "deaf" speaks of the body and its failings; it does not invoke a vibrant, subaltern culture with a language, community, and history of its own. It means deaf and not Deaf, or Deafhood, as it does for so many Deaf people.

This tremendous gap in perception, this imaginative audiological divide, shapes our present as Deaf and hearing people, much as it did our past. Arguably, today, the gap between Deaf and hearing people is wider than ever. It is a distance that can be traced to our shared history as deaf and hearing people. Scholars of various disciplines have begun to trace that shared history more closely, in an increasing number of books in recent years. Most works explore the history of the American Deaf community from its origins in the nineteenth century into the early years of the twentieth century. This study relies heavily on the work of those scholars and, indeed, could not have been written in their absence.[1]

The outlines of this history are well established. The Deaf experience of the nineteenth century is the story of two interrelated and interdependent narratives. First, it is the story of the emergence of a Deaf community, created when deaf people were brought into contact with one another in large numbers for the first time in the nation's history, when residential schools for the deaf were founded. Those schools followed the manual method; that is, they employed sign language in the classroom to teach their students. Physically deaf people, learning a signed language together in school, transformed their common experience of physical deafness into, first, a marker of their membership in a larger community, a deaf community, and then into Deafness, as a recognizable and distinct culture, one grounded in many ways in the use of this minority and gesturally based language.

Second, it is a story about the war of the methods in deaf education, a war triggered by the events of the first story. Manualists, supporters of the sign language, soon found themselves challenged by oralists, supporters of the exclusive use of speech. It is, for many scholars, a story of decline, in which deaf people lost ground as their language, sign language, was slowly forced from schools. The oralists won the war of the methods, and as a result, by the time of the First World War, over 80 percent of deaf children were taught by the oral method, without any sign language. That oralist victory proved pyrrhic; historians and linguists alike concur that the wholesale switch to the oral method undermined the quality of deaf education. By the time educational testing emerged as a pedagogical tool in the 1960s, deaf high school students were found to read, on average, at a fourth grade level, a result that would remain stubbornly consistent for the rest of the twentieth century.

If the results were so dramatically poor, why did oral education remain the standard for deaf children until the 1970s? Or, to put it another way, if it did not have the promise of educational success going for it, why did oralism win the war of the methods? Historians such as Douglas Baynton and Susan Burch have pointed to oralism's cultural appeal.[2] Oralists framed signing deaf people as foreigners in their own land, as people whose different language, sign language, alienated them from the mainstream of American life. A signing-based education was making deaf people more Deaf, oralists believed. They were using a communication system that visibly marked them as abnormal and handicapped people. Oralists were out to change all of that; as they understood it, they were on a quest to integrate deaf people into the normal (and hearing) mainstream. Oralists would bring the deaf into the hearing world, aiming in the process to eliminate the Deaf world altogether. Speech skills were meant to allow the deaf to abandon the Deaf world entirely. The power of speech would free deaf people from the supposedly narrow constraints of the Deaf community.

Deaf people understood this educational project quite differently, as an assault on their way of life, one that was determined to destroy their language, community, and culture. Unsurprisingly, they did not perceive themselves as people in need of rescue from their own community. They did, however, want to be integrated, on both deaf and Deaf terms, into the hearing world. But their understanding of their community and its needs was disregarded by oralist educators, whose educational mission depended on maintaining their own view of deafness as pathological.

This history is nearer to the surface than either side imagines. It can be seen in 2011 most sharply in Indiana. The issue of deaf education has reemerged into the national news, as the Indiana School for the Deaf faces both financial and pedagogical challenges. The Indiana School for the Deaf has a long and proud history. It was founded in 1843 by William Willard, a native of Vermont, who was educated at the American School for the Deaf in Hartford, Connecticut. The American School is the oldest school for the deaf in the United States, having been founded in 1817. William Willard became deaf at a fortunate time in American history. Going deaf at the age of six, Willard arrived at the American School at the age of fifteen, and attended the school from 1824 to 1829. He was therefore among the first deaf Americans to receive an education. He was a pupil of the school's most famous teacher, its Deaf cofounder, the Frenchman Laurent Clerc. Willard went on to become a teacher himself, working at the Ohio School for the Deaf from 1831 to 1841. He moved to Indiana and founded the school for the deaf there in 1843, making the Indiana School for the Deaf the first state school to be founded by a Deaf American.

As with all American schools for the deaf at that time, the Indiana School employed what today would be called the bilingual-bicultural method of deaf education. That is, American Sign Language (ASL) was the language of instruction in all classes, and that language was used in turn to teach deaf students English. Teachers understood that their pupils would come to have a Deaf identity and would become culturally Deaf while at school. They would also be fluent in both English and ASL, and the aim of their education was to allow them to take their place in society as Deaf Americans. Chapters 1 and 2 address the arrival of the French method of manual education in the United States and its transformation into the bilingual-bicultural model, first adopted at the New York School for the Deaf in 1833.

I argue that the schools for the deaf were not simply "manual," as they have always been described.[3] In the antebellum period, the bilingual-bicultural approach to deaf education became the common standard of deaf education, and was in fact the American innovation in a system of education largely imported here from France. The first residential school for the deaf in the United States opened in Connecticut in 1817. The Connecticut Asylum for the Education and Instruction of Deaf and Dumb Persons, as it was originally known, eventually changed its name to the American School for the Deaf.

The opening of this and other schools began a fundamental transformation in the lives of deaf Americans, as those who came together as students would begin to transform deafness into Deafness over the course of the antebellum period. Historians have known about this process of cultural emergence for some time, and many have pointed in particular to the decade of the 1850s as the period when the subaltern Deaf culture emerged for the first time into the broader American cultural landscape.[4] The rise of Deaf culture is at the center of this history, both metaphorically and literally. Chapters 3 and 4 are devoted to exploring the Deaf world of the nineteenth century, both in and out of its birthplace, the residential school.

Deaf people were at the center of their own history in the nineteenth century, for the war of the methods was a direct response to the unexpected transformation of deafness into Deafness. It is surely the case that many forces shaped the course of these educational events and, in turn, influenced deaf lives in the nineteenth century. But the primary force that drove events was Deaf culture. Both sides, manualists and oralists alike, had to confront Deafness, and they made pedagogical decisions as a result of that confrontation. Physically deaf people, as they engaged in the cultural work of Deafness, directly influenced events around them. The rise of cultural Deafness is at the heart of the story of nineteenth-century Deaf history, and it holds the key to understanding the war of the methods that followed its creation. This work seeks to trace these events.

In the field of Deaf Studies, the term "Deaf," with the upper-case letter, is used to refer to those physically deaf people who came together to form a distinct community with its own language, culture, and mores. As Christopher Krentz puts it, "Deafness, as an identity, extends far beyond audiograms and eardrums."[5] As the nineteenth century opened, there were largely only "deaf" people, with the lower-case letter, in the United States, people with varying degrees of audiological deafness, scattered across the country and mostly isolated from each other. They had as yet had no opportunity to form a community.

The formation and growth of Deaf culture was in itself a surprising victory for deaf people. They discovered a common people in meeting other Americans with hearing loss and made common cause with those people by forming a self-consciously Deaf community. But this Deaf awakening brought with it a corresponding hearing awakening. Hearing people close to these cultural events recognized that these self-identified members of a Deaf culture gathered in a community that defined itself in contradistinction to hearing norms, norms that had not even necessarily previously been understood as "hearing."[6] To borrow literary scholar Christopher Krentz's useful term, a new sense of "Hearingness" arose together with "Deafness."[7] As the two communities, deaf and hearing, came into close contact within residential schools in the antebellum period, the hearing community clearly changed its mind about the Deafness that it found there as the century wore on. Hearingness was reasserted as the normative value for American society, and Deaf ideas about deafness, especially ideas that departed from hearing norms, were rigorously attacked.

For disabled people to define the meaning of their disability for themselves was culturally threatening and remains so today. This is the case in no small measure because a positive image of a disability challenges the ableist norms of the able-bodied mainstream society. Able-bodied society assumes that a disabled life is a lesser life. In fact, it takes for granted that this must be the case. How could it not be? If a disabled life is not worth less than an able-bodied life, how can we be sure that an able body is, by definition, better than one that is disabled? Disability studies, as a discipline, has fruitfully explicated the cultural roots of ableism; it is time to turn to Deaf history with this work in mind.

Some disabled activists of the nineteenth century understood quite well the threat that they raised to ableist constructs of the body. As Deaf writer John Flournoy insightfully and succinctly remarked in 1858, "When we would claim equality, it offends."[8] The cultural superiority of the able body depends necessarily on the inferiority of the disabled body. If those with a disabled body refuse to play their cultural part, if they claim their disability as a point of pride and assert their equality with the able-bodied, they are bound to encounter a negative response.

This is exactly what happened to the Deaf community. Even as it came together, it was immediately attacked by oralists. Chapter 5 outlines the first public arguments in favor of oralism as offered by Horace Mann and Samuel Gridley Howe in the 1840s. Their opposition to Deaf culture is explored as well. Chapter 6 covers the manualist breakdown that followed this oralist challenge. As we will see, the manual side dissolved into factions, with some manualists continuing to support the original mission and beliefs of the field, as others, also calling themselves manualists, sided with the cultural concerns of the oralists. Again, these factions can be identified by their language choices. The bilingual-bicultural manualists still supported and defended what they called "the sign language" and what we call now American Sign Language (ASL). The new manualists demanded the use of "methodical signs," or signing in English word order. The oralists demanded English only and only in spoken, not signed, form. That the battle over Deafness would be fought with linguistic weapons is no surprise. Attacks on Deafness have long gone hand in hand with attacks on the sign language. To defend one was to defend the other. To attack one was to attack the other.

Paddy Ladd, in his ground-breaking work *Understanding Deaf Culture: In Search of Deafhood*, has theorized the cause of the Deaf as part of a larger struggle against linguistic colonialism. He points rightly to both oralism and artificial sign systems as assaults on signed languages, such as ASL, and on their users. As Ladd puts it, modern-day users of artificial sign systems, the descendants of methodical signs, are in fact covert oralists.[9]

In the mid-nineteenth century, signing in English word order appealed to certain hearing educators precisely because it promised to undermine the newly emerging Deaf culture. With a language of their own, American Sign Language, Deaf people became a community of their own. With methodical signs, they would not become Deaf at all. Rather, they would remain culturally hearing. Arguments over manual language systems were not arguments about pedagogy at all. Much as Ladd would have predicted, such arguments were instead arguments over the emerging sense of Deaf identity. The oppression of American Deaf people is intimately linked to the oppression of their language, American Sign Language.

In the end, methodical signing paved the way for oralism's entry into deaf education. As methodical sign supporters made clear their uneasiness with Deafness, they increasingly shared the cultural concerns of the first generation of oralists. The continued use of such signs allowed oralists to ask, Why stop with signing in English word order? Why not demand that the deaf speak, and not sign, in English? Speaking in English would seem to guarantee their transformation into culturally hearing people even better than methodical signs. Chapter 7 accordingly explores the fight to found an oral school in Massachusetts, one of the first in the nation's history, the Clarke School for the Deaf.

The threat that Deaf culture posed to the ableist status quo had to be countered immediately and in the strongest possible terms. The bilingual-bicultural manualist era can now be seen as the brief historical moment when deaf people were able, with the help of hearing collaborators, to shape their own understanding of deafness and, in turn, Deafness before other hearing people raised concerns about this entire cultural project. These concerns harkened back to far older and deeper trends in Western history, as far as deafness goes. For in the West, speaking has long been privileged over other forms of communication, and the inability to speak has long been seen as an indicator of a person's general inferiority and lack of intelligence. So bilingual-bicultural manualism represented a brief period of countercultural rebellion, with oralism constituting a return to the cultural status quo. The brief challenge of Deafness was beaten back and, with it, the prospect of similar rebellions by disabled citizens generally.

The disabled community today still faces many of the same challenges the Deaf community faced in the nineteenth century. In this way, the example of the Deaf community has much to teach us about the ways in which American culture has handled questions of the body, disability, and diversity over the course of its history. Like Krentz, I wish to make clear that "nineteenth-century deaf people were the first disabled American group to receive special education, the first to organize in a widespread way, the first to contest lack of access, prejudice, and pathological views of their difference."[10] This work is but a chapter in a larger American narrative about disability history. For the story of nineteenth-century deafness, and its transformation into Deafness, is a story about the possibilities and limits of living a disabled life in the United States, a story we need to know more about as we try to understand what limits still impose themselves in our society today.

Those limits continue to be largely linguistic. The events in Indiana revolve precisely around which language deaf people will use.[11] Indiana governor Mitch Daniels has filled four slots on the school's board of trustees with supporters of the oral method. Three of the new members are hearing, while two are active members of Hear Indiana, a group that supports the use of speech and listening in deaf education, to the exclusion of sign language. Deaf parents of Deaf children are protesting these appointments and the potential shift in school policy. The Indiana School for the Deaf is one of the very few state schools for the deaf that currently use the bicultural-bilingual method of deaf education.[12] Will that approach be abandoned as the composition of the board changes? As the reporter asked, more broadly, "Will sign language and the nation's separate schools for the deaf be abandoned as more of the deaf turn to communicating, with help from fast-evolving technology, through amplified sounds and speech?"

Both sides believe that it will. Hear Indiana released a statement in support of the governor, arguing that his appointments represent "a long overdue inclusion of the views of people who use technology like cochlear implants"—people, in other words, who use speech, and not sign, to communicate. Marvin Miller, the president of the Indiana Association of the Deaf, also fears that sign language will be abandoned. "Speaking and listening classrooms across the nation are known for their forced exclusion of ASL and expressly forbid any contact with culturally deaf role models."

Readers offered their views of the situation in Indiana, and the ghosts of deaf education history were very much in evidence. Twenty-first-century writers offered arguments that would be familiar to nineteenth-century oralists and their manualist allies. For instance, several commentators denied that American Sign Language is a language at all, a common nineteenth-century oralist argument. Others argued that children cannot learn as well with ASL; for example, pediatric audiologist Jane Madell declared that "children who learn language through hearing have much better language than most children who learn using ASL." Samuel Gridley Howe would undoubtedly appreciate such a statement about the importance of hearing and speech. After all, Howe wrote, in 1867, "Speech is essential for human development . . . there can be no effectual substitute for it."

Melissa Chaikof, the hearing mother of two deaf daughters and cofounder of the blog Auditory-Verbal Parents, a roundtable for parents who chose cochlear implants for their deaf children, argued that implants and speech-based education provide deaf children "the option to be fully participating members of the entire world and not of just one small piece of it." Using sign language "takes away their options for the future." Horace Mann made similar remarks in 1844, arguing that those Deaf people who are bilingual, who sign ASL and write English, will nonetheless find that as soon as such a person "passes out of the circle of those who understand that [sign] language," he or she will be "as helpless and hopeless as ever. The power of uttering articulate sounds, of speaking as others speak, alone restores him to society." Or, in the language of 2011, sign language takes away their future.

Another commentator displayed the hearing contempt for the Deaf view of deafness. Identifying herself only as a mother, who also chose implants for both her sons, she wrote in support of Chaikof, saying, "After many years, I can no longer tolerate the complete ignorance of the Deaf culture and their ravings. Cut the budgets for deaf schools, mainstream, implant—and listen to children talk and be a part of society." Hers is an opinion that nineteenth-century oralists would recognize. Samuel Gridley Howe argued in 1867 that the point of deaf education should be "to make [deaf children] as much as possible like other children." Again, Mann had argued that "speaking as others speak, alone restores [the deaf] to society." Deaf arguments to the contrary reflect "complete ignorance," as this mother would put it. What, after all, do deaf people know about living a deaf life?

What started as an article on the Indiana School for the Deaf quickly turned into a forum on Deaf culture, a conversation that was dominated by hearing voices. Many hearing people clearly assume that living a life as a Deaf person is to live a limited life. Only speech, Chaikof implies, will allow her daughters to live as "fully participating members of the entire world"—or, as Horace Mann would add appreciatively, as fully human beings, for speech, he noted in 1844, has "an extraordinary humanizing power," as those who have learned to speak, not merely read and write English, "have a far more human expression of the eye" than their signing peers.

Still, there were some readers who argued, as Deaf of Deaf commentator A.B. did, for "a deaf child's right to be deaf." Amica wrote, "With a solid foundation in ASL, children will have the world in their hands." Tim Riker, a Deaf of Deaf Californian, hit the mark when he observed that the problem facing Deaf people today is not the growing use of cochlear implant technology; rather, it is the way such assistive technologies "are used as tools to advance and politicize an anti-ASL agenda by proponents of a century-old ideology." It is that ideology, as Riker sees so clearly, that continues to frame debates like the one playing out in Indiana.

Ours may be a neo-oralist moment, but it was not always so in American deaf education. For a brief historical moment, professional educators embraced, rather than shrank from, Deaf culture, and the result was a period alive with possibility, most significantly the possibility that deaf people might become full citizens as Deaf Americans, claiming their Deafness while taking equal pride in their Americanness—the possibility, in other words, that disability would prove no barrier to equality in the United States.

Deaf people, as a community, have frequently been uncomfortable with claiming the label "disabled" for themselves, preferring to claim that their linguistic, and not physical, difference lies at the heart of their Deafness. But, it seems to me, the first historical claims for cultural Deafness were grounded quite passionately in the embrace of physical deafness. The turn to Deafness was made possible by deaf people making their own judgments about the meaning of deafness. Deaf culture reflected in no small part their collective determination that a deaf life was a life worth living.

Claiming disability, to use the phrase of pioneering disability scholar Simi Linton, was the necessary first step to claiming Deafness.[13] That was also the event that sent shock waves through the hearing world, in turn. How could deaf people be happy to be deaf? Didn't they really wish they could hear? How could they enjoy a disabled life? These are questions disabled Americans today still face from their able-bodied peers. It is in recovering the Deaf historical experience precisely as that of the first disabled Americans to engage in a public struggle over the meaning of their disability that allows us to explore Deaf history as a case study of disability, a case study with which we can probe the limits of acceptance and tolerance for disabled bodies in the American body politic, in our shared past, and, quite possibly, in our common future.

1

Thomas Hopkins Gallaudet and Laurent Clerc

A Yale Man and a Deaf Man
Open a School and Create a World

Why then are we Deaf and Dumb? I do not know, as you do not know why there are infirmities in your bodies, nor why there are among the human kind, white, black, red and yellow men. The Deaf and Dumb are everywhere, in Asia, in Africa, as well as in Europe and America. They existed before you spoke of them and before you saw them. . . . I think our deafness proceeds from an act of Providence, I would say, from the will of God, and does it imply that the Deaf and Dumb are worse than other men?

—Laurent Clerc, addressing the Connecticut
State Legislature, 1818

Beginnings

They were an unlikely pair to start a revolution in American education. Thomas Hopkins Gallaudet (1787-1851) was a hearing American, a minister by training, a graduate of Yale. Laurent Clerc (1785-1869) was a Deaf Frenchman, a fluent signer, a gifted teacher at his former school, the National Institute at Paris. A series of fortunate events brought the two together from an ocean's distance. Their meeting has slipped into legend in the Deaf community, but it is worth recounting the tale here. For with their partnership, they founded not just a school but an American community, a Deaf world.

It was not Gallaudet's lifelong plan to enter the field of education at all, never mind deaf education. How could he have considered deaf education as a career path? After all, there was no school for the deaf in all of North America in those years. Wealthy families sent their deaf children abroad to be educated, mostly to Britain. Deaf children from families of lesser means were left to develop their own idiosyncratic gestural systems in order to communicate. They created so-called home signs to communicate at least on a rudimentary level with their families, but they went without a formal education. Accordingly, most deaf children never gained access to English, to the language of a community, in other words, wider than home.

The fact that no school existed in the country does not mean that Americans were wholly ignorant of the possibility of educating the deaf. Many American newspapers and periodicals printed articles about deaf education in Europe throughout the early years of the nineteenth century. Most of these reported on the work being done to educate the deaf in France. The French system had been staunchly manual in orientation since its inception in the eighteenth century. The Abbé Charles-Michel de l'Epée began working to educate the Parisian deaf community in the years before the French Revolution. He is widely credited with inventing the manual method of deaf education, choosing to use signs and gestures with his students rather than speech.

In this way, he was bucking the European trend at the time, which was largely running in the direction of the oral method, most strongly in England and Germany. He published several works on his method, including *The Method of Educating the Deaf and Dumb Confirmed by Long Experience*, which was originally published in French in 1784 and translated into English in 1801. He also argued strenuously with the German oralists for the superiority of the manual method. Before he died in 1789, he gained the support of the emerging revolutionary government, which vowed that his then private school for the deaf would not die with him. The nationally funded National Institution for the Deaf at Paris subsequently opened its doors in 1791.[1]

The works of Abbé de l'Epée and his successor, the Abbé Roch-Ambroise Sicard, were well known, especially in the North in the United States, and their use of the sign language was widely and specifically lauded in the American press. Remarking upon the sign language in 1805, one writer called it that "silent representative language, in which the eye officiates for the ear, and communicates the charms of science, and the delights of common intercourse to the mind, with the velocity, facility, and certainty of sound."[2] Praise for the sign language as a language with the same facility as that of a spoken language was not uncommon in the American press in these years.

Given the general praise for the sign language, it comes as no surprise to learn that the American press gave little attention to the oral method of deaf education. While Sicard and the National Institute at Paris were frequently mentioned, the schools of England, dominated by the Braidwood family, received far less attention. The Braidwoods ran two academies, one in Edinburgh and one in London, and both adhered to the oral method.[3]

For all the attention heaped on the French in the American press, the fact remained that wealthy Americans with deaf children were most likely to send their children to the Braidwoods to be educated, presumably less out of any particular support for the oral over the manual method than for the shared language of the two countries. One such father, Francis Green, published a treatise on the oral education of his deaf son, Charles, entitled *Vox Occulis Subjecta*. A notice of publication appeared in *The Panoplist, or The Christian's Armory* in 1805 and the author wished the elder Green much success in his efforts to found a similar school in America. Significantly, the article did not particularly recommend oral education, though at the time Green did, but it did support the cause of opening a school for the deaf. As the author remarked, "Considering the number of deaf and dumb people among us, such an establishment seems highly desirable, and we wish the attention of the publick, in these prosperous times, may be turned to an object so deserving their patronage."[4]

There is some evidence to suggest that there was a weighing of the methods being conducted in some circles in the United States in the early nineteenth century. An 1807 article described a public demonstration of the results of oral education. A reporter recalled his response to the presentation of a young orally trained deaf girl: "There was a something in her voice extremely distressing," the reporter commented, "without being absolutely discordant; a plaintive monotonous sound, rather tending to excite melancholy than pleasure."[5] Rather than being impressed with the uncommon sight of a deaf girl speaking, this observer was struck instead by the inferior quality of the girl's voice. The act of speaking did not alone transform this girl into a hearing person, providing instead a pale and rather pathetic imitation of one. The rest of the article dwelled favorably on one of Sicard's public demonstrations, describing the impressive presentation of his favorite student, Jean Massieu, using only the "language of gesticulation."

Another part of the explanation may lie in the popular understanding of deafness in the period. At this time, it was widely believed to be in the nature of deaf people to communicate by gestures, for two reasons. First, it was natural because deaf people could not hear, and so of course they would gesture rather than vocalize to communicate. Second, it was assumed that God had provided these natural gestures as a mechanism for his deaf children to communicate in spite of their deafness. That is, where the human body had failed, God had provided. Hence, God's deaf creatures quite naturally used gestures, as God had so arranged. The use of a more highly developed sign language in a classroom setting was accordingly viewed as appropriate for deaf students.[6]

Founding a School

The founding of a school for the deaf in the United States did not depend initially on the attractiveness, or lack thereof, of any particular educational theory. It depended mostly on the deafness of one young girl, Alice Cogswell. The daughter of Mason Fitch Cogswell, a prominent Hartford, Connecticut, physician, Alice had lost her hearing to meningitis soon after her second birthday. Unwilling to send his daughter abroad to be educated, Cogswell instead decided to persuade the state that a school for the deaf was needed in Connecticut. Using his social connections, Cogswell persuaded the General Association of Congregational Ministers in Connecticut to commission a census of the deaf in the state.[7]

In June 1812, the association reported that it had counted eighty-four deaf people in Connecticut. From this result, Cogswell estimated that there were some four hundred deaf people living in New England alone and probably two thousand in the country as a whole. He used the census figures to begin a publicity campaign to convince the public and the state of the need for a school for the deaf. Cogswell also organized a group of his friends, many also wealthy New Englanders, to raise funds to send Thomas Hopkins Gallaudet on a fact-finding mission to Europe.[8]

Gallaudet and Cogswell knew each other even before the campaign for a school for the deaf began, as the Gallaudet family home was neighbor to the Cogswells'. Gallaudet had left Hartford for New Haven to attend Yale University, where he graduated first in his class at the age of seventeen in 1805. He received a master of arts from Yale in 1807 and subsequently worked there as a tutor. In 1812, he went to Andover Theological Seminary to prepare for a career in the ministry. Graduated in 1814, he was ordained a Congregational minister. He was always rather sickly, and illness found him recuperating at the family home, where he took an interest in the Cogswell family's efforts to educate Alice.[9]

At this time, 1814, those efforts included attending a local private school.[10] Wealthy Hartford resident Daniel Wadsworth urged Lydia Huntley, a family acquaintance and schoolteacher, to open a school in his mother's mansion. He personally invited fifteen girls, drawn from Hartford's elite families, to attend. The Cogswell sisters, Mary, Elizabeth, and Alice, all received invitations.

Huntley had no experience with deaf pupils, and she was dismayed to find that there were no readily available books on the subject in the United States, either. Nonetheless, she found that Alice came to the school using "animated gestures" and, it seems, an early form of American fingerspelling, referred to as "the old alphabet" and related to the two-handed British manual alphabet. How could the Cogswells have come to know a form of fingerspelling? Apparently, Mason Cogswell's father, James Cogswell, knew the deaf portrait painter John Brewster and may very well have learned it from him.[11] Huntley was able to incorporate these communication systems into her classroom and used them to teach Alice. By the time Gallaudet was recruited into the effort to open an American school for the deaf, agreeing to go to Europe on a fact-finding mission in the summer of 1815, Alice was already busily acquiring English.

Gallaudet, for his part, went first to Britain, where he hoped to learn about deaf education from the Braidwood family and planned to visit both of the Braidwood academies of London. The Braidwoods offered to take Gallaudet on as an apprentice at their London school, where he would teach handwriting to the students while he learned the Braidwood oral method, as long as he promised to stay in London with them for three years. Gallaudet was unwilling to agree to these terms.[12]

As it happened, the Abbé Sicard was in London, giving a public demonstration of the manual method and touring with his two best former students, now teachers in their own right, Jean Massieu and Laurent Clerc. Gallaudet attended the London exhibits and met privately with the abbé, who urged him to visit the school at Paris and promptly offered to instruct him in the manual method there.[13] While Gallaudet had been, by his own admission, impressed with the demonstration, he still decided to head to Edinburgh first, to visit the Braidwood Academy there.

While in Edinburgh, Gallaudet met Dugald Stewart.[14] Stewart, a Scottish philosopher of the common sense school, was a fierce critic of oral education, believing that oralist teachers were fools because they confused speech with reason. Articulation, he argued, was akin to teaching parrots to talk. In an address to the Royal Society of Edinburgh in 1815, he openly criticized the oral schools of Britain. Stewart explained his support of the manual approach of the Abbé Sicard, declaring that its purpose was "not to astonish the vulgar by the sudden conversion of a dumb child into a speaking *automaton* but . . . to convert his pupil into a rational and moral being."[15]

Stewart admitted that, at least among European audiences, the use of the manual method rarely excited the imagination of the masses as much as the sight of a deaf child speaking. But, when Gallaudet met with Stewart in Edinburgh in 1815, the philosopher urged Gallaudet to abandon altogether his quest to learn oral methods. Stewart insisted that Gallaudet should follow up on the invitation of Sicard and proceed directly to Paris in order to learn the French method of manual education and adopt it for exclusive use in the new American school. Following Stewart's advice, Gallaudet was inclined to look at manualism with new enthusiasm. Upon seeing first-hand the results that Sicard was having with his students, Gallaudet swiftly decided that the manual method was the best one to bring home to Hartford, and he abandoned his early ideas of trying to combine the two methods.

God, Country, Yale

Gallaudet's educational background contributed to his admiration for Stewart, for he had studied Stewart's writings as an undergraduate. This exposure made it more likely that he would take Stewart's point of view seriously. His school days had also helped to prepare him to embrace manual education. It is not insignificant that Gallaudet attended Yale. Yale wielded an extraordinary influence over early American deaf education. In the first twenty-five years of the American School's life, 1817-1842, there were twenty-five instructors. Of these, six were deaf; and, with the exception of Laurent Clerc himself, all were graduates of the American School. This is a high percentage of deaf teachers overall; 24 percent of the group under examination here was deaf. The remaining nineteen instructors were hearing, and of these, eighteen were Yale graduates.[16]

The influence of Yale on the development of deaf education in the United States goes even further than these numbers would suggest. The first six principals of the American Asylum were all Yale graduates. An analysis of the schools and instructors of the deaf, conducted and published by the *American Annals of the Deaf* in 1900, revealed that the "roll of graduates of Yale University who have entered the profession of teaching the deaf is long and illustrious. Twenty-nine graduates of Yale alone . . . have taught at the Hartford school. . . . The New York Institution . . . has enrolled sixty-three college graduates in its corps of instructors . . . one-third of whom were Yale men."[17] When Yale's president visited Gallaudet College in 1879, then Gallaudet president Edward Miner Gallaudet introduced him by saying, "And so we may greet President [Noah] Porter of Yale College, if not as a teacher of deafmutes, certainly as a teacher of such teachers; while he is a master at whose feet not only we of this College, but all who work at our side in the broader field of general education gladly sit as disciples."[18]

Yale's influence in this fledgling field was quite extraordinary. One possible explanation for the presence of Yale graduates in the field in such disproportionate numbers begins with Yale's classical curriculum. One of the achievements of the classical world was a highly refined sense of the power of gestures. "As it happens," historian Douglas Baynton reports, "pantomime was a highly developed and well-respected art form among the ancient Romans, a fact that fascinated the manualists." He concludes that, for these Yale men, the "use and cultivation of the sign language in the present was to them the revival of a high Roman art form. . . . a way of entering a world of the past, of sharing in what the ancients had themselves cultivated and revered."[19]

Still, why would so many Yale men choose, throughout the antebellum period, to go into deaf education? After all, here was a field with a steep learning curve; they would all be required to learn sign language, a language of which they were all entirely ignorant, a language Yale had done nothing to help them acquire. The field may indeed have offered them an opportunity to connect with the greatness of civilizations past, but it would seem to have attracted young Yale men with somewhat more concrete rewards in mind. Each made a career in an emerging field, instead of pursuing a safer path into a more established field of endeavor. Why?

Perhaps part of the answer lies in Timothy Dwight, president of Yale from 1795 to 1817. After all, five of the early teachers in the field, Gallaudet, Woodbridge, Orr, Weld, and Turner, had attended Timothy Dwight's Yale. Gallaudet, Weld, and Turner would also serve in turn as the first, second, and third principals of the American School, allowing them to most directly shape the life of the institution. Orr would also direct a second deaf institution, leaving the American School to become principal of the Central Asylum for the Instruction of the Deaf and Dumb in Canajoharie, New York. Yale's influence spread, then, beyond just the American School. Perhaps looking more directly at the Yale these men attended will provide an answer to the question, "Why Yale?"

One influence from Yale is immediately obvious. In the *Sixth Report of the Directors of the American Asylum at Hartford for the Education and Instruction of the Deaf and Dumb*, a seventeen-year-old student offered the following description of academic life at the school. "Mr. Gallaudet begins to make signs," the young man wrote, "teaching us about Mr. Tytler's book of the history, when each of us attends to his signs, then each of us stands and writes a long lesson on each of our slates for two and a half hours."[20] Tytler's *Elements of History* was the standard history text at Yale. All Yale undergraduates read it in their sophomore year.[21] Gallaudet was using the elements of his own education to build a curriculum at the American School. Granted, he was presenting the ideas of the text to them in the sign language, and was not expecting the students to read it themselves, but using it at all suggests a willingness to treat the academic capabilities of his students with respect. He believed that the deaf students were intellectually capable.

A Godly Federalism

But there is more to Yale's influence on Gallaudet than just the selection of textbooks. Timothy Dwight had offered to Yale undergraduates a vision of social life in America. Call it a godly federalism or call it the New England way, it amounted to a particular notion of what society should be like.[22] As Christopher Grasso argues, Dwight believed in "the superiority of New England's social and cultural institutions." For Dwight, he continues, "the New England way was both the 'true means of establishing public happiness' in this world and the best means for preparing . . . men and women to receive the Spirit and look forward to the next world."[23] Dwight worked hard to prepare young men, through their Yale education, to go out into New England to enact this vision of citizenship. He took every opportunity to school his students in his vision. Yale students heard Dwight lecture on theology each week, for the forty weeks of the academic year. And each day in their senior year, students listened to his lectures both in rhetoric and in moral philosophy.[24] "So Dwight preached the faith to his Yale boys," Grasso notes, "for they would need to reawaken New England, before New England could awaken America, and America could redeem the world."[25] Gallaudet and other Yale men would bring Dwight's message of public happiness, citizenship, and redemption to the deaf of New England.

Dwight was also convinced, as his intellectual biographer John Fitzmier reminds us, that "the social institutions that made up American culture rested on the foundation of individual morality and were entirely dependent on that morality for their well being."[26] One can imagine, therefore, that deaf education was a missionary effort in two senses. First, schools, like other American institutions, provided the setting in which to create the vitally important virtuous citizen. Second, if American institutions depended on individual morality for their success, it followed that all citizens would have to be made moral. All citizens would participate in the institutions of American life, and these institutions could not afford immoral members. Deaf citizens were included in this rhetoric, both insofar as they were not explicitly excluded and insofar as Yale graduates were willing to work to bring them into the circle of virtuous citizenship.

But could deaf people achieve this kind of citizenship? Were they perceived as capable of becoming virtuous citizens? Could disabled people be virtuous citizens or was this role only to be filled by the able-bodied? Dwight's ideals had to meet reality head-on. It would seem that the education Dwight's Yale provided had prepared Gallaudet to view an educated, moral citizenry as the basis for a good society. But as Gallaudet studied in Paris, he received a second education, one that explored the capabilities of deaf people. Truly, this education had begun in London, where Gallaudet saw Sicard's exhibition and met educated Deaf people for the first time. That education included not only seeing the language of signs in action but also learning a bit about Deaf attitudes.

Significantly, at that London demonstration, Clerc had been asked if the deaf were as unhappy as the hearing frequently believed them to be. He replied,

> He who never had anything has never lost anything; and he who never lost anything has no loss to regret. Consequently, the deaf and dumb who have never spoken have never lost either hearing or speech, and therefore cannot lament either the one or the other. And he who has nothing to lament cannot be unhappy; consequently, the deaf and dumb are not unhappy. Besides, it is a great consolation for them to be able to replace hearing by writing and speech by signs.[27]

Here Clerc indicated directly what Deaf people largely believed about themselves. They were as happy as the hearing. They considered the language of signs as the equal of speech. And they believed that literacy was an adequate substitute for hearing. As Clerc understood it, for the deaf, literacy provided the key to their inclusion in the wider society.

Still, Clerc's assertions aside, did not Dwight's emphasis on rhetoric present problems for adopting the manual method? Could Dwight's virtuous citizens also be a signing people? Rhetoric does by definition mean speaking, but, as historian Christopher Grasso has noted, "We should not refer to separate print and oral cultures, at least for eighteenth-century New England, where speech, print, and handwritten messages were interwoven in complex webs of communication."[28] Print and handwriting would clearly give deaf people the means to enter into this web of communication, even if they could not speak. And Dwight himself would not have made a tremendous distinction between print and oral cultures, given his functional blindness. Orality and print became increasingly interchangeable for him; he wrote as he spoke and he spoke as he wrote.[29]

Through print, deaf people would in effect gain access to oral culture. Most importantly, perhaps, they would gain access to newspapers. As historian Kenneth Cmiel argues, "The newspaper was as important to the nineteenth-century mind as television is to ours."[30] Gaining literacy, deaf people would gain the necessary tools to read and write their way into the mainstream of public life, exactly as Clerc had already explained.

Finally, Dwight's influence could quite possibly have prepared his students to see the deaf, like other minority groups, as worthy of attention and education. Although Dwight never addressed the question of deaf citizenship specifically, he did address the place of other minority groups in Connecticut. He wrote about Connecticut's Native American population, as well as its African American citizens. He believed that the traits that seemed to characterize the black community of his day, like ignorance, were the direct result of the deprivations of slavery and not indicators of inherent, biologically grounded, racial limitations.[31]

The connections to deaf education are clear. Though physically different from other citizens, deaf people did not have to be viewed as inherently and fatally flawed. Rather, like African Americans, they were historically lacking in opportunities to learn and to improve themselves, but education promised to change all of this. Dwight's godly federalism provided an ideological framework that opened the door for a disabled population to take its place in mainstream society. And Dwight's Yale graduates would be just the men to provide the education that would prove the key to inclusion. In this way, hearing people would have an important role to play in the story of the deaf community's formation.

Recruiting Clerc

In the summer of 1815, Gallaudet may not have been thinking about transforming deaf Americans into Timothy Dwight's virtuous citizens. In letters home to Alice Cogswell, he simply expressed his hopes in the potential of manual education itself to transform the lives of the deaf in the United States. Although increasingly homesick for Hartford, he wrote to her, "I shall stay here for some time. I do not know how long. I must learn all that Abbé Sicard can teach me. Then I shall be able to teach you in the best way."[32] Although he believed that

Alice deserved the best education he could provide her, after two months in Paris, Gallaudet reached the unhappy conclusion that he would not be able to master all he needed to know in a timely fashion. He needed to learn both French Sign Language and the French educational method, and this was an impossible task in a short period of time. His benefactors, however wealthy, would not pay for an indefinite stay abroad. He therefore asked Laurent Clerc, a graduate of the National Institution and a teacher there, to accompany him back to Connecticut and aid him in establishing the new school.

Clerc, then thirty years old, had been at the school since he had arrived as a student at the age of twelve. Gallaudet was asking him to leave not just his job but his home. But Clerc apparently had a taste for adventure and a feeling of obligation for his fellow deaf, in America and elsewhere. Clerc had been bitterly disappointed when an earlier opportunity to work as an instructor in St. Petersburg, Russia, had fallen through.[33] As he recalled the events that brought him to the United States years later, Clerc remarked, "I had a great desire to see the world, and especially to make my unfortunate fellow-beings on the other side of the Atlantic, participate in the same benefits of education that I had myself received."[34]

Without him, it was unlikely that the proposed school would succeed. Gallaudet was not yet familiar enough with the French method, or the sign language, to implement it easily in a new institution, never mind train other teachers in it. He clearly needed help. Clerc agreed to provide it, negotiating a three-year contract before the two men left Paris.[35] Sicard initially opposed this move, not wanting to lose Clerc, but finally relented, writing the bishop of Boston, "[Clerc] carries with him the regrets of his pupils and of the whole establishment. He was its glory and honour, but everything yields to the good he will accomplish. In order to console myself for his departure, I love to think of him as the apostle of the Deaf Mutes of the New World."[36] Thus anointed, the pair set sail for Hartford on June 18, 1816.

In the years to come, the American Deaf community would recognize the impact of this man, this act, and this date. By the end of the century, Job Turner, a man taught by Laurent Clerc at the American School who would in turn became the first deaf teacher hired at the Virginia School for the Deaf and the Blind, would write of Clerc's "sacred name." Another admirer told Clerc's son, Francois, "Gallaudet never showed more sagacity and tact and wisdom than he did in securing Clerc to accompany him to America."[37]

Or consider the words of the Deaf educator James Denison, who addressed the crowd that gathered at the American School for the Deaf to dedicate a memorial raised in Clerc's honor in 1874.

It would appear at this distance of time to have been the most trying, as it was the most momentous, act of Mr. Clerc's life to *decide* to accompany Mr. Gallaudet to America. He must bid farewell to home, friends, and relations—to aged parents on the verge of the grave; . . . he must abandon Paris, with its palaces and gardens and fountains, its libraries and art museums, its unrivalled resources for esthetic and intellectual enjoyment, so dear to the heart of the true Frenchman; he must prepare to see buried beneath the dust of disuse . . . his precious French, his only written language, mastered with the heavy tax of time and effort laid upon the deaf-mute; he must tear himself from his beloved teacher and friend, Sicard. . . . Yet, from all we can learn, Mr. Clerc did not hesitate in making his decision. . . . [H]e took prompt leave of his friends, and the scene of his labors and triumphs, and on the 18th of June he embarked for America with Mr. Gallaudet.[38]

So many years later and still Denison vividly painted the scene of the most important act in American Deaf history, an act that did not even occur on American soil. He stressed not the date when the American School opened, or even the date when Clerc arrived in America, but the date that made the school's opening possible, the date when Laurent Clerc chose to board the ship that would take him to the United States. That decision, that day, June 18, Denison held up as the date that changed not just one man's life but the course of the lives of all deaf people in America. To them, on that day, Clerc left on a journey that would change history.

Meeting Alice

The return trip took fifty-two days. During that time, Gallaudet taught Clerc English and Clerc taught Gallaudet French Sign Language. After docking in New York, they left for Hartford, finally arriving on August 22, 1816. Here Clerc met Alice Cogswell, the girl whose deafness had sparked these events, for the first time. He described their meeting:

> She had one of the most intelligent countenances I ever saw. I was much pleased with her. We conversed by signs, and we understood each other very well. . . . I had left many persons and objects in France endeared to me by association, and America, at first, seemed uninteresting and monotonous, and I sometimes regretted leaving my native land; but on seeing Alice, I had only to recur to the object which had induced me to seek these shores, to contemplate the good we were going to do, and sadness was subdued by an approving conscience.[39]

In early September, the two men embarked on a five-month fundraising tour, beginning in Boston. Clerc embraced public speaking, signing eloquently while Gallaudet acted as his voice interpreter. When the funds came together with the necessary legislative approval, the school, the American Asylum for the Deaf, opened its doors on April 15, 1817.[40] Leaving Lydia Huntley's school behind, and with a firm educational foundation upon which to build, Alice Cogswell was the first pupil to enroll.

Learning the Lessons of Deafness

Gallaudet had learned first-hand that deaf people could become Dwight's virtuous citizens, that they were indeed capable of attaining the skills of citizenship for themselves if educated properly. If Gallaudet found that his Yale education had uniquely prepared him for this vocation, his second education in Deafness, at the hands of Laurent Clerc, was also crucial for firmly establishing the manual method in the United States. Gallaudet would come over time to absorb the Deaf lessons of his teacher well. They were frequently challenging. While Gallaudet could fairly easily absorb Clerc's commitment to manualism and to literacy, other Deaf values were harder to learn.

Clerc claimed that the deaf were the equals of the hearing. In his address to the Connecticut legislature on May 28, 1818, just over a year after the American School opened, Clerc reminded his audience, "Every creature, every work of God, is admirably well made; but if any one appears imperfect in our eyes, it does not belong to us to criticize it." Perhaps, after all, such perceived imperfections are just that, reflections of our own limited perspectives and nothing more. "Perhaps that which we do not find right in its kind turns to our advantage, without our being able to perceive it," Clerc mused.[41]

A crisis occurred for the two men when Clerc took a deaf wife. In 1819, Clerc married Eliza Boardman, a former student at the Hartford school. They were married in Troy, New York, close to her relatives, by Rev. Dr. Butler, the chaplain of the U.S. Senate, whom Clerc had met on one of his fundraising tours in Albany. When he announced the news of his engagement to Gallaudet, Thomas was initially upset. He abruptly announced that deaf people should not marry each other; they should only marry hearing people, if they marry at all. Society was likely to disapprove of such a match, and it could result in deaf children. (As it would turn out, all six of the couple's children would be hearing.) Clerc was angered by his response.[42]

But, as the two men were bound together by the institution they had founded, they continued to work side by side. Over time, Gallaudet came to realize that he had been wrong to oppose this specific marriage and deaf-deaf marriages in general. By setting such a powerful example, to Gallaudet and other instructors in the antebellum period, Clerc helped to demonstrate that the deaf students in their care would have life patterns identical to those of their hearing peers. They too would graduate, find work, marry, and raise children. In this way, deaf lives could and would look like hearing lives.

This was so well established a principle in manualist circles that the directors of the Virginia Institution could confidently write in 1851, "In our favored country, the cheapness of living and the abundance of all things encourage intermarriage, and almost universally, when our mutes have married at all, they have married among themselves." Even the possibility of such unions producing deaf children, the officers continued, "is not sufficient ground for denying deaf mutes the chief earthly happiness" of marriage.[43]

Gallaudet came to understand this so well that he too married a deaf woman and a former pupil, Sophia Fowler, in 1821. Sophia Fowler communicated exclusively in American Sign Language and written English; she never developed a speaking voice. She and Thomas raised eight children, all hearing, but of course the language of daily life in the household was the sign language. All members had to use the sign language to communicate. When he married Sophia, Gallaudet knew that his, like Clerc's, would be a Deaf household. He married a deaf woman knowing that she could not speak. But this inability did not strike Gallaudet as an obstacle to marriage. He did not expect her to be able to pass as hearing in order to be seen as marriageable. Though able-bodied himself, he had learned enough to see a disabled woman as a suitable partner, wife, and mother, quite a countercultural stance both then and now. Here, in his own marriage, is a picture of Gallaudet putting both his Yale and his Deaf lessons into practice.[44]

These events, these dual educations, help to explain why Gallaudet, and in turn other young Yale men, embraced the manual method. Trusting that Gallaudet had thoroughly investigated the matter and found the best method for the first American school, Mason Fitch Cogswell and his benefactors likewise accepted manual education. The question remains as to why the public accepted manual education and supported it.

The fundraising tour that Gallaudet and Clerc embarked upon when they returned from France probably had a great deal to do with this acceptance. The first educated Deaf man to tour the United States, Clerc delivered speeches in sign to American audiences throughout the Northeast, with

Gallaudet acting as his voice interpreter. Clerc was, as Gallaudet knew, an impressive example of the benefits of manual education. He provided living proof that deaf people, through education, could become virtuous and capable citizens. A product of the manual system of deaf education, Clerc also convincingly demonstrated on the lecture circuit that the sign language was a successful teaching tool and that an investment in deaf education would be well worth it. Clerc served in antebellum America, as John Vickrey Van Cleve and Barry A. Crouch have argued, as "an exemplary model of what a deaf person could become—educated, industrious, socially skilled."[45]

Clerc's role in brokering the acceptance of the manual method in the United States cannot be overestimated. He was a far more powerful public symbol than Gallaudet could have been. After all, Gallaudet was hearing, and so he would have to argue for the method's effectiveness in the abstract. Clerc could simply demonstrate it. "All skepticism upon this subject will be put to rest," one advocate declared, "by a mere perusal of Mr. Clerc's address."[46]

Clerc's first public addresses concerned themselves with two major themes, dispelling myths about deaf people and convincing Americans to support the cause of deaf education. An 1816 address found Clerc lamenting that the United States was neglecting its deaf citizens. The zeal for reform and improvement was obvious to Clerc, as he noted the presence of numerous institutions to improve society, including common schools, hospitals, and poor houses. Yet, there was nothing for deaf people, which struck Clerc as a great shame, for it would be "a great benefit . . . to restore them to society, to their families, to the cultivation of their understanding, in the same degree as if they could hear and speak."[47] Here as elsewhere, Clerc emphasized that deaf people possessed intelligence equal to that of hearing people and could be educated similarly.

The Philadelphia Story

In a speech in Philadelphia, Clerc built a multilayered argument in favor of deaf education. He appealed to his audience's patriotism, urging them not to fall further behind the Europeans in this area; to their civic pride, asking them to support their fellow countrymen in their quest for education; to their Christianity, explaining that the deaf were cut off from the comforts of religion; and even to their sense of self-preservation, posing the hypothetical scenario that they might have deaf children of their own one day and would undoubtedly want to see them educated.[48] Again, while emphasizing the ability and intelligence of deaf people, Clerc would use every argument at his disposal to persuade audiences to support his cause.

The audience in Philadelphia, for its part, resolved to devote itself to fund-raising and specifically thanked Clerc "for the opportunity which he has kindly afforded them of witnessing the efficacy of that system by which he has been instructed."[49] Other published reports similarly reflected on Clerc's powerful example of what the educated deaf might achieve. As one put it in 1818,

> The Rev. Mr. Gallaudet returned to his friends, a qualified instructor upon the French system. He brought with him as an assistant, a most interesting man, Mr. Clerc. This person never heard a sound or uttered a word, being deaf and dumb from his birth. Yet he is so quick and intelligent, that he has become acquainted with both the French and English tongues, which he writes with grammatical accuracy. . . . In him we have an example of the ability of a person, himself deaf and dumb, to give the necessary instruction to others labouring under similar disabilities.[50]

Clerc's poise and intelligence undoubtedly won many viewers over to the cause of deaf education, and more specifically to manual education. As an educated Deaf man, he demonstrated the possibilities for deaf people to his largely hearing audiences. His accomplishments impressed even those hearing Americans still skeptical about the possibilities of educating born-deaf people.

The audience in Philadelphia questioned Clerc about his capabilities. In an open question and answer session after his address, Clerc was asked directly, "By what means do you judge whether the operations of your mind are similar to those of persons who can hear and speak?" It was a critical question. Clerc asserted repeatedly in his public speeches that deaf people could be educated "in the same degree as if they could hear and speak." He did not recognize a hierarchy of ability here, one that separated the deaf from the hearing. He believed in the fundamental equality of the deaf and the hearing. Was this true? And, perhaps more importantly, would hearing audiences believe it? Clerc answered the question: "I can express my own ideas by writing, and as what I write is what you speak, I can judge that I possess the same faculties of the mind as you do."[51]

Clerc based his response on the grounds of language acquisition, in this case, English. He knew he had a mind like the hearing because he could write as they could speak. This would seem to privilege English over the sign language and, in some ways, perhaps it does. But if one assumes that the nineteenth-century audience for this answer would not have widely believed that English and sign language were linguistic equivalents, one sees immediately that it would not have been expedient to claim that the deaf and hearing had equal minds because one could learn the sign language while the other learned English. That would only have emphasized their basic difference. Their claim to equality had to lie elsewhere, and it had to lie in the fact that both groups could share a language, a common language, in this instance, English. The path to equality for deaf people, paradoxically, was to be found in claiming the language of hearing people as their own.

Significantly, this claim did not require any disavowal of deafness or of the sign language. Clerc himself was always recognized as a deaf man, and not as someone who was successfully passing as hearing. He never developed a speaking voice, nor was he known as a skilled lipreader. He was a signing Deaf man. In this exchange in Philadelphia, questions "were proposed to Mr. Clerc by the Ladies and Gentlemen present, in *writing* and by *signs*, which were answered by him in *writing*, with a promptitude rarely equalled by those possessing the full command of their speech."[52]

Even as he stressed English language acquisition, this was a bilingual performance. Clerc could claim English only through the sign language, and he would only write it, not speak it. He had a mind equal to that of the hearing, but he was not hearing. The deaf and the hearing could learn the same language, but they would not use it in the same way. Restoration to and integration into society for the deaf would come by learning English, certainly, but also by using it in deaf, and not in hearing, ways.[53]

His status as a signing, nonspeaking user of English precisely enabled Clerc to stand in for the rest of the deaf community, demonstrating their potential capabilities through the display of his own realized capabilities. As Clerc explained, among educators of the deaf in France, it was well understood that "this artificial speech, not being susceptible among the deaf and dumb of complete improvement, nor of modification and regulation, by the sense of hearing, is almost always very painful, harsh, and discordant and comparatively useless. It has neither the rapidity nor the expressiveness of signs nor the precision of writing."[54] By behaving in recognizably Deaf ways in public, always signing and never speaking, Clerc also provided hearing witnesses with a set of expectations with which to regard other deaf people.

At this crucial moment when deaf education was just being established in the United States, the cultural expectations for deaf people were being defined in Deaf terms. Marriage and child rearing were both to be expected for deaf graduates, even deaf-deaf marriage, as Clerc and Boardman demonstrated. Learning English in its written form via the sign language, exactly as Clerc had, was the path to integration in the wider society. Mastering spoken English was entirely unnecessary.

Hearing Acceptance

These were the goals for the wider deaf population as Deaf people like Clerc understood them, but it was not only deaf people who argued for these positions. Again and again, hearing commentators in the early nineteenth century also stressed that the deaf could, through manual education specifically, be restored to society and made useful and happy members of it, participating as equals in the moral and intellectual life of the community. These may have been Deaf terms, but they were also embraced by hearing professionals in the new field of deaf education. Both groups, deaf and hearing, worked together to implement the manual system of education, which resulted both in the creation of a Deaf world and in the integration of the Deaf in the hearing world.

From the very first years, antebellum teachers recognized that the schools served a larger mission than even education. They knew that the shared school environment helped to shape their deaf students into a distinct community, one in which their first language, the sign language, would always come first. As the American Asylum's directors put it in 1828,

> The system for teaching the Deaf and Dumb was introduced into the United States about eleven years since by the establishment of the American Asylum at Hartford. It is now extending throughout the Union and it is desirable that a uniform system should prevail that the Deaf and Dumb, who form in some measure a distinct community, should have a common language.[55]

This is a remarkable statement, coming so soon after the founding of deaf education in the United States. Hearing educators acknowledged that the deaf "form in some measure a distinct community." The statement is especially surprising given that, prior to the foundation of schools for the deaf, there is no indication that hearing people acknowledged the deaf as a community of any kind. This statement implies that the teachers grasped the importance of the residential school in creating a recognizable Deaf community by bringing deaf people together in large numbers for the first time.

They also understood that the common language of that community, the sign language, was disseminated through the residential schools. Since this distinct community, scattered nationwide, would need a common language, this too was to be an important function of the manual schools. As the manual system spread, so too would one common signed language.[56] In fighting for the spread of the manual method, teachers, both hearing and deaf, knew that they were contributing to the creation of a new community on the American scene, a Deaf community.

It was a world that Deaf people would, of course, develop further after they graduated. But it was a world with its roots firmly planted in the residential schools. The residential schools were quintessentially Deaf places, even if staffed with significant numbers of hearing people. In the antebellum period, those hearing teachers expected that their students would largely choose to live as signing people in an extended Deaf community; they sought to give them the tools to participate in the life of the hearing world as well.

Gallaudet believed that the deaf were owed access to manual education by the hearing community. In 1818, Gallaudet argued that "the sterner voice of justice" called for community investment in deaf education. He explained,

> New England lavishes her public bounty upon her colleges, academies, and schools. It is her glory and her strength, that the streams of useful learning run through her obscurest villages and reach her humblest cottages. The parents of the deaf and dumb, nay, in many instances the deaf and dumb themselves, have for years been obliged to contribute, from their own private sources, to supply the great fountain from which these blessings of human and divine knowledge flow; and all around them have drunk deeply of its thousand springs. It is the hand of justice, then, rather than of benevolence, which should extend to their thirsty souls the simple cup of refreshment which they so earnestly crave.[57]

Gallaudet framed his argument for deaf education not on the grounds of benevolence, as his readers might have expected, but rather on the grounds of justice. Hearing people, much like Clerc's inquisitors in London, made assumptions about deaf people. They were seen as unhappy, perhaps even deserving of pity. Here, Gallaudet rejected this depiction. He would not cater to prevailing hearing prejudices by appealing to hearing people's sense of their own superiority, their ability to exercise their benevolence. He did not want to excite hearing pity.

Rather, Gallaudet challenged his hearing audience by demanding justice for the deaf. Benevolence suggests that one privileged group extend its generous hand on behalf of the less fortunate. Justice, by contrast, demands reciprocity; both groups, deaf and hearing, owed something to each other. Again, as Gallaudet tried to persuade his hearing readers to support deaf education, he chose to paint a picture of deaf people as essentially equal to hearing people. Hearing did not imply superiority nor deafness, inferiority. Through education, for which both had an equal capacity, equality would prevail.

Whig Support for a Manual Future

The early results of the new system seemed to confirm these hopes. Perhaps the most significant reason the public supported manual education in the antebellum period is that it returned results. The successes of the early years of the American Asylum were crucial in establishing broad-based support for the manual system. "The advances made by the pupils at Hartford, as appears by the different reports of the directory, and more particularly by the specimens of the composition accompanying the second annual report," one reporter commented, "are truly gratifying and wonderful."[58]

Publishing students' compositions proved a critical success. The students' work demonstrated the "rapidity of comprehension" of the deaf, as well as their "active ingenuity."[59] By reading these student essays, the public had the opportunity to see the deaf making their way "into the pale of society" as they learned English. The manual system that had produced Laurent Clerc quickly showed its worth in the United States. Like Clerc, American deaf students were demonstrating, through their success at the American Asylum, "that they [were] capable, not only of becoming useful and happy members of society, but of grasping the most sublime and intricate truths."[60]

This vision of deaf education, which emphasized the basic equality of the deaf and the hearing and the potential of the sign language to realize it, was not limited in its reach. It was not to be found merely in the annual reports of schools for the deaf themselves. Other journals with wider readerships also portrayed deaf education in this light. The *North American Review* published an article on the founding of the American Asylum. A Whig publication, the *North American Review* covered a variety of reform movements. Educational reform was only one of many reform opportunities, and deaf education was a field of narrower interest still. Yet the *Review* approached the topic with a great deal of interest.

As the *Review* described deaf education for its readers, it noted that through manual education, the deaf "can be put in use of faculties of mind, of the possession of which, they had before been unconscious; and thus— from being objects of pity, shut out from the intellectual world and its inhabitants—they can be admitted to a participation of most of the pleasures of science and letters."[61] The work of the American Asylum forcefully demonstrated that the deaf need no longer be "objects of pity."

The *Review*'s rejection of pity for the educated deaf draws attention to the prevailing cultural attitude that the deaf and other disabled Americans faced. Pity and charity, as well as fear and rejection, the flip side of condescending sympathy—these were common reactions to the disabled, in the antebellum world and perhaps in our own as well. Deaf people have, historically speaking, been on the front lines in the fight against "pity" as the dominant lens through which disabled people are culturally perceived. Through the years of the rise of manual education, they shared that fight with hearing allies.

Those allies, like Gallaudet, did not expect Deaf people to give up their sign language in exchange for English. They would use both languages. Teaching grammatical written English was the principal goal of educators at the American Asylum. But even as Gallaudet described his profession's primary mission, he challenged the expectations of his hearing audience, forcing them to move beyond their stereotypes. As he wrote in the school's second annual report,

> This is the only avenue to the various departments of knowledge which books contain, and which must, forever, be inaccessible to the deaf and dumb until they become familiar with the powers and use of letters in their various forms and combinations. This also is necessary even for the purposes of their common intercourse with mankind, most of whom know nothing of the manner in which thoughts can so easily be expressed by signs and gestures.[62]

Rather than portray deaf people as outside of hearing society, requiring English to gain entry into the hearing world, Gallaudet described hearing people as the outsiders, largely ignorant of signs, and unable to communicate in the Deaf world. In a neat rhetorical reversal, Deaf people, it turns out, have to use English in order to accommodate the linguistic ignorance of hearing people. Once more, Gallaudet placed deaf and hearing people on equal footing. Just as deaf people could not be expected to learn how to articulate, hearing people could not be expected to learn to sign. What both groups could be expected to do was read and write English. A sign-based education would be the mechanism to bring English to deaf people.

2

Manual Education

An American Beginning

The system for teaching the Deaf and Dumb was introduced into the United States about eleven years since by the establishment of the American Asylum at Hartford. It is now extending throughout the Union and it is desirable that a uniform system should prevail that the Deaf and Dumb, who form in some measure a distinct community, should have a common language.
—*Twelfth Annual Report of the American Asylum*, 1828

Linguistic Choices

Manual education promoted classroom instruction in the sign language. That would seem straightforward enough. But which language was this? The phrase "the sign language" was invoked in the nineteenth century, along with "the natural language of signs" and "natural signs." And so-called natural signs were later contrasted by educators with "methodical signs" or "artificial signs." The cluttered vocabulary of the nineteenth century can make it difficult to understand exactly what language choices educators faced, or what those choices meant to them.

Given the existence of many different kinds of signing, it is important to understand how hearing educators perceived their choices. The linguistic choices that they made influenced the development of Deaf culture in crucial ways. If today Deaf culture is marked by the use of American Sign Language (ASL), we must understand how that language survived into the twentieth century. After all, by the late nineteenth century, oral education would have as its explicit goal the abolition of the sign language. Oralists believed that if they could succeed in removing sign language from the classroom, the language would eventually go extinct.

The failure of oralists to eliminate the sign language from the life of the Deaf community needs explanation. Deaf people themselves played a crucial role in keeping the language alive, in spite of the onslaught of the hearing teaching establishment. They continued to use ASL despite widespread cultural disapproval. But the efforts of the earliest teachers have largely been overlooked. Yet, their educational choices, and their corresponding attitudes toward the sign language of their students, were crucial in providing the opportunity for ASL to set down deep and lasting roots in the United States. By investigating how the sign language was treated at the residential schools, we can begin to glimpse how the Deaf community would come to claim ASL as its birthright and later fight to preserve its linguistic heritage.

"The Sign Language"

The term "sign language" did not refer to one language alone in the nineteenth century. Throughout the nineteenth century, various sign systems existed simultaneously. Typically, though again not in every case, the phrases "the sign language" and "the natural language of signs" referred to what in the late twentieth century would come to be called ASL. The sign language was generally recognized as the natural language of deaf people, both as the language that they most commonly used among themselves and as the language that originated from the deaf community itself. "This beautiful language," one observer wrote, "is their own creation and is a visible testimony to the activity of their intellect. It is a language of action, full of force, full of animation, full of figurative expression, oftentimes full of grace."[1]

One antebellum author tried to explain the origin of the natural language of signs. Deaf children were said to use "natural signs" at home; they invented them in an effort to communicate with their hearing families. "Natural signs," the explanation went, were those that nature prompted deaf children to make, in an effort to communicate with the hearing people around them. Natural signs were not a language in and of themselves, but they had the potential to contribute to the natural language of signs as it developed at the residential school. Educators claimed that signs "employed by the deaf and dumb before instruction" were "almost entirely destitute of pronouns, conjunctions, adverbs, and the moods and tenses of verbs."[2] Students came to them, they continued, with only a "limited and imperfect natural language of signs, and in this they universally express their thoughts in a very different style and idiom from ours. They must be brought, by slow and patient steps, to change this style and abandon these idioms, for those of a refined language."[3] How can these statements about the apparent paucity of the sign language be squared with the educators' statements of praise for the sign language?

The answer lies in the nineteenth-century manualist concept of the cultivated versus the uncultivated language.[4] All of the above remarks include mention of the language in an "uncultivated state" or "before instruction." These natural signs were in part natural because all human beings, deaf and hearing alike, were thought to have recourse to this language; hearing people, for instance, were said to use such natural signs when they met other hearing people who did not share their spoken language. In the absence of a common spoken language, even hearing people resorted to using gestures and natural signs.

This natural language, however, was uncultivated. Verbal languages were known to have evolved over time. Standardization, in terms of pronunciation and grammar, occurred over the course of this cultivation. The natural language of signs, on the other hand, had not yet had such an opportunity to develop. Individual deaf students arrived at the school possessing only the language in its uncultivated state. They could express their immediate wants but few ideas. They used natural signs with only a hint of grammatical structure, having no way to mark verb tenses or other parts of speech. By bringing deaf children together in one place, the school allowed the cultivation of natural signs to begin. By the lights of manualists, deaf children would here engage in the work of cultivating their native language, exactly as speakers of languages had done over the ages. Once more, deaf and hearing people were treated as essentially the same in manualist theory.

At the residential school, the natural signs of the students would become the natural *language* of signs. The students abandoned their own individual idioms and embraced a more cultivated language. By bringing uniformity to the language of their students, hearing educators and deaf students, working and signing together, would "elevate to as high degree of excellence as possible the natural language of signs employed by the Deaf and Dumb." Educators did not doubt that over generations deaf people would "construct a visible language, equally copious and equally perfect with the languages now in use"; nor was it inconceivable that deaf people in time "would add to this a corresponding system of ideographic writing."[5] Through these efforts and over time, this perceived "distinct community" would gain "a common language."

Antebellum observers tried to describe this process of cultivation as they witnessed it. At the residential school, a deaf child confronted a signing community. "He abandons his own signs for those which he finds in use," as one writer explained, "not because they appear to him more appropriate, but because they are universally intelligible." This language that the newcomer finds in use is the "joint production of teachers and pupils."[6] Together, the two groups spun the natural signs of the students into the natural language of signs. Both contributed to the creolization process.

While families may have previously understood the individual signs of their child, they would quickly find themselves unable to understand this new language. The new creation deviated substantially from purely mimetic signs. An author in 1834 called this process "reduction."

> However accurate originally may be its imitations, however striking its analogies, it invariably undergoes, in the hands of the dumb, a species of abbreviations. . . . By the institution of these abbreviated signs, usually denominated signs of reduction, the language of action becomes singularly elliptical, as well as figurative.[7]

This process of abstraction, of moving signs away from pantomime and imitation, educators perceived, would continue through the generations. "That the language of action is capable of being reduced to system and advanced to the perfection of spoken language is a truth self-evident," this author wrote, "at least to those who have been accustomed to its use."[8]

The signs of reduction would bring the sign language into its own, allowing it to develop along the lines of its own linguistic principles. Manualists stressed that these signs of reduction in the natural language of signs were not to be confused with methodical signs. The sign language was "not reduced . . . to conformity with a language which must be understood before the conformity can be comprehended."[9] Methodical signs were not natural signs. But they were another type of sign system that existed in the nineteenth century and they need to be explained here.

"Methodical Signs"

"Methodical signs" referred specifically to a type of signing invented by hearing people. The French educators, Abbé de l'Epée and Abbé Sicard, had created these methodical signs for the purpose of signing grammatical French. The goal of methodical signs was to present French gesturally. The pair invented signs to indicate the part of speech and case of each particular word. As Harlan Lane describes it, in Epée's system, "even the simplest sentence took on enormous complexity. One example: a line from Racine, 'To the smallest of the birds, He gives their crumbs,' required forty-eight signs from Epée's pupils. 'Gives' alone required five signs: those for verb, present, third person, singular, and 'give.'"[10]

Renate Fischer, in another analysis of de l'Epée's methodical sign system, has further expounded on its character and complexity. To introduce his deaf students to the French phrase *"je crois"* (in English, "I believe"), de l'Epée's system, as Fischer describes it, presented explanations of the words in both written and gestural forms. The written explication presented *"je crois"* as containing four distinct meanings at once: "I say 'yes' with my mind. I think that 'yes.' I say 'yes' with the heart. I like to think that 'yes.' I say 'yes' with the mouth. I have not seen, and do not see now, with my eyes." The accompanying signed explanation de l'Epée described as follows:

> first, I make the sign for the first person singular by pointing towards myself with the index finger of my right hand, its point directed toward my breast. Then I put my finger on my forehead, the domed part of which is supposed to encompass my mind, that is, my intelligence, and make the sign for "yes." Then I make the same sign for "yes" by putting my finger on that part which is usually considered to be the seat of what we call our heart, in the spiritual sense, i.e. our ability to love. . . . Subsequently, I make the same sign for "yes" on my mouth, moving my lips. Finally, I put my hand over my eyes, and show, while making the sign for "no" at the same time, that I do not see anything. Now I have only to make the sign for "present tense," and one writes "I believe."[11]

Although all of these grammatical concepts, including the present tense that de l'Epée so pointedly signed, also existed in French Sign Language, the language did not of course exactly parallel French, hence the perceived need to invent a way to sign French in order to teach the national language to deaf students. It is not entirely clear whether or not Clerc and Gallaudet adopted the whole system for use in their new school, including the elaborate written explanations that de l'Epée preferred. It seems more likely that they adopted simply the usage of methodical signs themselves, for the same reason de l'Epée had, in order to present English gesturally.[12]

Early Deaf Education

The early reports of the American Asylum provide invaluable insight into the opinions of early educators of the deaf. The perspective of the American Asylum on deaf education was especially weighty because the Asylum became the training ground for teachers and principals of other schools. As the first school for the deaf in the country, the American Asylum set the pace for deaf education for the entire antebellum period. Prospective teachers came to the American Asylum to learn the methods of the manual system. Laurent Clerc offered lessons in the sign language there. Teachers trained at the American Asylum went on to found or work at schools in other states. For instance, the first deaf teacher hired at the Ohio School for the Deaf in 1830, Danford Bell, was trained at the American School. Rev. Joseph Tyler, an experienced teacher at the American School, was hired to be the first superintendent of the Virginia School for the Deaf in 1839.[13] Schools that found themselves floundering frequently called on the American Asylum for help. Laurent Clerc briefly took over as principal of the Pennsylvania School, for instance, when it experienced an administrative collapse that threatened to close the school.[14]

As early as 1819, the American Asylum outlined its teaching efforts. The primary goal of the school, according to its directors, was to teach the students written language. Four different methods were employed to attain this goal. The first method, "on which all the rest are founded, and without which every attempt to teach the deaf and dumb would be utterly vain and fruitless, is the natural language of signs, originally employed by the deaf and dumb in all their intercourse with their friends and each other."[15] The second method was the methodical signs. The officers of the American Asylum described the methodical signs as

the *same* natural language of signs, divested of certain peculiarities of dialect which have grown out of the various circumstances under which different individuals have been placed, reduced to one general standard, and methodized, and enlarged by the admirable genius of the Abbé de l'Epée and . . . the Abbé Sicard, so as to accommodate it to the structure and idioms of written language, and thus render it in itself a perspicuous, complete, and copious medium of thought.[16]

Clerc and Gallaudet believed they had succeeded in transforming Sicard's French model of methodical signs into a system useful for presenting English on the hands. Methodical signs would present English in a medium, namely, a visual and gestural medium, that deaf students would be best able to understand. This kind of signing was considered best for use in the classroom, especially for teaching English, while the natural language of signs was considered the best language to use to convey general information and to teach religion.

The third mode of communication used in the early years of the school was the manual alphabet. The manual alphabet was, and is, a system of twenty-six different handshapes. Each handshape corresponds to an individual letter of the English alphabet. The advantage of the manual alphabet, according to American Asylum instructors, was that it offered a way for deaf people to communicate precisely using English words with the same speed as written language. Instructors encouraged hearing people to learn the manual alphabet in order to bring deaf people more tightly into common society. Clearly, it was unrealistic to expect everyone in the country to learn the sign language. But even "a person of common understanding can very soon learn this alphabet, and it affords to all who will bestow the trifling pains which are necessary to acquire it, a ready, easy, sure and expeditious mode of conversing on all subjects with the deaf and dumb."[17]

Finally, the fourth mode of communication that instructors promoted was simply writing. Writing, according to early reports, is "habitually employed in the schoolrooms, and by it the pupils are taught the correct orthography of our language, to correspond by letters with their friends, and to derive from books the vast treasures of knowledge which they contain."[18] Instructors regarded teaching English through reading and writing as vitally important to the future of deaf students. Deaf students, they realized, would be cut off from passing conversation. They, more than others, would need access to books for crucial practical information as well as for enjoyment.

The only method not used in the school was oral training. Articulation was not taught to any deaf students in the early years of the school. An early report explained that the principal of the school and his associates had decided "not to waste their labour and that of their pupils upon this comparatively useless branch of the education of the deaf and dumb. In no case is it the source of any original knowledge. In few cases does it succeed so as to answer any valuable end."[19] In support of their decision, the school cited the published opinions of Dugald Stewart.

Very early on, a picture of the meaning of deaf education comes into focus. Deaf education was meant to bring deaf children into contact with the wider intellectual world that hearing people occupied by teaching them to read and write English. The use of sign language, in both natural and methodical modes, was considered crucial to this project. Deaf children could not be expected to learn English without the use of the sign language in the classroom.

The method used to introduce the students to English was relatively straightforward. A teacher would start with simple objects, holding up, for instance, a hat in front of the class. He would point at the hat and produce a sign for it. Getting the class to imitate the sign, they soon made the connection between the object and the sign. Once he was confident the association had been made, he would write the word "hat" on a blackboard and begin in this way to introduce the students to written English. Simple verbs, actions that could be acted out for the students, usually followed next, with adverbs and adjectives to come.

Teachers tried to draw from their students' knowledge of the sign language in order to teach them more English, each language building upon the other. New concepts were regularly introduced and discussed first in the sign language since "a great deal of knowledge is communicated to them by mere signs, long before they have acquired such a command of written language as to be able to express their own thoughts intelligibly and correctly in words."[20] In addition, students' fledgling efforts to compose their own sentences in English were not taken as indicators of the extent of their knowledge of English since "it is abundantly easier to converse in a new language, or to read it in books, than to write it correctly, as the experience of all will testify, who have studied the dead languages or who have acquired foreign ones."[21] Antebellum teachers had a clear sense that deaf students learned English in the same way that hearing children learned a second language, that is, in fits and starts, and with language comprehension frequently outstripping production.

Teachers knew the fight to bring English to their students was a difficult one. They understood that English would always be the vernacular of the hearing while the sign language would be the vernacular of the deaf. More important, they understood why this would be so. The sign language would always be preferred in the Deaf community as a "medium perfectly intelligible."

The sign language was regularly used in the school and in the classrooms. The natural language of signs was considered from the first a proper language of instruction. "By the freedom of communication which it establishes," one writer noted, "it will . . . render the pupil, in a measure, the architect of his own intellectual edifice; for it will enable him to profit by his own independent reflection. He possesses the means of interrogating his master—a means he will not fail to employ."[22]

As students progressed through the grades, they would often be expected to reply to their teachers using the methodical signs, in order to demonstrate their grasp of English and their ability to use it colloquially. At no point, however, was the natural language of signs abandoned. It was widely believed that the natural language of signs was the students' first language, the one they would use regularly with their friends and families in everyday conversation. Students were not expected to use methodical signs outside of the classroom. They were understood to be a classroom tool. Educators recognized that deaf students were native users of the sign language; what they hoped to do was add English to their linguistic repertoire.

Effective Teacher Training

Officials at the American Asylum believed that the only way teachers could be effective in the classroom was to know and use the sign language correctly. "How are the teachers of the deaf and dumb to become thus qualified?" Laurent Clerc asked, and then answered his own question. "It must be by bringing them together as well as the pupils at one institution which, from its size and numbers, will furnish the opportunities and the means necessary for this purpose."[23]

The residential schools themselves provided the crucial training ground for fledgling teachers. Such newcomers to the field were expected to learn the natural language of signs there in order to communicate effectively with students. "In the province of pantomime they are themselves the master," noted one educator, "and those who hold intercourse with them must be content to receive the instrument at their hands."[24] In some ways, prospective teachers were expected to be trained by the deaf students. Teachers were expected "to learn all their various modes of expressing their ideas by the natural signs, which [the deaf] themselves have invented."[25]

If they were to have a future in the field, hearing teachers would need to master this unfamiliar language, and they could learn it only at a school for the deaf, ideally directly from deaf people themselves. As the directors of the American Asylum explained, "This singular, living, moving, acting language . . . can only be obtained by actually witnessing it. Books cannot portray it. Even the glowing touches of the pencil can but approximate it. Nothing but the human countenance . . . can exhibit it."[26]

Clearly, Deaf students had a lot to teach and hearing teachers had a lot to learn before they could be competent in the classroom. And now, administrators coupled that advice with a more sophisticated linguistic argument about the natural language of signs. The language was understood to be of Deaf origin, with idioms and other constructions very different from those found in English. And the natural signs truly belonged to Deaf people; they were the only ones who could properly teach it.

Educators were very clear on this point.

The first essential of all instruction is . . . that a medium of reciprocal communication shall exist between the instructor and the instructed. To the former, we suppose pantomime a novel language. He is incapable of holding a connected conversation with his pupil, for he can neither understand nor make himself understood. The parties must therefore, for the time, change places. The first requisite to his own instruction must be supplied by the pupil himself. He must give the lessons and the master must become the learner.[27]

Natural signs were of Deaf origin and had to be learned from the Deaf in order to be learned well.

The Sign Language as the Native Language of the Deaf

But what did this natural language of signs look like? How was it organized? What kind of language did hearing educators believe they were learning? Early annual reports of the American Asylum offer the first clues.

> Signs and gestures, combined with the endless varieties of the expressions of the eye and countenance, is the native and favourite language of the deaf and dumb. For some time, it is the only medium of intercourse which their instructors have with them. It is the foundation of all their improvement. It is the vehicle, strange as it may seem, of almost all the information, both on human and divine subjects, which, in the early stages of their education, can be communicated to them. It is the constant interpreter of the words and phrases which they learn. It is their living dictionary, to which they, of necessity, resort in every emergency.[28]

This brief paragraph provides much insight into the early nineteenth century's understanding of the natural language of signs.

Educators, at this point in the life of the profession mostly hearing, deemed the sign language "the native language" of deaf people, in spite of the fact that most deaf children had hearing parents, themselves unfamiliar with the language. It was called "native," even though most deaf children did not grow up using a sign language. How could such an unorthodox process of language acquisition be deemed "native"? The answer may lie in a different understanding of the word itself.

The sign language was understood to be the native language of the deaf because it was native to deaf people, not necessarily as individuals but as a group, as a community. Linguistic competence and community membership went together. To the extent that hearing educators recognized this connection, the residential schools would remain places where Deaf culture could blossom and grow.

It was the native language of the deaf because it was organized along linguistic principles structured to deliver language visually to people who would use their eyes and not their ears to acquire it. All deaf people were visual people, so the sign language was, in this way, their true native language.

Finally, because it was their native language, the sign language could act as "a living dictionary." With a firm footing in their native language, students could confidently expand their linguistic competency in English. They could display their growing competence in both languages by demonstrating an ability to translate phrases and sentences from one language to the other.

The whole thrust of deaf education at the American Asylum, and its sister antebellum schools, rested on this complex understanding of the sign language. The teaching of the deaf was conceived to be identical to teaching any child a foreign language. That is, the teacher of the deaf could "give a translation, by signs, of any phrases, or sentences, or succession of sentences, into the natural language of the pupil, or receive his translation of the same, as the evidence of his understanding their import."[29] This emphasis on bilingual education was the reason why the success of a teacher rested on his or her ability to use the sign language well.

The asylum's directors hoped that their system of manual education, together with the practice of on-site teacher training, would spread to schools across the country; recall that they commented, "it is desirable that a uniform system should prevail, that the Deaf and Dumb, who form in some measure a distinct community, should have a common language."[30]

That common language was to be the sign language. They announced that their intent was "to elevate to as high a degree of excellence as possible the natural language of signs employed by the Deaf and Dumb, so as to make this language itself a complete medium of communication between the instructor and the pupil on all subjects."

Significantly, as we have seen, this wish to "elevate" the language did not mean a desire to turn it into English. Instructors were talking about the sign language here, not methodical signs. These comments, then, can only mean exactly what they say: a desire to see the sign language nationalized, its structures regularized and codified, and its vocabulary ever expanded to make it in itself a "complete medium of communication." Linguistic competence in both ASL and English was the goal of deaf education in the early nineteenth century, with the understanding that such competencies would not just promote language learning but build the Deaf community.

The New York Difference

Other schools for the deaf participated in this community building as well. The New York Institution was founded a year after the American Asylum, but it remained in a very unorganized state until 1830, when one of the American Asylum's premier teachers, Harvey Prindle Peet, took over as superintendent. Additionally, two new teachers were hired in 1830: Leon Vayesse, a hearing man who had been a teacher at the school for the deaf at Paris, and John Burnet, a Deaf man.[31] The changes in the school's staff quickly resulted in changes in its pedagogy and philosophy.

The goal of deaf education, as understood by the officials at the New York school, was to "put it in the power of every deaf mute in the State to obtain the education necessary to render him a useful member of society."[32] The question was what method of education would be most likely to guarantee this outcome. Educators took this question seriously and complained in New York of the perceived lack of a "well defined system."[33] By 1833, the New York school had decided on a new course. It published its reasoning in its annual report of that year. Soon, even the American Asylum would decide to follow New York's lead.

The bold new plan? The New York school had decided to break with the French method. "As an instrument of instruction," the directors announced, "methodical signs have been abandoned in the New York Institution."[34] The school had already adopted in its place a bilingual approach to deaf education; this "important change . . . has been gradually introduced within the past few years," the directors acknowledged. Here, they were announcing publicly that this transition to bilingual education had "been finally consummated."[35] The colloquial language of signs and the manual alphabet were the only signed systems in use in their classrooms. Both were used to teach English, which appeared in the classroom frequently in a written form. The officials of the New York school sought to make the reasons for this move clear. The school's 1833 report dwelled at length on the topic of methodical signs and laid out the case for their abandonment.

Like teachers at the American Asylum, officials at the New York school saw a new language emerging before them. They too believed that the deaf students arrived at school with their own idiosyncratic natural signs. These signs, from many different students, essentially underwent a process of creolization or, as nineteenth-century observers understood it, "[a student] meets many who, in like manner, have constituted their individual languages, but who by common consent, abandon them for the more copious dialect which results from the combination of the whole." This new combination of signs formed a language, one that soon constituted the "most valuable means" of communication available for students and teachers. In addition, "this language, like every other, so far as the dictionary of its signs extends, admits of direct translation." Concepts and sentences could be translated from the natural language of signs into English and back again. This native language of the students was therefore invaluable in the classroom.[36]

Methodical signs, however, had a completely different origin. They were not native to the student at all but were "presented to him only after his arrival at the institution."[37] That is, methodical signs were an invention of hearing educators; they did not arise from the interaction of deaf students themselves. As a result, they had to be formally taught. That would not seem, at first glance, like a reason to abandon them, but educators at the New York Institution argued that indeed it was.

Methodical signs were meant to introduce students to English. Educators now perceived that "however closely they may imitate the grammatical forms of written languages, they present these forms in a garb no more intelligible to the learner than the alphabetic characters themselves."[38] By using them, deaf students were forced to learn both the unfamiliar methodical signs and the English words and concepts they were supposedly presenting. Why, officials at the New York school finally asked themselves, do we not simply teach the students English directly?

In addition, since these signs were an invention that had to be formally taught, rather than an addition to the language of signs that sprang from the students themselves, they never became used colloquially by the students. "The name of a language," the New York teachers observed, "is therefore inapplicable to them since they do not possess the character of a medium of communication."[39] If the goal of deaf education was to teach the students language, they were not being well served by methodical signs.

In the end, educators decided, methodical signs did not even serve their stated purpose, which was to translate English into a signed form, a guise in which deaf students would supposedly find English more accessible. Methodical signs could not even be said to "admit of translation" for to say so was

a perversion of the term, if translation be understood in its widest and most important meaning. . . . To translate really is to enunciate the complete sense contained under a given combination of signs, by means of another combination made up of signs entirely different. When a school boy, by help of his dictionary, renders for each word of a Latin sentence a corresponding English word, without regard to the signification of his author, we do not think of dignifying his performance with the title of translation.[40]

In the same way, methodical signs did not, in fact, translate English. Instead of using them, the officials at the New York Institution argued, deaf students should be pressed to translate English directly into the natural language of signs in order to demonstrate that they have truly understood the meaning of the English words. They should also translate the natural language of signs into English in order to gain competence in both languages.

New York school administrators concluded that methodical signs ultimately added nothing to the project of language learning. The whole system of methodical signs had "become unwieldy in its material, and burdensome in its use, retarding the labor of the instructor and seriously impeding the progress of the pupil."[41] Instead, the instructors would rely upon "the language of action"[42] or "colloquial signs."[43] The addition of the description "colloquial" is significant. Methodical signs had been again and again rejected for colloquial use; an important objection leveled against them was the very fact that they were "never used in the daily intercourse of the deaf and dumb."[44]

Now, educators saw these methodical signs with new eyes, as "artificial and arbitrary signs."[45] They were "artificial" because they were hearing inventions, not springing from the deaf community, not originating naturally in a community of language users. These artificial creations were simply no longer needed in the classrooms of the New York Institution, especially when a natural sign language, a language as natural as English, was readily available for teachers to use with their deaf students. The choice in New York, as the administration there understood it, was to "adopt the colloquial sign language of the deaf and dumb" or to "affix a definite sign to every word in spoken language." The choice for colloquial signs was clear.

A year later, the school reported its satisfaction with its decision.

And the board feel happy in being able to state that the results of the instruction communicated since the change took place, have been such as abundantly to satisfy their highest expectations. They are convinced that the employment of the signs used by the deaf and dumb themselves, as a means of explaining and dictating words and sentences is as much superior, in fact, to the use of artificial signs invented by the teacher, as it is more plausible and philosophical in theory.[46]

Such satisfaction and success soon convinced other schools to follow New York's example. The American Asylum too dropped methodical signs from its curriculum. As the decade of the 1840s opened, most schools for the deaf in the United States were moving to drop methodical signs and to teach by using the natural language of signs alone in the classroom.

The New York school concluded,

> Thought and language, then, are essential to each other's existence, and must advance together, hand in hand. Let either be isolated . . . and it is feeble and well nigh powerless. But unite it to its natural ally, and it instantly becomes progressive in character and mighty in results. A child who has no language must necessarily possess but few ideas. A child who is acquainted with words and sentences merely, and neither thinks nor knows what they mean, is no better than a parrot. He alone can truly be said to possess a knowledge of language whose stock of ideas and means of expressing them are respectively parallel and equivalent to each other.[47]

They believed that their new pedagogy, employing the colloquial language of the deaf, would provide a superior education for deaf students.

Teachers offered their support for this new pedagogy. As John Burnet described it, the New York School now stands for "the rejection of methodic signs, that is to say, of all signs which are not colloquial among the pupils, which do not represent ideas but words, and which are not the work of the deaf and dumb themselves, but devised by the teacher to render the language of signs parallel to that of speech."[48]

F. A. P. Barnard agreed. Barnard, who would later become the president of Columbia University, spent his early years in education as a teacher of the deaf, first at the American School for the Deaf and later at New York. His progressive deafness, which increased while he was a student at Yale, was probably an aid to his quickness in picking up the sign language. Barnard was also a keen observer of the sign language and of pedagogy. He welcomed the departure of methodical signs from the classroom and in fact taught at the New York School during this time of transition; he worked there from 1832 to 1838. The whole trouble with the methodical method, as he saw it, was that it forced the teachers to spend more time explaining the meaning of these unfamiliar signs, instead of using that time to explain words. Barnard complained that the methodic sign system presented the deaf student "with a set of unintelligible elements, arranged in an unintelligible order." Barnard did not mince words: "Truly the system of methodical signs is an unwieldy . . . machine, and a dead weight upon the system of instruction in which it is recognized." Such signs "remain without a plausible excuse for their continued existence"; he trusted that they would disappear entirely "with the next generation."[49]

Linguistic Choices and Cultural Consequences

Antebellum educators understood that making the natural language of signs the language of instruction in residential schools would enable the Deaf community to grow. They did nothing to interfere with the growth of this community or with the development of Deaf culture. Instead, they declared that deaf people could attain social equality with hearing people precisely through the pursuit of bilingual education. Bilingual education would enable the deaf to learn English, the language they would need in order to enter the social mainstream. To learn English, Deaf people did not have to give up the natural language of signs at all. Rather, the cultivation of their own deaf language was itself the key to learning the language of the hearing. And, in keeping with the burgeoning sense of equity between the groups, hearing people had to do precisely the same; they had to learn first the language of the deaf in order to introduce to them the language of the hearing.

These linguistic issues were not simply pedagogical considerations for educators. The linguistic theories of antebellum educators shaped their reaction to the prospective Deafness of their students, as well as their self-understanding of their profession and its meaning. Through the development of their understanding of the nature of the sign language, antebellum educators came to believe that their students did not have to abandon their Deafness and become culturally hearing. Rather, they could become Deaf while also coming to take their place as citizens, as American; Deaf people could be bilingual and bicultural; they could be Deaf Americans. Educators would use the colloquial language of signs themselves to make possible this transformation from isolated deaf individuals into members of a Deaf community.

By setting deaf education on this path, and doing so with an understanding of what that meant pedagogically, linguistically, and culturally, the American system of manual deaf education broke decisively with its French roots in 1833. It brought bilingual-bicultural education to deaf Americans for the first time. It also made the burgeoning deaf community and the school system allies, and not adversaries, in the birth of Deaf culture in the United States.

Some outside observers of deaf education responded positively to this situation. N. Southward, the editor of a juvenile religious magazine, *Youth's Cabinet*, described his visit to the American Asylum in 1840. He told his readers that here a deaf child will "acquire a knowledge of Arithmetic, Geography, Grammar, History, &c., and will become so familiar with language that he can read and understand the Scriptures." He stated that all of this learning was done through the medium of the sign language, and explained that a teacher would offer a lesson in signs and the students were then asked to offer English translations of the teacher's lessons on their slates. "I was much pleased with this mode of giving instruction," Southward wrote, "and with the interest the scholars manifested in it."

In particular, he told his readers, his attention was drawn to "one little red-haired boy. . . . He was about 13 years old, and was the smallest boy in the room; but he seemed the most eager to get instruction and the quickest to learn." But it is Southward's depiction of him that draws the attention of modern eyes: "He may yet exert an influence over millions who can hear and speak."[50] Deaf education would, it seems, offer boundless opportunities to deaf children, well beyond the borders of the Deaf world. Not only would this education prove individually beneficial, enabling the deaf child, as Southward put it, "to live happy and useful as a farmer or a mechanic."[51] It would also enable the deaf child to take his or her rightful place in the American community, and perhaps that rightful place would be one of great leadership, even leadership and influence over hearing people.

Admittedly, praising the education of the handicapped was a common trope in juvenile literature in the antebellum period. As historian John Crandall reminds us, the celebration of the nation's humanitarian efforts on behalf of the disabled was "unequivocal" in nearly all juvenile literature of the period. Institutions like the American Asylum were regularly singled out for praise. The work of such schools was promoted to young people with regularity to inspire the pride of budding patriots.[52] Still, Southward went further than most. He not only strongly approved of the project of deaf education, but he implied that through such education, the deaf could attain social equality with the hearing.

And this red-headed boy himself? How did he and his peers perceive their education, their community, and their life options? For those answers, we need to journey into the residential schools and investigate the world they were creating from the Deaf point of view.

Learning to Be Deaf

Lessons from the Residential School

But when anybody tells me that he is sorry because I am a deaf and dumb boy, I am not so sorry, because I think that I am as smart as a speaking boy.

—Herman Erbe, 1870

Nineteenth-century educators watched as deafness was transformed into Deafness before their eyes in residential schools for the deaf. Most of them witnessed this metamorphosis with hearing eyes. How did deaf people understand both their deafness and their Deafness? What did the emerging world of Deaf culture look like from within?

The annual reports of various schools for the deaf offer a tantalizing glimpse into this fledgling culture. In the nineteenth century, such annual reports regularly included samples of students' writings. These samples, including letters home, school assignments, student essays, and valedictory addresses, provide insight into Deaf culture from the very places it first emerged and from the people who brought it into being.

That being said, a few caveats about this material are in order. First, school officials, typically the principal, selected the writing samples that would be included in each report. This obviously means that they had tremendous incentive to pick samples that would portray their schools in the best possible light, favoring those sure to demonstrate both the academic success and the progress of their students. However, school officials in fact pointedly left the samples uncorrected and many examples include ungrammatical English sentences. The samples, in other words, are not suspiciously perfect. Officials selected a wide range of students' works, publishing samples from students of various grade levels, ages, and competencies. The samples could still be construed as being the work strictly of bright young Deaf elites, but of course *any* educated deaf person could be considered elite in this period, as it is estimated that only half of all school-age deaf Americans attended residential schools in the nineteenth century.[1]

Second, while officials might select what they considered the best samples, the students still provided the content themselves. They were asked to describe what their lives were like before they came to school, or to discuss their perception of the condition of deafness. It is likely that school officials did not choose to publish every student's answer to those questions. Yet, even though this is a selected pool of answers to open-ended questions, it nonetheless offers a valuable window into the world of deafness, as nineteenth-century students understood it.

Third, most, though not all, of the samples offered here are from students from the American School for the Deaf. From 1817 to 1877, some twenty-one hundred students came to Hartford from twenty-four states, the District of Columbia, and Canada. By looking most closely at the American School for the Deaf, we gain access to a cross-section of the deaf population from around the nation.

Fourth, the schools included more or less information about the composer of each piece as the century wore on. Some schools began the practice by keeping the identity of the students anonymous; later, some included the writer's initials and some personal information, such as the age when the student became deaf. I have noted as much information as I possess on any particular sample.[2]

What follows is an introduction to life in the residential schools from the point of view of the students themselves. Here, deaf people emerge into their own history, in their own words. Here, we see the ways that deaf people thought about their lives, their deafness, their emerging sense of Deaf identity, and their education.

Arriving at School

In 1817, I arrived at the Asylum which was in Hartford. I was much astonished to see many the deaf and dumb, who were lively to talk by signs which I could not understand. They were very cheerful and happy to live there and were very active to learn their lessons. . . . My sisters and I were conducted to examine the chambers and rooms, which were very neat and clean. We visited each of the classes and we were much interested in seeing them. While Mr. G taught them by signs I could not understand them, but I wondered that they could understand them very fast. O! I did not know how to make them and I was in great confusion in studying about things.

I thought I should never improve very well. . . . I said that I would not live with the deaf and dumb because I was a stranger and disliked to live there for several years. I was melancholy to stay with them. . . . My father said that I should stay with the deaf and dumb the next day and he would to be separated from me. I felt very sorry and was homesick. The girls were happy to talk with me about the news by signs. In a few weeks, I was willing to live there and I became well acquainted with them. . . . Mr. W.C.W. would soon teach me by signs. I attended to acquire them.[3]

Arriving at school was a significant event for most students. Most could recall their emotions, their excitement, even their trepidation, clearly. Some could even remember the exact date, acknowledging the importance of the event, as this was the day when their lives changed. This was a turning point, they knew, and most students could sharply distinguish two distinct time periods in their lives, the years before they went to school and the years after. Where a single arrival story is just one person's memory, a group of such recollections tells the story of the birth of a community.

Nancy Dillingham recalled in 1824, "I was born deaf and dumb in Lee [Massachusetts]. . . . I supposed that my deaf and dumb sister and I were the only deaf and dumb in this world, and that all could hear and speak."[4] Harriet Knapp recounted a similar misconception. "When at home," she remembered in 1847, "I thought I was the only deaf and dumb girl in the world, before I had seen any other one."[5] And in 1854, Ellen A. Richardson wrote, "When I was an ignorant girl, I often thought that my two sisters and one brother and I were the only deaf and dumb in the earth, but at last I found many deaf and dumb persons in the United States and other places. How ignorant!!!"[6]

The story of discovery is strikingly consistent across the years. Many young deaf people, throughout the antebellum period, grew up mistakenly believing that they were the only deaf person on earth. It is no wonder that, unacquainted with any deaf adults, living in hearing families, surrounded by hearing and speaking people, they each believed themselves alone. It is estimated that, in the nineteenth century, one American out of every 5,728 was born deaf.[7] This fact would account for the isolation most American deaf children felt in their largely hearing homes and communities. Coming to school changed all of that.

The residential school created a community that many students immediately recognized as their own. As Fisher Spofford wrote in 1824, "I sadly thought that I was the only deaf and dumb person in the world. . . . I went to the Asylum and was much surprised at seeing so numerous deaf and dumb and was very glad that I was as deaf and dumb as them."[8] The happy discovery of a shared deafness is what would eventually create cultural Deafness in these residential schools. Cultural Deafness was grounded in the physiology of deafness. That is, without deafness, there would be no Deafness. The one gave birth to the other, in the residential school setting. Indeed, the one was a precondition of the other. As deaf people found each other, they would bond together and celebrate their difference, transforming it along the way into Deafness, an identity they would claim with pride. For many a deaf student, coming to school was indeed to find that he or she was, as Thomas Hopkins Gallaudet put it, "among his countrymen."[9]

For some students, the American Asylum represented their first educational experience. But other deaf students recalled the frustrations of attending the common school before finally arriving at the school for the deaf. Nancy Dillingham recounted her early years in the following way. She remembered, "I did nothing at home but play," and her parents wanted more than that for her. Her father was especially keen to have her learn to write, and he finally insisted that she attend the local common school.

Here, however, her situation did not much improve. She wrote dismissively of her common school experience, "The school house at which I did nothing, but I looked." The teacher looked at her "with pity," Nancy thought, "on account of my deafness and dumbness," but managed finally to teach her how to knit. Though her mother reportedly admired this newfound skill, her parents were nonetheless disappointed that she had not made any academic progress.

They enlisted her hearing brother and cousin, who both attended the school, to help her in class. Her hearing cousin, Lucy, helped Nancy practice writing the letters of the alphabet, but she remained unhappy at the school, convinced that the other "scholars were looking at me while I wrote on a desk." She was probably correct to think so. As literary scholar Rosemarie Garland Thomson reminds us, "[Be]ing looked at is one of the universal social experiences of being disabled."[10]

Nancy's complaint at being so singled out by her classmates' stares gives us a rare historical glimpse into what Thomson theorizes is a significant part of the process by which disability is and has been culturally constructed. She writes,

> Staring is the social relationship that constitutes disability identity and gives meaning to impairment by marking it as aberrant. . . . The staring dynamic constitutes the starer as normal and the object of the stare as dif-

ferent. The exchange between starer and object witnesses both the ano-
nymity that confers agency on the starer and the singularity that stigma-
tizes the one who is stared at. In this context, then, staring is the ritual
enactment of exclusion from an imagined community of the fully human.[11]

Nancy clearly sensed her exclusion in the face of the stares of her hearing
peers. Even as she tried to observe the same classroom norms as her hearing peers, their stares marked her as different. Given her unhappiness at the
common school, Nancy must have been delighted to discover that her father
had read in the local paper of the opening of a new school dedicated to the
education of deaf children and that he planned to send his deaf daughters
there. He first sent Nancy's deaf sister, Abigail, who left, Nancy recalled, on
April 6, 1817. Nancy herself followed soon after. "My brother accompanied
me to the Asylum on the 18th of October 1819, when I was about eighteen
years old."[12]

While Nancy's father learned of the existence of a school for the deaf
through the medium of the newspaper, as the century wore on, others
learned through the example of those who had gone before. In 1859, William D. Hickok recalled that his parent met a deaf man at church, most likely
James Austin. Austin explained to them that he had attended the American
Asylum. "He was very smart and intelligent," Hickok remembered. "My parents thought that I had better go to school in Hartford to write and read."[13]

He needed to go to Hartford because, as the Dillinghams had discovered,
most local school teachers were not prepared to teach a deaf child. They did
not know how to accomplish the difficult task of introducing a deaf student
to written English. Several nineteenth-century deaf students chronicled their
frustrating experiences at the common school. Charles Augur, a young man
born deaf in a hearing family in Milford, Connecticut, described his life
before he came to the American School in 1846. Like Nancy Dillingham, he
had attended a local school; like her, he had found it disappointing. Though
nearly thirty years separate their experiences, they remain remarkably
consistent.

Previous to my connection with the American Asylum for the deaf and
dumb as a pupil, I was in a state of ignorance and unhappiness. During
my early childhood, I could be taught by neither my parents nor my relatives how to learn to read, on account of my deafness. Another reason was
that they were not acquainted with the language of signs. . . . At the age
of five years, I was put in a school, not distant from my father's residence

and took lessons in penmanship; however I could not understand the sentences which I copied. . . . After having left school, I was put under the instruction of a lady . . . to take lessons in drawing. . . . I had a natural taste for drawing but I had a passionate desire to be taught the construction of the English language.

What emerges here is an explanation for the failure of the local school to provide him with an education, as Charles interpreted it. While he acknowledged that his deafness played a role in this failure, he insisted that it was not the cause of it. It was not because he was deaf that he was unable to read. The true obstacle was his community's lack of familiarity with the sign language. He would be able to read, deafness or no, if only the people around him knew how to teach him.

However, once a teacher decided it was not possible to teach written language to a deaf pupil, another task was substituted. In Nancy's case, knitting seemed easier to teach, and in Charles's case, drawing was offered up. He clearly viewed this as a poor substitution.

In desperation, at home, Charles resorted to trying to teach himself to read.

One evening I took a newspaper and tried to read it in imitation of my father, but I could not understand a word. So I asked my father to make signs for the word "the," but he did not know how. Some evenings my parents, brothers, and sisters sat in a circle and spent much time enjoying themselves in agreeable conversations, while I was sitting out of the circle with my eyes fixed upon them, thinking of their intelligence and my ignorance. I sometimes felt so envious of their lives of light as nearly to burst into tears.

Whether or not Charles was literally sitting out of the circle, he, like so many other deaf children, felt like an outsider in his own family.

Given that he had endured so much frustration, it comes as no surprise to learn that, like Nancy, Charles recalled exactly when he was finally able to receive the education he so desperately wanted. "At the age of ten years my father received a letter from Mr. Weld in respect to my future education at the Asylum," he wrote. "On the 12th day of May 1846, I set out for Hartford with my father and when we got there, we found the Asylum for the deaf and dumb pleasantly situated."[14]

There, he would meet his classmate, Charles Steere, who came to Hartford from Gloucester, Rhode Island. Unlike Charles Augur, Charles Steere had lost his hearing due to childhood illness when he was six years old. Yet he too remembered being just as isolated in his hearing family. He referred to his childhood as a time of darkness, and he begged his family to send him to school, because he wanted to learn "to read as well as my parents could." But his family informed him that this was impossible. "They answered and told me that no one could teach me how to read," he wrote. "Then I wept fast and asked them why I could not read as well as they could. They replied, because I could not hear. I asked why I could not hear as well as when I was a little boy. Because it is mysterious." When the family learned of the existence of the American School, they made plans to send their son, who "was exceedingly glad and I desired them to hurry and prepare for me to go there. . . ." Arriving at Hartford before the start of the school year, Steere waited impatiently. "When two days had passed away, the school began and I was glad of it because I wished to learn fast before I became a man."[15]

Surprisingly, his story shares much in common with those of the other deaf children discussed here, despite the fact that Steere had not lost his hearing until he was six years old, while many of the others were born deaf. In spite of his added years of experience with spoken English, his family apparently still felt ill equipped to teach him to read, much like the parents of the congenitally deaf children. Steere's parents also seemed to believe it was impossible for him to learn to read on account of his deafness. When he lost his hearing, his parents apparently viewed him as leaving behind the language of the hearing. Unfortunately, there is not enough information from the parents' point of view to fully examine how they interpreted the meaning of their son's deafness. If Steere's account is accurate, their belief that his deafness was an absolute barrier to English is striking, and it points to the difficulty the deaf population faced in laying claim to English, perceived exclusively as a spoken and a hearing language.

This sense of isolation, of apartness from the rest of the world, ran through students' recollections. It reveals more than their individual discomfort. As Thomson reminds us, there was a larger cultural process at work here. "[D]isability is a culturally fabricated narrative of the body," she writes. "Disability, then, is a system that produces subjects by differentiating and marking bodies."[16] In knowing some bodies as "deaf," others come to know themselves as "hearing" and accordingly as superior to the perceived defective, deviant, disabled body.

Very rarely, some nineteenth-century deaf observers wrote about their perceptions of the power relations at work in the dynamic relationship between deaf and hearing bodies. John T. Southwick, the valedictorian for the New York School in 1847, invoked in his valedictory address the deaf experience of growing up among hearing people. "[The deaf] are often despised," he wrote, "especially by their parents, who feel sorry, and some-times despair of having them get learning." He continued,

> Having done nothing to displease their parents, nor committed any crime, yet they are in cases, miserably shut out from the presence of other people, so as to deprive them of knowledge and in their mental darkness seem idiotic. This, some parents do in a most cruel manner, and appear like the savages, thrusting their pitiless daggers through the bosoms of little inno-cent children crying out for mercy.[17]

He vividly described the isolation of being a deaf child in a hearing family, but this time with a twist. In a graphic departure from most deaf writers, Southwick blamed the hearing parents directly for allowing this isolation to persist. Whereas most writers, like Charles Augur, blamed the combination of their deafness and their parents' understandable ignorance of the sign lan-guage, Southwick seemed to think that hearing parents themselves were at the heart of the problem.

Southwick's argument, that hearing parents secretly despise their chil-dren for their disability, may seem shocking. But there are hints that other nineteenth-century deaf people shared Southwick's assessment. For instance, P. F. Confer, a deaf man from Indiana, argued in 1858 that living largely scat-tered among a hearing population made the deaf cultural targets of sorts, "despised by hearing men," as he put it.[18] It also seems telling that Southwick chose his words for a valedictory address. It would seem to indicate that he believed they would find a receptive, rather than hostile, audience.

Southwick's comments were shaped by the common deaf experience of growing up deaf in a hearing family, for in the nineteenth century, most deaf children had hearing parents. Even today, most deaf children, an estimated 90 percent, are born to hearing parents. That leaves a small minority who are born into deaf households. They have a quite different experience of growing up.

Evidence of their passage in the historical record is difficult to find, yet glimpses emerge, like the one offered here from Paulina N. Marsh, a student at the American Asylum, in 1858. She came from a deaf family; both of her parents, her brother, and her sister were deaf. Her story about growing up is one of inclusion and communication. She remembered a childhood incident, in which she disobeyed her mother, ran off with her playmates, and suffered a minor injury. When her father arrived home, it fell to him to make sure that his daughter understood the lesson of this event. Paulina recalled, "My father came into the house & saw me, & asked me what was the matter. I answered. . . . My father was very sorry. He advised me not to disobey my mother because she was wiser than I."[19] This is a thoroughly typical childhood story, and nothing in it speaks to Paulina's difference as a deaf girl at all. Its very ordinariness is what makes it different. She, and a handful of others like her, experienced quite a different childhood than that of most of their deaf peers.

And some of those from hearing families did not find themselves as isolated in those settings as John Southwick feared. Many clearly had strong bonds with the hearing members of their family and worried that those bonds would snap under the pressure of the long-distance relationship that boarding school life imposed upon them. For some deaf students, such separation was not easy and they clearly worried that their families were forgetting about them. As a girl of thirteen wrote home to her parents in April 1843, "My dear parents—I wish to write a letter to you. . . . I have not forgotten my brothers and little sister Helen. I try to improve in learning my lessons every evening. I wish you would write a letter to me about the news."[20] Another young woman complained in a letter home in 1842, "I often think about my parents, brother and sisters, but I do not hear from you longly. You often find letters from me. I wish you would write now a long letter to me."[21] Another expressed confusion at the silence of her sibling: "My Dear Brother. I am very happy to write a letter and send it to you. I have not heard from you for a long time. . . . Why have you not written a letter to me for a long time? . . . I wish you would write a long letter to me soon."[22]

Most nineteenth-century student writing suggests that students were excited to receive the opportunity to attend school. John E. Crane remembered that he was working on his family's farm in Maine when "one day I was informed of there being an Institution in Hartford for the Deaf and Dumb, and it made the blood run through my veins to think of it, for I desired very much to get an education."[23] This is not surprising. Most deaf children were keen observers of their surroundings. They saw that the people around them could generally read, which, given the rising literacy rate in the antebellum period, meant they could perceive in some way their outsider status in an increasingly literate society. They could see that other children, perhaps their own hearing siblings, went to school. Many of them also tried going to school, but found no one there who could or would teach them. They could see the rest of the hearing members of their family communicating easily, while they were excluded from everyday conversations. Many understandably took that exclusion quite hard, as the tears of Charles Augur and others would testify.

Attending school promised to change all of this. There, the students would find each other, coming out of the isolation of hearing families and into a new community. There, they would not be left out of conversations anymore and their questions would get answers. There, they would learn to read English and be rid of their "ignorance," as many of them put it. And all of this would happen through the medium of the sign language.

Seeing the Sign Language

I arrived here on the first day of February 1868 safe and sound, but when I was out among the pupils, I thought myself better off at home, for I could not understand one word they said. It seemed very curious to see them express their ideas to each other by the action of the hand called signs. They made their hands fly about their head in such a manner that I thought they were fighting mosquitoes, but I soon got acquainted with the sign language, and in looking back to the day on which I entered school, I perceive that I have made great improvement.[24]

As John Crane's surprise above would indicate, most of the students who arrived at the residential schools in the antebellum period did not know the sign language and had in fact never seen it before. When George arrived at the Pennsylvania School for the Deaf, he was taken to the school's chapel to see a lecture. As he remembered, "[M]r. —— was lecturing to the pupils. I was much surprised to see him making signs instead of speaking."[25] While most deaf children certainly had home sign systems, idiosyncratic gestures they used to communicate basic needs to their hearing parents, like George, they had never seen a signed language used to communicate in the same way that hearing people used spoken language. It must have been an astonishing sight for most of them.

Other students, of course, did arrive with more elaborate communication systems and were accustomed to the idea that gestures could be used to carry on conversations. Deaf siblings Nancy and Abigail Dillingham signed with each other. As Nancy said, "My d&d sister talked with me often about things."[26] Still, their code, like others that were surely created by deaf siblings, was intelligible only to themselves. It was not recognizable by deaf people outside the family. At the residential school, the students would learn a common language, what the nineteenth century called simply "the sign language," and most learned it before they learned English.

One group of students at the American School, however, did arrive with a signed language all their own. They came from Martha's Vineyard, for there, one out of every 155 residents was deaf. Nora Ellen Groce has identified "at least seventy-two deaf persons born to Island families over the course of three centuries. At least a dozen more were born to descendants of Vine-yarders who had moved off-Island."[27] The Vineyard was the single largest source of schoolchildren at the American Asylum in its early years. The first students from the Vineyard, Lovey Mayhew, Mary Smith, and Sally Smith, arrived together in 1825. Seventeen more would follow them in the years before the Civil War.

These students came to the American Asylum from the only place in the country where deaf and hearing people were apparently on equal social foot-ing. Groce reports that the island deaf were fully integrated into island life.[28] They were as evenly distributed as their hearing peers across the socioeco-nomic scale. They took on the same occupations as hearing people. They participated in island politics; all adult deaf men were allowed to vote and to serve in the local militia. Several were regularly elected to various town offices. They married at an equal rate with their hearing peers and were as likely to marry a hearing person as a deaf one.[29] After the American Asylum opened, deaf islanders were among the best educated people on the island; the state funded their schooling, and so most completed a full course of study, whereas many hearing children left school early to go to sea to help their families.

As much as the asylum gave to the Vineyard deaf, they offered just as much in return to the culture of the fledgling school. These students came from a place where deafness was common and perfectly unremarkable, a place quite different from the mainland, with its largely negative attitudes toward deaf-ness. These students therefore wore their deafness lightly. How lightly is dem-onstrated in the student writing samples. Of those I have been able to identify as having been authored by a student from the Vineyard, none has the narra-tive quality of the other students. None of the Vineyard students wrote about their lives before coming to the asylum in terms of their isolation or loneliness. When asked to write a narrative about their lives before coming to school, the Vineyard students produced stories about life on Martha's Vineyard, stories that could have been written by any child who grew up on the island. Many wrote about interacting with the Native American population there. Others wrote about the African American fishermen they knew. Some wrote of the fishing industry, and outlined the process of drying cod.[30]

While other students put their deafness at the heart of their life stories, frequently lamenting the way their deafness ostracized them within their hearing families and interfered with their efforts to get an education at the common school, for the Vineyard students, deafness makes virtually no appearance in their reflections, beyond an occasional reference to signing with their families. In most places in nineteenth-century America, deafness mattered a great deal. But this was not true on the Vineyard, and the students' essays reflect that fact. These Vineyard students therefore offered to the others a very different attitude about deafness.

It is hard to know precisely what the impact of their example meant to the other students. Not only had most of the other deaf students never met another deaf person; they had certainly never met any so nonchalant about being deaf, so comfortable in their own skin. It has recently been argued, given the way that deaf and hearing lives were so intertwined on the Island, "that [the Vineyard] Deaf person may not feel like a crucial link in the chain of Deaf heritage."[31] The Vineyard Deaf, it can be argued, lacked class consciousness and wore their deafness so lightly that they did not even perceive their deafness as being of particular cultural importance. As Harlan Lane, Richard Pillard, and Mary French write, "What we are suggesting is that it takes a 'them' for an 'us' to develop, and the blending of hearing and Deaf lives on the Vineyard, because of shared family life and language (underpinned by genetics), discouraged the construction of hearing people as 'them.'"[32]

While that argument is persuasive for explaining the culture of the island, it remains the case that when these students left the island for the residential school, a quite different environment, they encountered other deaf people who had very different experiences of deafness. For those deaf people from the mainland, deafness had indeed separated an "us" from a "them." It would have been a revelation for most of the deaf students from the mainland to discover that this did not have to be the case. Here, the Vineyard deaf would have been cultural leaders, offering a powerfully different example of another way of being deaf.

Most importantly, the Vineyard students came from a place where signing was as natural as speaking. Unlike the other students, the Vineyard deaf brought a signed language with them, Martha's Vineyard Sign Language. The language is most likely linguistically related to a signed language used in County Kent, England, where most of the original settlers on the Vineyard came from.[33] This was the language that Groce argues all the Vineyarders, deaf and hearing alike, knew and used daily. The Vineyard deaf, in all likelihood, were the only deaf Americans to arrive at the school with a *language*, not merely a gesture system.[34] Bringing that language to the American Asylum, the Vineyard students contributed to the creation of American Sign Language. The Martha's Vineyard Sign Language came into contact with the French Sign Language brought to the school by Laurent Clerc. In turn, these two languages encountered the various gestural systems and home signs of the other deaf students. Out of all of this contact was eventually born what the nineteenth century would call simply "the sign language" and what the twentieth century would come to know as American Sign Language.[35]

But how did most of the students learn this sign language? Teachers at the various residential schools insisted that they did not formally teach the sign language to their students. Rather, they said, they used the sign language to teach the students English and other subjects. The students learned the sign language from one another. In some cases, it would seem that this was a formal process. As Abigail Dillingham, a member of the inaugural class at the American School, wrote to a friend in 1818, "I wish to stay here. I like the Asylum very much. . . . I am very happy with all my friends the deaf and dumb. Every noon I am teacher and make signs to my two pupils."[36] Most frequently, however, students seem to have picked up the language simply by being at school, surrounded by signing people. For some, this was a very easy process. As Eliza Morrison assured her cousin Robert in 1820, "I am very happy to talk with the deaf and dumb because we understand each other by signs. It is very easy to learn signs."[37]

Such assurances aside, it did not prove easy for all. Charlotte Conklin in 1850 wrote that, when she arrived at the New York Institution, the teacher, Jacob Van Nostrand, "made signs" to her. "I did not understand his signs," she wrote, "but I soon learn them. I tried to make signs and I tried to learn to read and write and make signs and improve."[38] William Hickok recalled that when he entered the American School in 1855, "I saw them making signs with their arms. I could not understand them. . . . I began to study my lessons in Mr. W's class. He taught me how to spell with my fingers and I was happy with him but I could not understand his signs. But after a few months I could understand them. Now I am happy to study and improve."[39]

While deaf people recognized the importance of learning English and strove to become literate, they clearly regarded it as a second language. Overwhelmingly, deaf people preferred the sign language to English—as did this student, who, when asked directly, "Which do you consider preferable, the language of speech or of signs?" responded forthrightly, "I consider to prefer the language of signs best of it because the language of signs is capable to give me elucidation and understanding well."[40]

The movements of hands proved more easily understandable to deaf eyes than the elusive movements of lips. And the use of the sign language built up the deaf community out of students who arrived at school as strangers to each other. Signs are not easily captured on paper, but still students attempted to describe their signed language in print for hearing readers. George Loring offered the following description of the language of signs in 1822.

> The language of signs is the action of some members of the body, with the arms; and the expressions of the face or the counterfeit of the feelings. This language is generally accompanied with the expressions of the face or the counterfeit of the feelings. . . . The expressions of the real or counterfeit feelings are indispensable to the language of signs. If the expression of a real or false feeling were not used with the sign of a feeling, the sign would be vague. The signs generally resemble what is seen in the mind. The signs, when used in conversation, have but few arrangements, but words must be in arrangement. The gestures are very easy to use in conversation and are quicker than writing. I believe that speaking is quicker than they. These actions must be clear and should be used according to the proceedings of the circumstances. The language of signs belong to the deaf and dumb; and some persons who can hear and speak converse by signs. The deaf and dumb understand the words through the signs which a person makes to express the words.[41]

This description underscores the beliefs that guided manual education. First, while the grammars of sign and English are different, both have grammatical rules. For sign, an important one is the role of facial expression; even in 1822, it was understood as carrying meaning in a signed conversation. Second, though hearing people may converse by signs, the language of signs "belong[s] to the deaf and dumb." Finally, through it, they come to know English. This deaf boy confirmed what hearing teachers of the manualist school had hoped, namely, that fluency in one language led to fluency in the other.

Though most of the deaf students did not learn the sign language until they arrived at school because they had not grown up with it, they still recognized it as being uniquely theirs. The sign language could not rightly be said to belong to speaking people. In learning the sign language, all deaf people who came to school in the nineteenth century were coming into their language. It might have been long in coming, for some of them, but it was nonetheless a linguistic homecoming. It brought them two languages, as they acquired sign and English side by side. To apply Deaf Studies scholar Ben Bahan's insight, learning both languages meant that deaf students could recognize that "B is for door."[42] In other words, they learn the English letter "B" and simultaneously learn that the /B/ handshape forms the basis of the ASL sign, DOOR. "B is for door" precisely captures the vision of the nineteenth-century Deaf community claiming its linguistic place in the American scene.

Deafness in White and Black: Race at the Residential School

From the beginning, and without much public fanfare, both the American School and the New York School were integrated.[43] The schools did not comment boldly on their racial admission practices, but neither did they turn away black deaf students who wished to enroll there. At the American School, the first African American student, Charles Hiller, arrived from Nantucket in 1825. He was fifteen years old, and he was the only free black student in the school. At the New York School, the first African American student to enroll was Horace Crawford. He came to the school in 1818 when he was eleven years old. He was joined by ten-year-old Sally Robinson the following year, as she became the first African American female to attend the New York School.

These black deaf children represent a very fortunate minority of the overall African American deaf population. An analysis of the 1890 census suggested that, even then, "only 20 percent of African American deaf males and 13 percent of deaf African American females even attended school."[44] Securing an education made these students a rarity in the African American community, and a minority within the minority community of the deaf.

At the American School, between 1829 and 1870, eleven more free black students followed Charles Hiller's footsteps. Integration was the norm at the American School. In fact, in all those years, there were only seven years when the school was all white. In most academic years, white and black deaf students attended classes together. All the black students at the American School came from northern states. They were Reuben Jones, Horace Way, Cyrus Randall, Henry Simons, Adam Hill Metrash, Sarah Taylor, Susan Cisco, Samuel Graham, and the Boardwin siblings, Delia, Susan, and George.[45]

Meanwhile, at the New York School, the list of free black New Yorkers includes Horace Crawford, Sally Robinson, Paul de Grass, John Johnson, Elijah Jones, Margaret Ryass, John Anthony, James Tim, Joseph De Hart, and Aaron Cuffee. In addition, Elizabeth Pepinger came to the school from New Jersey, Salina Green from Kentucky, and Isaac Cheney from New Orleans, apparently brought north to the school by a sympathetic Union officer. The school also welcomed David Hill; he was a Native American, a member of the Onondaga tribe.[46]

Thomas Hopkins Gallaudet supported the abolitionist cause and so did others on his staff, like Lewis Weld. Weld, a member of the prominent New England family, graduated from Yale in 1818 and immediately went to work as an instructor at the American School. After three years there, he left to serve as principal of the Pennsylvania School for the Deaf from 1822 to 1830, but he returned to Hartford when Thomas Hopkins Gallaudet stepped down as principal. Weld then served as the American School's principal from 1830 to 1853. Weld's brother was Theodore Dwight Weld, a leading abolitionist and the husband of Angelina Grimké, the prominent abolitionist and feminist. Given Weld's involvement with the school, it is unsurprising that he would firmly establish a policy of race-blind admissions at Hartford, as most of the free black students attended the school on his watch.[47]

We also know that the American School, unlike the New York School, chose to publicly identify its students as deaf only and never by race. In 1854, the New York School published a cumulative list of students from 1818 to 1854. It added the notation of "colored" in its "Remarks" column to publicly identify the African American students in its ranks. The American School also periodically published lists of its pupils, but their race was never mentioned and all the students were simply listed alphabetically, white alongside black.

In particular, it is significant that the American School never published two lists of students, white and black. This was a common practice in Hartford during Weld's time there. In the 1840s, when the greatest number of black students was attending the school, the Hartford City Directory continued to segregate its citizens, publishing a list of citizens of Hartford, understood to be white, and another, separate list of "colored persons."[48] To discover the race of the students requires a trip to the American School to consult the original student entry journals, and here again, students are not separated by race but rather are simply listed in the order in which they enrolled in the school. Alice Cogswell is student number one. Only by reading through the notes on each student can one find any discussion of his or her racial background, and in most cases discussion means simply a phrase, "colored student." In its public representations of itself, the school was home simply to deaf students, and they were all equally deaf together, male and female, black and white.

It could be argued that the school was not claiming some higher ground here but was simply hiding its racial practices from public view. That is certainly possible. Why a committed abolitionist like Lewis Weld would hide his racial politics is not as clear. The New York School, by contrast, publicly identified its students as "colored," thus making clear for all to see that it welcomed black students alongside white.

In any event, practice in this case is arguably more important than appearances. In 1825, when Charles Hiller enrolled at the American School for the Deaf, most schools in Connecticut were segregated. After the American Revolution, the state had passed legislation to gradually abolish slavery and emancipate its slaves. Any child born to slave parents after 1784 would become free at age twenty-five, an age later reduced to twenty-one. As a result, by 1830, of the roughly eight thousand black people living in the state, only twenty-three were still enslaved. Of the free population, many of them were former slaves. Together, those eight thousand people represented about 3 percent of the state's population. Connecticut was an overwhelmingly white state. Its free black residents faced discrimination at every educational level.[49]

Even after Hartford had welcomed Hiller, New Haven had voted down an educational effort directed to African American men. A proposal came to the town in 1831 to establish a vocational training school for young black men, but it was voted down by a vote of seven hundred to four.[50] More famously, when Prudence Crandall turned her school in Canterbury, Connecticut, into an academy for African American girls in 1833, it provoked a firestorm of public protest and mob violence in northeastern Connecticut. Still, students came from all over the state, as well as from Boston, Providence, New York City, and Philadelphia. To fight the school through legal means, the state passed what became known as the Black Law, in May 1833. The law absolutely prohibited the establishment of schools for African Americans from outside Connecticut unless the host town gave its approval for the venture, and it was written specifically to provide a statute by which Canterbury could act to close the Crandall School.

But its wording was broader than that and could have been used to stop the American School's integration. It mandated

[t]hat no person shall set up or establish in this state any school, academy, or literary institution for the instruction or education of colored persons who are not inhabitants of this state; nor instruct or teach in any school . . . in this state . . . or harbor, or board, for the purpose of . . . being taught . . . in any such school . . . any colored person who is not an inhabitant of any town in this state, without the consent in writing first obtained of a majority of the civil authority.

The Crandall School was shut down in 1834, and the law was repealed in 1838. The American School was therefore quietly offering an education to black deaf children during a particularly contentious time in race relations in Connecticut's history. It would maintain that commitment to integration for the rest of its history.[51]

This commitment to equal racial access presents us with surely one of the more unusual images of the nineteenth century, that of white deaf southern children attending school with free black peers. There was no school in the South until the Virginia School opened in 1839, and no school in the deep South until the South Carolina School for the Deaf opened in 1849. Southern states, much like the other New England states, entered into arrangements with the American School to send their deaf children to Hartford to be educated. Virginians continued to attend the school until 1838, and South Carolina sent students until 1848; they numbered about thirty altogether. A handful of students also came from North Carolina and Alabama, with Georgia contributing another twenty-six students, most coming like the others in the 1830s and 1840s. It is difficult to imagine what these students made of going to school, for instance, side by side with the Boardwins for six years.

It is fairly easy to imagine what their hearing southern parents would have thought. As historian Hannah Joyner, discussing deaf life in the South, explains, southerners were deeply concerned about the abolitionist inclinations of northern teachers and administrators. They increasingly feared that their deaf children would be influenced by these northern beliefs, and fail to develop a firm sense of southern identity. "When loyalty to the white South grew in importance during the late antebellum period," she concludes, "Deaf educators and Deaf individuals became tainted with danger and treason."[52]

Joyner describes, in particular, how unhappy David Tillinghast's white, slave-holding family in North Carolina became as he increasingly began to espouse abolitionist views during his time at the New York School for the Deaf. They would have been even more dismayed, had they known, that he had black classmates. David Tillinghast attended school with Salina Green and Ann Williams.[53] If exposure to northern ideas in school came to be seen as increasingly problematic for white southerners, how much more dangerous, even treasonous, it would have been to them to see their deaf children attend school with free black peers.

And even New Yorkers might have blanched, had the practice been well known. While the abolitionist leanings of the New York School were well known, it is not clear how much publicity their integrated stance received. It is widely assumed in the secondary literature on education in New York that the schools of the city were segregated in the nineteenth century.[54] Like the

Hartford School, the New York School may have been integrated and regularly welcomed students of color, but its stance on race was not very public.

This is not entirely surprising, given the state of race relations in the city during these years. The New York School opened in 1818 but, as the city moved into the 1820s, it entered, in the words of one scholar of African American history, "a dark age in New York's race relations as racialist thinking spiraled downward to new lows."[55] After slavery was abolished in New York, racism arguably increased, creating worsening conditions for black New Yorkers, culminating in the outbreak of anti-abolitionist riots in 1834. Even as late as the 1850s, white racism was believed to be too virulent to attempt integrating the schools in the city.[56]

Broadcasting its integration in this period might have been dangerous for the New York School for the Deaf. But its policy of racial integration in the nineteenth century indicates a long-standing commitment to serving the deaf of New York, regardless of color or race. Such integration must have been crucial to building a sense of Deafness as a bond of fellowship that overrode the growing sectional impulse that increasingly divided hearing people.

Once southern schools were established, this racial mixing ended for white southern deaf children. Pulling out of northern residential schools, they attended southern deaf schools, which were always racially segregated. "From the middle of the nineteenth century until desegregation began in 1955," Carol Padden and Tom Humphries report, "every school for the deaf in the southern states made 'separate' arrangements based on race. Almost every southern state and the District of Columbia had separate campuses for Black deaf students; the rest, like Arkansas and South Carolina, had separate buildings on the same campus."[57]

The segregation of southern schools comes as no surprise. The extent of integration in other northern residential schools requires further investigation. We also need more research to learn how black and white deaf students viewed one another, to discover what happened to these black deaf students after graduation, and to ascertain whether or not their experience at integrated schools shaped the racial attitudes and practices of the larger antebellum Deaf community.

Learning Deaf History

Nineteenth-century deaf schoolchildren were well-versed in the story, however hagiographic, of how the sign language came to America and how they in turn came to be educated. The story of the Abbé de l'Epée was told and retold;

its persistence through the years demonstrates a certain historical understanding on the part of the deaf community. First, they knew their roots. They recognized that the French story applied to them in the United States, and was as much their history as Americans as it was the history of the French Deaf. There is a nascent transatlantic quality to the Deaf community here. Second, they believed the story was worth passing on through the generations. All deaf children needed to be introduced to it and to embrace it as their history. Third, telling this story is a way of marking the historical progress of the Deaf community. The story makes clear that the community knew that there was a time in the not so distant past when deaf people were left uneducated, and its telling indicated that they were grateful that those times had passed. Fourth, knowing these stories marked the members of the community as Deaf. They claimed a history different from that of the hearing people around them, with heroes and narratives largely unknown to the hearing world. Finally, the Deaf community recognized the important role that hearing people played in their world. They recognized, arguably in a way that the wider hearing community did not, that the history of both communities overlapped. The Deaf had their own heroes, yes, but they also knew that some of them were hearing. The history reinforces the connection between the Deaf and hearing communities. Culturally, they were parallel communities, but they were not completely segregated from each other. Their worlds did connect at certain crucial junctures.

As hearing teachers were the ones who first introduced the students to these tales, the existence of these stories also reveals much about the mindset of the hearing people at these schools. They apparently believed that they were witnessing the birth of a community at the residential schools. In passing on the stories of the roots of deaf education, these same teachers demonstrated that this community needed to know its history. Though American citizens, the American School's founding teachers seemed to understand that their deaf students also claimed citizenship in a larger Deaf community, a community that stretched across the Atlantic. De l'Epée's story, in other words, was their story too. A look at the Deaf stories of deaf education provides a glimpse into the imaginative world that deaf students and their teachers occupied in the nineteenth century.

The stories began circulating while both Thomas Hopkins Gallaudet and Laurent Clerc were still teaching at the American Asylum. Early accounts of the story of the Abbé de l'Epée suggest that students not only absorbed the history lesson offered them but also took away lessons about their own potential that the history would seem to indicate. Here is an 1827 version of the story, as told by an eighteen-year-old boy at the American School.

Many an opinion has long been held that the intellectual powers of the Deaf and Dumb are obtuse, and that it is difficult for them to learn. This thought must have been not judicious. First because as efforts can flow out of the condition of difficulties, so the efforts to make signs have been successful, and were, at first, established by the venerable Abbé de l'Epée; and afterwards used by the Abbeé Sicard, the successor of that valuable man, and now by the present teachers who are well skilled in signs; among them is Mr. Laurent Clerc, a deaf and dumb French teacher, whose late teacher was Sicard. By his abilities which distinguish him in the most shining parts of a great scholar, the Deaf and Dumb can boast of him. Secondly because belief is admissible to the capacity of the Deaf and Dumb to learn, and incredulity would be foolish. . . . And thirdly because the minds of the Deaf and Dumb are intelligent as well as those who can speak and hear.[58]

This young man traced a direct line of succession, from de l'Epée to Sicard to Clerc, and finally from Clerc to the American deaf. The American Deaf community was linked in this way directly to the French community; it sprung as a branch from that root. The French past was his past. And this past had shaped his present. As the manual method made its way across the ocean, and American deaf flourished accordingly, it proved that the deaf were as intelligent as the hearing.

Other students were similarly quick to use the story to offer their own interpretations of the meaning of deafness. Elvira Derby, a student at the American School, told her version of events in 1831.

Mr G. [Gallaudet] found that a girl was deaf and dumb in this city and pitied her, because she was ignorant. He soon became thoughtful and wished to teach her how to read and write but he did not know. Therefore he endeavored to obtain the means of going to Europe. They gave Mr. G much money for his passage, that he might learn the signs from the deaf and dumb of Paris. When he returned from Paris with Mr. L.C. [Laurent Clerc] they established a school for the deaf and dumb here and instructed the pupils who made good improvement. When some of them had finished their instruction, they returned home and are now capable of conversing with their friends in writing and with their fingers. A part of the men of the United States imitated and founded institutions for the Deaf and Dumb.[59]

Elvira's story provides interesting details. She believes that Gallaudet pitied the deaf girl, Alice Cogswell, not because she was deaf but because she was "ignorant." While her deafness could not be corrected, her ignorance could, so framing the story in this light would suggest that the distinction was important to determining the outcome of the events. If Gallaudet had pitied her for her deafness, Elvira suggests, he might not have acted at all. As it is, he "became thoughtful" and went to Europe to find a way to help Alice overcome her ignorance.

Significantly, in Elvira's telling of the tale, she imagines that he goes to Paris to learn the sign language "from the deaf and dumb of Paris." Here the language comes to America from the deaf directly, not from hearing people. Not only are the French and American deaf communities linked by a shared history, as other students' tales indicated, but they are also bound together by a shared language. Clerc assumes a position of tremendous importance. He serves as the transatlantic link between two deaf communities, one reaching out in solidarity to aid the other.

This transatlantic link, between the American and French deaf communities, was stressed repeatedly. It appears in this story, as told in 1832 by an eighteen-year-old girl who was a student at the New York Institution, again providing evidence that this was a tale told not only at the American School but as a part of deaf education more broadly.

The Abbé De L'Epée, who was a priest, lived in Paris. One day he called at a house of a stranger on business. But the lady was absent from home. When he knocked at the door, a servant heard it and opened it. She let him in and he was shown into a parlour where two young ladies were sitting down, engaged in sewing. One of them invited him with a motion of her hand to sit down, but she did not speak to him. He wished to converse with the ladies while he was expecting that the lady would return home. Then he asked questions to the two ladies but they did not answer him. He was very much surprised that they continued silent. He felt almost offended and imitated their silence. He waited for the mother who soon came home again. She met him and introduced her daughters to the priest and spoke to him with a sad countenance, informing him that they had never spoken since they were born. He pitied them because they did not know of the religion and worship of God who has created all the universe. He was in a great affliction at this intelligence of the deafness of the two ladies. Then he left and went home. He thought what means he could invent to instruct them. For several days he failed in this. He again went to the same house and told the mother that he felt greatly desirous to teach her daughters to understand the signs and therefore they could converse by writing. The mother was very happy to hear this. So every day he taught them and made them improve. In some years they became intelligent and they could express their ideas in writing. They were always very happy. The priest thought that there were several deaf-mute persons in Paris and so he found them. They entered his own house to be educated. He always was an instructor till his death.[60]

The story contains important details. The two girls are deaf, but are clearly educable; they can sew and they know how to greet a houseguest. They are not merely sitting stupefied in their mother's parlor. Once again, the story asserts that the hearing protagonist, in this case, the abbé, pitied the girls not for their deafness but for their ignorance. To bring them out of this ignorance, he invented a means to instruct the girls; he would teach them signs in order to teach them written French. How he knew the sign language in the first place remains unclear in this story, though in others it was said that the abbé invented the sign language.

As Carol Padden and Tom Humphries point out, the story is not about the historical figure of the abbé at all. "Instead it has come to symbolize, in its retelling through the centuries," they write, "the transition from a world in which deaf people live alone or in isolated communities to a world in which they have a rich community and language. This is not merely a historical tale but also a folktale about the origins of a people and their language."[61] While the tale may contain more myth than history, the importance of this story, passed on through generations at the residential schools, cannot be underestimated. Gallaudet, together with Clerc, continued the work that the abbé had started; they brought the written word, via the sign language, within the reach of the American deaf people. The American Deaf community responded by embracing the de l'Epée story as their own.

Judging Their Teachers

The teacher endeavors to establish some kind of intercourse with him by showing him objects by signs and asking him their meanings and uses. He commences by forming letters with a pen. He is taught the manual alphabet representing the letters on the different positions of the hand. The teacher writes the names of objects and draws their illustrations on a large slate. He points his finger to them and asks the pupil what they are. Words are combined in simple sentences. . . . He is taught the inflections of nouns and verbs. He writes the qualities and properties of objects on his slate. By-and-by phrases are combined into compound sentences. The sentences are lengthened until they become narratives. The pupil can write as the speaking person and his mind becomes independent. When he has completed his education, he leaves the school and goes home, and his parents and friends are very happy to converse with him by writing on his small slate.[62]

Deaf students largely believed that the sign language enabled them, finally, to learn English. Many students, as we have already seen, suggested that the reason they did not learn to read while they lived at home was that no one in their family knew the sign language. Given their previous academic experiences, including the widespread failure of the common schools, most deaf students were quick to compare the common schools to the residential schools, and attributed their current academic progress to their teachers' mastery of the sign language and to their superior pedagogy. Some even directly remarked on the issue of their teachers' qualifications. A young woman wrote to a friend in 1823, "I am now very happy to have come to the Asylum and to have a good opportunity of being favored with instructors who are qualified and capable of teaching me by signs on the various subjects of religion and other things. Indeed, I can understand them distinctly."[63]

If teachers were qualified in the sign language, it was because they learned it largely from deaf people. As discussed earlier, teachers were encouraged to observe closely the ways in which students used the language. John E. Crane could remember his teachers learning the sign language in exactly this way. He recalled seeing two young, new teachers, A. S. Clark and Job Williams, who boarded on campus together, "learning signs by talking with the boys in the backyard from the window" of their room.[64] Other students went so far as to comment on their teacher's academic training. A young man wrote in 1830, "Mr. Washburn taught me well, had been at Yale College in New Haven."[65] He referred to Elizur Washburn, who graduated from Yale in 1826. And many students over the years singled out Laurent Clerc for special praise, as did this young man in 1843, who declared, "He is one of the most respectable teachers."[66]

American Deaf students occasionally tried to describe how the manual method worked, for the benefit of those unfamiliar with the process of teaching the deaf. One boy at the American Asylum stated in 1821, "I did not know many words that I copyed some words at the slate. Mr. O taught me but I did not know all the words. . . . I began to learn the words by making signs."[67] The sign language, as the students described it, became the vehicle for learning English. Signs came quickest, easiest, and first.

Knowing the signs, students were led slowly to make the association between a concept in sign and that same concept as expressed in English.

The method, as students experienced it, was designed to lead pupils slowly from signs to words. It built upon past successes. Individual signs for objects were translated into English words. The words were combined into simple phrases, the phrases into simple sentences, the simple sentences into complex sentences, and finally the complex sentences were combined into paragraphs and whole narratives. The deaf students used their knowledge of the sign language to master English. The result, deaf students argued, was that they could "write as the speaking people." One young deaf boy declared this system of education "very admirable."[68]

This bilingual approach to deaf education, using American Sign Language to teach English, did not, apparently, foster a resistance to acquiring English in antebellum deaf students, as was later charged by late-nineteenth-century oralists. Similar arguments were still used in the late twentieth century to argue against returning ASL to the classroom and for retaining English-based sign systems in deaf education. Students need English, not ASL, the argument goes; if they are exposed to ASL, they won't learn English because ASL interferes with English acquisition.

If anything, these student writing samples from the early nineteenth century would indicate that precisely the opposite was the case. Nineteenth-century deaf students seem to have achieved greater success in learning English, by using the sign language to learn English, than their late-twentieth-century counterparts generally demonstrated. Most modern studies have concluded that the average deaf adult reads on average at a fourth-grade level. And, instead of resisting English and favoring only the sign language, most nineteenth-century deaf students expressed a great desire to learn English. They knew that acquiring English was crucial for their social and economic independence. In the late twentieth century, the Deaf community's relationship to English was highly charged and rarely so straightforward.

This modern ambivalence toward English is a legacy of the oralist triumph in deaf education. By making the acquisition of English, and especially spoken English, the overriding goal of deaf education, oralists succeeded in making those deaf people who could not speak feel like "oral failures."[69] By denigrating the sign language and making it the language of "oral failures," oralists created a deep suspicion of English among signing Deaf people, who began to suspect that oralists were using English as a weapon to destroy ASL. Since this was indeed the mission of oralists, Deaf people were correct in their suspicions. But the resulting situation left Deaf people unable to claim English as their own, as a language that could be used by both Deaf and hearing people. It became a "hearing" language as oralists tried to eliminate both ASL and Deaf culture.

But in the early nineteenth century, Deaf people could be unabashedly bilingual. Most importantly, their teachers were models of this goal. Both hearing and deaf teachers were expected to be bilingual; they had to know both English and ASL. Since they had worked hard to master the language of their students, they could with fairness encourage their students to do the same. Deaf students could work hard at learning English, secure in the knowledge that they were not being asked to choose one language over the other. After the methodical sign systems were abandoned, deaf students knew that they did not have to sign in English. To encourage the students to use English more colloquially with one another, the hearing teachers did not ask them to use signed English. Rather, they asked the deaf students to fingerspell to one another more frequently. As one young girl explained in 1843, "Mr. Weld told the pupils that they must spell with their fingers to each other because they would improve very much. I try to spell with some of the pupils with my fingers."[70] By appreciating the differences between ASL and English, hearing teachers demonstrated respect both for ASL and for their deaf pupils. That respect, in turn, encouraged their deaf students to try to make English their own.

The manual method was the only method that deaf people could possibly support in the nineteenth century. It was the only method that demonstrated respect for the natural language of signs, a language that hearing teachers themselves called the native language of deaf people. The editors of the *Deaf Mute Pelican*, the school newspaper of the Louisiana School for the Deaf, were clear. They believed that the "natural tendency" of all the deaf, semi-deaf, semi-hearing, and born-deaf alike was to communicate by gesture. All would allow their articulation skills to lapse, once teachers ceased hounding them to speak.[71]

And the editors of the *Pelican* viewed this behavior as completely natural. Oral communication could never be for the deaf what it was for the hearing. Only the natural language of signs could serve the deaf well. As the editors understood it,

> An oral language could never be as natural . . . the sign language is rapid—as rapid as spoken language with hearing persons; it is sure, almost always intelligible without repetition; it is exceedingly flexible, so that it may be varied to express the nicest shade of thought or emotion; it is capacious, complete, a full formed language as any. How natural then that the deaf and dumb use it in spite of every restraint of incentive to the contrary! They will use it; they must. It contains the elementary forms of their thought; it embodies their poetry and their song; their comedy and their tragedy; their wit and their wisdom.[72]

An oral language could never be as natural for deaf people as a signed language. For a people that cannot hear, an oral language must always be secondary to a visually accessible language. For this reason, manualists acknowledged that oral communication would never become the primary method of communication for their deaf students. It could never embody, the way that signs literally can, the wit and wisdom of the Deaf community.

Deaf students also had practical reasons for choosing manualism over oralism. It produced results. Most deaf students were in school to get an education, and naturally, they favored the method that actually delivered on its pedagogical promises. As Joseph Sanger remarked about a visit to the American School,

> There are about two hundred pupils, the greater part of whom had made rapid progress in the knowledge of written language in proportion to their time spent in this acquisition. I was surprised that several of them being deaf from birth had made more rapid improvement in their studies and in conversing on their fingers. I had almost persuaded myself that they had once lost the sense of hearing, but they had done it by sense of their perception and diligent and undivided study and owing to the youngness of their minds, easy to commit words to memory.[73]

The better part of two hundred students making rapid progress—this was why deaf people favored manualism.

Most hearing teachers for the better part of the nineteenth century were therefore unsurprised that the oral method enjoyed little support among deaf people. A student from the Pennsylvania Institution, William, perhaps put it best in 1870. "The people who are deaf mutes are taught in Massachusetts [at the Clarke School for the Deaf, an oral school that opened in 1867] by the form of the lips which they are learned to do and they are also taught to speak like speaking folks," he explained, "but it is impossible for anybody to teach them to hear."[74] Oral education simply could not make deaf people into hearing people. It could only try to make them less Deaf. At the manualist residential schools, in environments that sanctioned the use of the sign language, deaf students like William slowly became Deaf adults.

Embracing Their Education

It is both possible and necessary, that notwithstanding his deafness and dumbness, one should be instructed in the language which those who hear and speak use. It is exceedingly advantageous that a deaf and dumb person should understand how to write his language and to read books. When he has acquired an excellent education, he will find unspeakable pleasure in reading good books with perfect ease and correctness. When he feels weary, having nothing to do, he takes a good book, and derives a great deal of amusement and spirit from it. He gains much information and interest by reading periodical publications as well, and acquires a great deal of knowledge by studying philosophy well and reading history well. He finds peculiar interest in perusing Scriptures; by which he is taught about God, the most important doctrines, and excellent precepts; informed that God made him and the world; about the most extraordinary and important events and actions; and that Christ came into the world and died for sinners; and invited to heaven; and he derives comfort from the Holy Book in trouble. To converse with persons intelligently by writing and to write letters well, are peculiarly amusing and edifying to a well educated deaf and dumb person. When he follows some occupation, having been well instructed how to write and to cypher, he can do business with others as well as those traders who hear and speak, and protects himself from being imposed upon by any one. A good education is one of the greatest blessings which the deaf and dumb enjoy and must be acquired with diligence and great exertion.[75]

Deaf students reflected positively on their school years. In 1847, Hannah M. Patten wrote to a friend from the New York Institution, "I am very happy to stay here and learn the different kinds of books in the school. I am very glad that God led me to come here and learn for my improvement. . . . I have enjoyed myself very much here because it is a great pleasure for me to learn and obtain wisdom and improvement."[76] In that same year, her classmate, Lucinda E. Hills, remarked that she was an "ignorant girl" who "could not read any books" when she arrived at the school, but she had been "willing to improve also" and now was pleased that she could read and write.[77] Mary Lackie reflected about what her life would have been like if she had never gone to school. "When I think of the state of my mind before I came here," she wrote in 1854, "it seems as if I should have led a very miserable life, if I had not been sent to the Asylum."[78] Another young lady commented in 1823, "I feel very grateful to God for . . . providing a school for me. My time has been much occupied with my studies every evening with much interest; and I have been particularly delighted to attend to geography and to the wonders of the world."[79]

Deaf people understood the importance of education for them and recognized that it was in some important ways even more necessary for them than for hearing people. As A., from the Pennsylvania Institution explained,

"Every child should have an education, but it is more important for the Deaf and Dumb for they can neither speak nor hear, and could not express their ideas well if they had not gotten a good education."[80] Another Pennsylvania student, M., elaborated. "Without the knowledge derived from schools, speaking people can be able to converse and be something; but not so with the deaf and dumb," M. wrote. "Unless they are educated they must be doomed to remain in the deep darkness of ignorance without being able to express their joy or sorrow to anyone. Oh! How deplorable is their lot!"[81] M. hits upon the real problem of deafness, which is less its auditory aspect than its social impact. Whereas "speaking people" could pick up English and many other points of information just by listening in on the conversation of others, deaf people had to be purposefully introduced to all these things.[82] One can imagine that from the point of view of a newly educated deaf student, the condition of uneducated deaf people would indeed have seemed woeful, deplorable, or doomed.

Understandably, deaf people cherished their schools and their teachers. Harriet Knapp declared, "The few years of my scholarship have been the happiest of my whole life."[83] Many would have agreed with the valedictorian of the New York School for the year 1850, who declared, "I am very grateful to God for having provided the Institution for us to be taught to read and write."[84]

Out of all the benefits that education offered them, deaf students stressed repeatedly that literacy was the most important skill that they had acquired at school. Gaining fluency in English, the language of their country, was important to most deaf students. They viewed literacy as vital for both their private and public lives. The ability to read represented the ability to participate in the culture of their fellow citizens. "The civilized world abounds in books, periodicals, and newspapers," a graduate of the Ohio school wrote in 1849. "[The educated deaf person] has access to them. Thus he is happy."[85]

The entire advantage of education could be understood as the advantage of literacy. Students held quite specific ideas about the benefits that literacy would offer them. As they understood it, literacy provided the pleasure of reading both periodicals and books. It provided the comfort of opening the Bible in times of trouble. It conferred the blessings of religion and the knowledge of God. It provided the power to correspond with people, both hearing and deaf. It would prove a useful skill when seeking employment. Literacy brought deaf and hearing people closer together. Sharing a common language enabled them to interact in ways that would otherwise have been impossible.

Deaf people knew that achieving fluency in English was not an easy task. They praised those deaf people who had achieved public recognition as writers. James Nack, a deaf poet, was often singled out for praise. John Carlin, the deaf poet and painter, was also frequently mentioned, in spite of his lack of support for the use of the natural sign language in the classroom. One observer noted Carlin's success with pride. "Mr. Carlin and some of our most distinguished deaf mutes write excellent like the speaking people," this writer noted in 1850. "They have got the acquaintance of language by practice and care in reading."[86] Other deaf people were urged to follow his example.

Having applied themselves in school, many deaf students felt they were in a position to offer advice to both the students and the teachers who would follow them. A young lady, upon graduating from the American Asylum in 1839, delivered a farewell address to her teachers. "Gentlemen," she stated,

> I am from the State of Connecticut. I have been here nearly five years. I shall leave here for home this spring and not return again. Before we came here, we were like beasts, ignorant of having souls, the existence of God, the creation and system of the world, and our duties; but since our admittance into the Asylum, we have increased in the knowledge of these things. Now we can read, write, and converse with others, and I think this makes us happy and free. We feel grateful to you all for having so long taken the trouble to teach us and to deliver us a great many different sermons in the chapel, and for your good advice. . . . I hope we shall never forget you all when we part with you. I trust that if you are constantly faithful, industrious, and ardent to teach your pupils, and that if they follow your good examples and also are very attentive to you, they will improve better than ourselves, and if so, indeed, I will rejoice and not be jealous.[87]

This author made several important points. She believed that without an education, deaf people were pitiful creatures, ignorant of the world and their place in it. But education made them "happy and free." Education and literacy succeeded in transforming deaf people completely. Gratitude toward those who had wrought such a transformation was the only appropriate response. But it was not an uncritical gratitude. This girl also believed that she was now in a position to instruct her teachers. She urged them to be "faithful, industrious, and ardent," while calling upon future students to be "attentive." By addressing both groups, she placed them in a reciprocal relationship. And she expressed an awareness of a Deaf community and understood the school as the source of that community. By attending the residential school, she became part of this Deaf community, one that would spread across generations.

If manualists believed that education, and especially literacy, enabled deaf people to participate in American life and culture, deaf people demonstrated time and time again that they shared this belief. "Education," as one graduate commented in 1859, "by making intelligent and capable citizens of us, has placed us under new responsibilities."

> We are required to bear our share of the burdens of society, and should consider it a privilege so to do. It is our duty to add, by our labor, to the aggregate wealth of our country, and to be examples of respectful obedience to the laws, which afford to us security of life and property in the same degree as to our speaking and hearing fellow citizens. And inasmuch as we owe to the sympathy and efforts of others most that we possess to make life pleasurable, we should ever be ready with heart and purse, to aid, as far as lies in our power, any one who, less fortunate than ourselves, may stand in need of help.[88]

Deaf people understood the power of education in their lives. In a democratic society, education confers the tools necessary to citizenship; by virtue of their education, deaf people became "intelligent and capable citizens." They would share in the responsibilities and rewards of citizenship alongside their hearing peers.

Remembering a time when deaf people in the United States went uneducated, the author acknowledged the debt that they owed to others for intervening on their behalf. He suggested that deaf people should in turn do the same and help those "less fortunate than ourselves" for, as educated people, the deaf could no longer be considered unfortunates. As one young deaf woman explained, they were unfortunate only "before having come to the Asylum" when "they could not talk with strangers by writing on paper or small slates, or by spelling with their fingers."[89] Of course, by asserting that one could "spell with the fingers" to communicate with hearing people, this author revealed her assumption that hearing people would make the effort to learn the manual alphabet in an attempt to do what they could to include deaf people in the social life of the larger community, just as deaf people were doing what they could, namely, mastering English, in order to be included as well. Many deaf people hoped that hearing people would try to master some skills to welcome them into society.

Understanding Deafness

Deafness means inability to hear. Many people lose their hearing in their youthful age, by disease of different kinds. Sometimes people are born deaf and have never heard a word. . . . But now there are many institutions for the Deaf and Dumb to get instructed in and anybody who wants to get knowledge, can get it, by going into the Deaf and Dumb Institution, but if they are lazy and don't try to learn in it, they will never become intelligent in it, but if they are industrious and anxious to learn, they need not be dunces. Many of the deaf people now are intelligent, and worth having about because they can do almost any kind of a trade as well as any of the speaking people. . . . I believe that deaf mutes are worth nearly as much as speaking people because they have got as much wit, if they are intelligent, and they also can do nearly as many kinds of trades as the speaking people. . . . You needn't think that deaf people are as dumb as beasts, but they are generally very clever and behave well and show good manners to people. But they are not worth more than speaking people who can hear and speak.[90]

In coming to the residential school and getting an education, many deaf students were moved to reflect on their deafness in new ways and tried to describe what they thought deafness meant and what it did not mean. As early as 1825, a Deaf understanding of deafness was suggested; deafness was described not as a handicap but as a linguistic condition. A deaf girl of fourteen revealed this interpretation of her deafness as she tried to answer the question, "Why did you learn to read and write?" She responded,

It has pleased God to deprive me of hearing and speech. I am deaf and dumb, and cannot understand those who speak, nor can they understand my signs. I am therefore required to learn to read and write, because I wish to understand what they tell me or what they write in their letters, and also wish to talk to them.[91]

In this account, both sides labor under a handicap. Neither side understands the language of the other. She wished to learn English, to read it and write it, as a way to bridge the linguistic gap between herself and the hearing. But it was this linguistic gap, and not their auditory abilities, that separated hearing and deaf people. Once both sides possessed a common language, the gap between them would disappear altogether.

Rather than assert the differences between Deaf and hearing people, deaf students tended to stress that deaf people were in many fundamental ways like speaking people. They could learn, if they worked hard at their studies. They could do almost all of the same trades as speaking people. They were just as intelligent and mannered and witty and clever. They just could not hear. Both sides, deaf and hearing, could meet each other essentially as equals. As historian of deafness Harlan Lane has argued, "Deaf leaders . . . have sought integration with autonomy, integration that seeks not to efface but rather to enhance Deaf identity."[92] This would seem to be precisely the vision that this first generation of deaf leaders, the first graduates of residential schools, put forward.

Others in the nineteenth century understood Deafness as a visual condition. As early as 1820, an observer of the deaf noted "the expression of their speaking eyes."[93] Deaf people commented on the importance of their eyesight. "The deaf mutes must work with their eyes more than speaking people," Herman Erbe explained. "I thank my Heavenly Father because I can see with my eyes."[94] Many Deaf people considered sight the most important of the senses. Just as some invoked God's will to explain their deafness, Thomas L. Brown applied a little biblical exegesis to explain why sight was the most important sense of all. He offered this reading of Genesis, explaining, "[T]he eye is more valuable than the ear in most respects. Adam was created to *see* first (after breathing) and the first thing Eve did was to behold her new husband. The second thing they did was to *hear*."[95]

Much like Brown, other deaf students remarked upon the importance they placed on sight. Asked to answer the question, "Which is the greatest calamity, to be deaf and dumb or blind?" Mary Toles did not hesitate. This student at the New York Institution responded immediately, "blindness." She even composed a story, with a mother and two daughters, one deaf and one blind, to illustrate her reasoning. In the story, the deaf daughter returns home to her mother after graduating from a school for the deaf. Her mother can scarcely recognize the girl, so transformed is she due to her education. The deaf girl had left home unable to express her thoughts at all, but now, Toles emphasized, she is bilingual, communicating fluently in both the sign language and in written English.[96]

Toles ended her story with a moral of her own.

And she no longer needs your pity. You have given her the means of instruction and those means have been employed to her present and future happiness; and now what is there to consistently prevent her being placed on an equal footing with those who hear and speak? Then pity the deaf and dumb in ignorance and if you pity, aid them. Give them every means of instruction in your power and they will be capable of high and holy feelings; yea more, they will be capable of expressing those feelings. They will tell you also that they are more fortunate than the blind since the birth of their mental sight, but had it been their lot to remain always in ignorance, blindness would have been infinitely preferable.[97]

Once again, a student submitted that education alleviated the condition of the deaf and placed them on an equal footing with hearing people. Toles argued that, with education, deafness became irrelevant. The important handicap that deafness imposed, by her lights, was a social handicap, and that could be effectively eliminated through education. Her fiction mirrored her real-life experience. Edward Allen Fay noted upon her death in 1901, "The loss of her hearing seemed to her parents . . . a terrible blow, the ruin of her life; but to her, as to many of the deaf, it proved a blessing in disguise, giving her opportunities for education she could not otherwise have enjoyed, broadening and elevating her whole future life."[98]

A Deaf point of view was emerging here. Educated Deaf people increasingly grew to view the handicap of deafness as a social construction. As John Burnet put it in 1835, "Their misfortune is not that *they* are deaf and dumb, but that *others* hear and speak. Were the established mode of communication among men, by a language addressed, not to the ear, but to the eye, the present inferiority of the deaf would entirely vanish."[99] Education gave deaf people the tools to reflect on their social position, and they were quick to conclude that cultural forces deeply shaped deaf life, perhaps even more so than physical deafness itself. They were the first disabled people in American history to claim that disability could be socially constructed.

But deaf students did not avoid the topic of physical deafness, either. Some nineteenth-century students suggested that physical deafness had its occasional advantages. As one student put it,

> The deaf and dumb boys cannot hear or speak, but they can speak with the dactylology and they can write on the slates as the people talk. The deaf boys cannot hear the noise of the carriages running on the road when they sleep by night. They have a peace. The people who can hear are interrupted when they sleep in the night. They are unhappy.[100]

This passage reflects an attempt to understand the sense of hearing. Even though it was very difficult, if not impossible, for born deaf people to understand what it was like to be a hearing person, it did not mean they were ignorant of the more general concept of sound. This deaf boy knew enough about sound to know that hearing it did not require active listening. Another boy, Herman Erbe, struggled to imagine what the experience of hearing music was like. "I can feel a noise easily instead of hearing it," he wrote. "When some of my friends play on pianos, I then put my hands on them and feel the sounds. The sounds make me feel sweet. I think that the speaking people hear the same which I feel."[101]

Most Deaf students did not dwell on a sense they lacked, however curious they may have been about the experience of hearing. They preferred to focus on what Deaf people could do. While hearing people could take pleasure in listening to music, one young man noted, "[the] deaf and dumb cannot enjoy music because they are destitute of the organ of hearing. But they should be contented because they can be moved by poetry while they read poems."[102]

Antebellum teachers noted the emergence of a distinctively Deaf attitude toward deafness. At the first convention of American teachers of the deaf in 1850, one participant remarked that the deaf "were not themselves inclined to consider the deprivation of their sense at all as a misfortune, though others, in possession of all their faculties, regard it as a great affliction."[103] There was a noticeable difference between the ways in which Deaf and hearing people thought about deafness.

Some deaf people did express unhappiness with their physical deafness. John Crane remembered how he felt after he went deaf at age ten. "After I lost my hearing," he wrote, "I could not seem to enjoy myself as well as I used to." He missed the sounds of daily life, including the voices of his parents and the singing of birds. But he also felt strongly the sting of social isolation. "As I would gaze on the people as they passed by with a close companion or companions, conversing with each other, with smiles on their faces, seeming to be in high spirits, I longed to be with them, but how could I engage in their conversation, deaf and destitute of learning?" Here, he recognized the socially constructed aspects of his condition. He was not necessarily cut off from conversation with these companions because he was deaf merely. He was cut off because he did not have a means to communicate with them, nor they with him.

After attending school, however, he reached new conclusions about his life and his deafness.

There is a wide difference between my education at the present day and when it was before I came to this Institution. What can be the cause of it? Have my ears been opened so that I can hear and speak as people do in general? No, it is only the influence of this Institution over me. It has instructed me how to use the manual alphabet and to read and write, that I may be able to converse with whom I please. Now I need not to be sorry or disappointed because I am deaf, for I can join with companions and enjoy myself, as well as I could before I was deaf. This Institution may be compared to a medicine. It cures the ignorance of deaf mutes.[104]

Other students similarly recognized that getting an education had forced them to rethink the meaning of their deafness. After attending school, a young woman concluded of the deaf, "To tell the truth, they are not at present unfortunate beings."[105] Harriet Knapp agreed, writing in 1843, "With a good education, I truly do not regard my deafness as a deprivation."[106] Like Crane, she was late-deafened and could remember her days as a hearing person. It is significant that the residential school experience enabled them to look at deafness differently. They were obviously just as deaf as when they entered, but they now perceived the meaning of their deafness in a new light.

Of course, not all deaf people felt the same way about physical deafness. Some late-deafened students particularly took their hearing loss hard. A young man who became deaf when he was six years old reported that he was "very sorry because my hearing is lost. . . . I should have many friends if I had not lost my hearing. I have very few now. They sometimes mock me because I am deaf."[107] Yet, it should be added that age of onset of deafness was not a consistent predictor of how deafness would be perceived. Not all deaf people who lost their hearing, and could therefore remember a time when they too were hearing people, felt sorry for their loss.

Herman Erbe, a student at the American School in 1870, remembered his childhood in this way. "Nine years ago, when I was five years old," he wrote, "I was a speaking boy." He described an accident, a fall in which his head struck a large rock.

> Some days afterward, my father spoke to me but I could not hear what he said because I had lost my hearing by the fall. Then all my friends were surprised and very sorry. But when anybody tells me that he is sorry because I am a deaf and dumb boy, I am not so sorry, because I think that I am as smart as a speaking boy. But I am sometimes sorry because I lost my hearing by a fall and because I was careless.[108]

The distinction he drew is an important one. He was sorry for his carelessness, not for his deafness. He was "as smart as a speaking boy." There was no reason to feel sorry for him.

His story also brings out another important distinction between nineteenth- and twentieth-century deaf experiences. This boy became deaf at age five. Yet he attended a manual school, learned the sign language, and identified himself as a deaf boy. By the twentieth century, such a path would become much more difficult. As a postlingually deafened child, he was just the sort of child whom oralists wanted in oral schools. They would recommend forbidding him to sign so as to make him work harder to preserve his speech. They would want him to conceive of himself as "a hard of hearing boy," as one more like hearing people than different from them, and not as a deaf boy. He would have been the boy oralists would want to save from certain Deafness.

But, as it was, Herman Erbe was a deaf boy, one as smart as a speaking boy, and his hearing parents could accept him as such. And in the nineteenth century, the born-deaf were frequently equally unapologetic. As Wilson Whiton commented in 1818, "I was born deaf and dumb. God made my deafness, I am complyed with God's will."[109] William Breg similarly declared in 1847, "I am 14 years old. . . . I have never heard and spoken. I am a deaf and dumb boy but I am not sorry. I will leave this school room. I will go home and work in a cabinet shop or meadow or corn-field or dig potatoes."[110] If Herman Erbe was not sorry because he was just as smart as speaking boys, William Breg was not sorry because, following his schooling, he would be able to support himself. Neither boy felt he had a reason to be sorry.

Because these boys felt they had to justify themselves, however, it is apparent that hearing people generally believed that deaf people should feel very sorry indeed to be deaf. A graduate of the Ohio School for the Deaf confronted this issue directly.

> Often have I been asked if I were happy, and if I wished to speak and hear. I have answered that I was as happy as any man and that I never wished very much to speak and hear. The persons who asked me these questions said, that if they were in my situation, they should be very unhappy. All the living creatures God has made are happy on account of his benevolence. Are deaf mutes excepted? No. He has provided means by which knowledge, so essential to happiness and virtue, can be imported to them. Is the condition of such deaf mutes as have been taught the Christian religion and various branches of knowledge . . . still as lamentable as it was previous to their being educated? Are they unhappy because they have not the inestimable sense of hearing which others have? He that says *yes*, in answer to these questions, is greatly mistaken.[111]

More of the difference between the Deaf and the hearing comes through here. The Deaf graduate discovered that hearing people found it difficult to believe that he could actually be happy, for they would be most unhappy to be deaf. The graduate found their assumptions perplexing. Why would they assume that he was so unhappy? He could only try to explain that his deafness was not a source of grief to him; in fact, he had never wished to hear. Hearing people probably found that assertion difficult to believe. But why would the born-deaf wish for something they had never had and could therefore not miss? This graduate tried to explain that, once educated, the deaf could not be anything but happy. It was their ignorance, not their deafness, that was a cause of grief, and their ignorance could be alleviated through the mechanism of the residential school. As John E. Crane said, the school acted as a medicine, for "[i]t cures the ignorance of deaf mutes." He was referring here to both the ignorance stemming from their lack of education and also, it would seem, their ignorance of what a deaf life would mean.

As the nineteenth century faded and the twentieth century opened, oralism exerted a firm and increasing control over deaf education. As the twentieth century progressed, the medical model became the preferred lens through which to view deafness. Deafness was assumed to be a medical problem in need of a solution, and more time, effort, and money was poured into finding a cure for deafness, first through hearing aids and then through cochlear implants.[112] Those whose deafness could not be cured were encouraged to work hard to pass as hearing, by using speech and rejecting sign language, and by seeking out the company of hearing people and avoiding deaf people. Oral education was supposed to make passing possible. In this way, oral educators believed that they were offering their own cure for deafness.

Oralists and medical professionals would have been mystified to discover that this is not what nineteenth-century Deaf people meant at all when they sought a cure for deafness. They wanted a decidedly low-tech approach, namely, the sign language and manual education. When Deaf people spoke of treating their deafness, they meant addressing and changing the social condition their deafness frequently placed them in. They meant alleviating the isolation and ignorance to which their deafness tended to subject them. They meant going from a world in which they were alone and deaf to one in which they joined a Deaf community.

Many deaf students assumed that by making this transformation, they would become equal members of the larger society of which they believed they were a part. As Deaf students left the schools that had educated them, they looked forward, with Thomas J. Chamberlain, to becoming "useful and respected citizens, and an honor to our 'Alma Mater.'"[113] Would the hopes of these Deaf students be realized? Would they have the opportunity to become "useful and respected citizens" as they assumed? What would it mean to lead a Deaf life in nineteenth-century America? What did life after the residential school hold?

The Deaf Way

Living a Deaf Life

It does not matter what may be thought of anything I now say, or of my saying it in this manner, by those who do not belong to our fraternity. I write merely for those who are deeply concerned in the subject of my letter. The time may come when I shall tell the public some of our secrets. . . . At present, I address only you; and as there is no need for us to tell our secrets to one another, there may be little here to interest any but ourselves.

—Harriet Martineau, 1834

Perhaps, from the outside looking in, deafness did appear as a kind of fraternity, full of secrets known only to the initiated.[1] After all, the Deaf world was not one that was much visited by hearing people during the nineteenth century. The organizations, practices, and people of the Deaf community were not widely known to antebellum Americans, and the history of the Deaf community remains largely unfamiliar to hearing Americans today. Here, then, is a kind of tour of the nineteenth-century Deaf world.

Organizations

The first deaf association in the country was the New England Gallaudet Association of the Deaf.[2] Founded in 1854, the New England Gallaudet Association of the Deaf drew members, both male and female, from all over New England. The association was the brainchild of Thomas Brown (1804-1886). Brown was one of the most important leaders of the Deaf community of the nineteenth century. His father, Nahum Brown, was the first deaf person in the Brown family, as far as anyone knew. He married a hearing woman and, with her, had two deaf children, Thomas and his sister, Persis. Thomas attended the American Asylum, entering at the age of eighteen in 1822; he remained there for five years, completing his course of study and learning a trade in carpentry. He stayed on for two additional years as a carpentry teacher at the school, but in 1829, at the age of twenty-five, returned home to work his family's farm in Henniker, New Hampshire.

As the deaf members of the Brown family began to get educated and then returned to New Hampshire, Henniker emerged as a center of Deaf life in New England. An estimated forty-four deaf people lived in and around Henniker in the nineteenth century. Henniker is a very small town; over the course of the entire nineteenth century, its population never topped two thousand residents.[3]

Many of this number were members of the extended Brown family. In 1832, Thomas Brown married a Deaf woman from Martha's Vineyard, Mary Smith, whom he had met at school. Smith was thought "an amiable woman, with fine sensibilities, large-hearted, intelligent, and industrious, and an ornament to society in Henniker."[4] Smith's parents were both hearing, but she had deaf grandparents on both her maternal and her paternal sides. This mixed hearing and deaf family mirrored the family life of most deaf Vineyarders, who lived with and among hearing people.[5]

This audiological mix also distinguished the deaf Vineyard experience from the deaf mainland experience. Where most deaf mainlanders found themselves living in hearing families who were largely ignorant of deafness and sign language, Mary had hearing parents who were fluent signers, thanks to the deafness of their own parents. The couple had a deaf son, Thomas Lewis Brown, in 1839. Thomas's deaf sister Persis married a hearing man, Bela Swett. The couple had deaf sons, who took deaf wives, and had deaf children in turn.[6]

Thomas Brown was a leading resident of Henniker, remembered as "one of our most intelligent, upright, industrious and respectable citizens."[7] He was described as "practical, methodical, deliberate and far-seeing." Well thought of in the larger Henniker community, Brown served as a delegate to the state's Democratic convention in 1851. It was Brown, "always willing to do his share, and more, to forward any plan which promised to promote the welfare of his class," who urged his fellow graduates in 1853 to form a society "to promote the intellectual, social, moral, temporal, and spiritual welfare of our mute community." The following year, in 1854, a group of those graduates, from every New England state, would gather at the Brown family farm in Henniker to draft a constitution for the new organization, which named itself in honor of Thomas Hopkins Gallaudet. Thomas Brown was elected its first president, a position he held for twelve years.[8]

It was the first formal organization of, by, and for Deaf Americans to draft a constitution. As historians John Vickrey Van Cleve and Barry A. Crouch point out, this constitution denied membership to hearing people, reserving membership to "mutes" and to those "only deaf." "Mutes" referred to deaf people, those born deaf or early deafened, who did not, could not, or would not, speak. The term "mutes" also suggested those deaf people who had attended a manual school for the deaf. "Only deaf" indicated individuals who had lost their hearing in adolescence or adulthood and had therefore retained their speech. They were not "mutes." The constitution added that such "only deaf" people may also "have never been in any institution for deaf-mutes." These were people who might have lived part of their lives as hearing people. They had not attended a manual school, and they might still speak. These, then, were the "only deaf." As Van Cleve and Crouch note, in 1854, most deaf people received no speech training in school. They were therefore likely to be mute and chose to identify themselves by their lack of speech, attaching no stigma to their inability to communicate verbally.

Van Cleve and Crouch further suggest that the New England Gallaudet Association of the Deaf decided to admit both "mutes" and "only deaf" to full membership because the "association realized that it was to the advantage of all deaf people to act in unison, not to be divided by the distinctions that hearing people were apt to apply. The fact of deafness, alone, was a sufficient characteristic to define a person's identity within the deaf community in the middle of the nineteenth century."[9]

But there were other reasons, beyond political expediency, why the New England Gallaudet Association of the Deaf chose to include all kinds of deaf people. The borders of nineteenth-century Deaf culture were drawn differently than those of the twentieth. In 1854, Deaf culture could comfortably include "mutes" (the born deaf, the early deafened), the "semi-mutes" (those profoundly deaf who used some speech), the "semi-deaf" (the hard of hearing), and the "only deaf" (those who had lost their hearing while retaining their speech).

Deaf culture was able to include this range of audiological diversity because hearing teachers did not divide deaf people along these lines of distinction in 1854. In 1854, all of these various deaf people attended the residential schools together. They lived together. They went to class together. They learned English together. They learned the sign language together. The schools that they attended were universally manual in method, as there were no oral schools in 1854. The differences among them, including age of onset of deafness, were certainly noted by educators, but only for the purpose of deciding which students stood to benefit from an after-school speech-training lesson, not to divide them into separate schools entirely. Nineteenth-century residential schools contained all kinds of physically deaf people and so the culture too sought to embrace all of the deaf. It was indeed enough to be deaf in the mid-nineteenth century.

The constitution of the New England Gallaudet Association of the Deaf reflected the values of Deaf culture. Thomas Brown was aiming even further than including people along the audiological spectrum; he also wanted to include people who were deaf but who had never attended a residential school. He wanted those deaf people to also feel welcomed into the larger deaf community. They were all physically deaf. Even though they had not experienced the acculturating influence of the residential school, joining this organization would provide them another path into the Deaf community. One suspects Thomas was here influenced by the example of his own father, Nahum, the recognized patriarch of the Deaf Brown clan, but a man himself not a product of the residential school. The New England Gallaudet Association signaled that there were many ways to be both deaf and Deaf, and deaf people of all backgrounds could find a home in the larger Deaf community.

The very language of the culture indicated the way that it perceived the world; people were speaking or mutes, not hearing or deaf. And deafness was taken as the center, with deviations marked from that center. Some people were deaf and some were semi-deaf. The terminology for those same populations in the twentieth century would be "deaf" and "hard of hearing." Identifying as "hard of hearing," of course, puts hearing at the cultural center, and indicates one's deviation from that perceived cultural norm. The term also indicates a sense of identification, declaring that one is more like the hearing than the deaf. People would rather be understood as "hard of hearing" today; what is the benefit to attaching oneself, politically or culturally, to the Deaf community as a "semi-deaf" person? This strikes me as the real reason a term like "semi-deaf" is seen as so anachronistic; it is articulating a different cultural understanding of deafness entirely.

Only in the Deaf community is this older, nineteenth-century usage sometimes retained. As Carol Padden and Tom Humphries describe it, in ASL the term A-LITTLE HARD-OF-HEARING can indicate someone who can hear only a little and VERY HARD-OF-HEARING can mean someone who can hear pretty well. They were puzzled at how the terms in ASL meant exactly the opposite of what they would mean in English until they realized the following:

This is the crucial element in understanding these "backward" definitions: there is a different center, a different point from which one deviates. In this case, DEAF, not HEARING, is taken as the central point of deviation. A-LITTLE HARD-OF-HEARING is a small deviation from DEAF, and thus is used for someone who is only slightly hearing. VERY HARD-OF-HEARING is someone who departs from the center greatly, thus someone who can hear quite well.[10]

The nineteenth-century Deaf community, before the rise of oralism, would seem to have organized itself along the lines that Padden and Humphries suggest. It too put Deafness at the center and noted the extent of difference from that center. It focused on communication preferences and assumed that Deaf people would largely be mutes. But the semi-mute and the only deaf were welcome, as long as they identified themselves as culturally Deaf.

The enrollment records of the American Asylum reveal the extent to which many people chose to identify themselves with the Deaf community. The records show many students who became deaf in childhood, well after learning English and knowing how to speak, who grew up to marry born-deaf persons. In spite of their own personal histories, they did not think of themselves as "speaking people" or as "hard of hearing people." They did not marry hearing partners to try to attach themselves to the hearing community, or try to pass as hearing. Their school experience enabled them, or perhaps even encouraged them, to develop a strong sense of Deaf identity.

A list of prominent Deaf figures of the nineteenth century similarly reveals this diversity of deafness. Fisher Spofford was widely hailed as one of the most eloquent signers of his day; his "orations" were famous in the Deaf community. He went deaf at the age of three. Thomas Brown was the undisputed leader of the nineteenth-century Deaf community. He was born deaf. William Chamberlain strongly identified with the Deaf community and became one of its leading journalists. He went deaf around the age of eight. William Swett, Chamberlain's journalistic partner and another well-known figure in the Deaf world, was born deaf. Henry C. Rider, a man who founded a school for the deaf and was among the first to call for a national organization for deaf Americans, an activist devoted to his community and tireless in his advocacy on behalf of its political rights, went deaf at the age of four. George Loring, the recognized leader of the Boston Deaf community and a leading light in the larger New England Deaf community, did not speak. Mary Toles, who went deaf at the age of thirteen, but who married into a family with prominent connections in the Deaf world, was said to have a beautiful speaking voice. There was a tremendous range of audiological experience in the nineteenth-century Deaf community.

From what I have found, none of these people found themselves attacked within the community for a perceived lack of properly Deaf credentials. Thomas Brown, for example, did not reject Henry Rider as somehow "not deaf enough." Nor was Brown especially noted as being Deaf of Deaf, or from a deaf family, in any deaf press coverage of him that I have seen. Both of these are later cultural concerns.[11]

For instance, historian Susan Burch, looking at the deaf press of the 1920s and 1930s, has found that "the community—when out of the public spotlight—continued to praise the . . . population of natural leaders: Deaf children from Deaf families, the 'Deaf of Deaf.'" These were "master signers who saw Deafness as the norm" and who "challenged the image of the hereditary Deaf as 'undesirable.'"[12]

It is not difficult to understand why the Deaf of Deaf gained more cultural cachet as time went by. During the years of the oralist control of residential schools, the Deaf of Deaf were best positioned to pass on the cultural values of the Deaf community to the deaf children from hearing families. They did so largely without the support of their teachers and administrators, and frequently did so in spite of overt opposition to the transmission of that culture. Increasingly isolated from contact with Deaf adults, the Deaf of Deaf in residential schools became ever more important to the survival of the culture and its language. They kept ASL alive and put it in the hands of the deaf children from hearing families. Arguably, the Deaf President Now strike of 1988 represented the height of their cultural power and influence.[13]

However, in the antebellum period, as Deaf culture was just coming into existence, the Deaf of Deaf were not yet reified in quite this same way. First, there were not that many of them. There would be more Deaf of Deaf families once more couples met at residential schools and subsequently married. While they were still a small percentage of the Deaf community, as only roughly 10 percent of deaf people have deaf parents, the numbers of Deaf families would increase accordingly over the course of the century. Second, the school system was manual and Deaf adults were active in it. Deaf children were not the sole cultural transmitters at work in the period. The rise of oralism had much to do with the subsequent cultural rise of the Deaf of Deaf.

Being deaf from a deaf family in the nineteenth century proved a *personal* advantage at school; those fortunate students arrived with a working knowledge of language and with a very different personal experience of growing up communicating with their family members. But in a time when Deaf culture was still coming into existence, it did not clearly give these students a *cultural* advantage. All deaf students, from very different personal and auditory backgrounds, lent a hand to birthing that community. And all laid claim to their Deafness as they chose to become members of that community and live their lives within it. So Henry C. Rider could be just as passionate about his community, even though he did not physically join it until he was four, as Thomas Brown, who had been deaf from birth. After all, Thomas Brown was born in 1804. There was no American Deaf culture we could point to in 1804, nor was there a recognizable American Deaf community. Being Deaf of Deaf in 1804 could not carry the meaning it would for later generations of deaf people. And not being Deaf of Deaf could not have been culturally stigmatizing, either.

Together, then, these were the people who joined Deaf associations like the New England Gallaudet Association of the Deaf. Possessing a new sense of a Deaf identity, they increasingly wanted organizations to foster and preserve their community. State organizations for the deaf quickly emerged as well. The first, the Empire State Association, was founded in New York in 1865. One of its most energetic presidents, serving for sixteen years, was in fact Henry C. Rider (1832-1913), who cited the residential school as the heart of the Deaf community.[14] Such organizations merely continued what the schools had started, namely, weaving a community together. As Rider put it, the residential school experience "engenders in our hearts the longing desire and almost irresistible impulse to meet with each other; and even though it be brief, to enjoy for a short season the society of our boon companions."[15]

The opportunity to enjoy such company led large numbers of Deaf people to attend the association's annual conventions. Alphonso Johnson, another president of the Empire State Association, explained why so many gathered together. "When at home, we are widely scattered, and must carry on conversation with our speaking brethren by the slow and laborious process of writing," he said, "but here we meet and our language of signs is brought into full play. Thought flashes from mind to mind, and we feel elated. . . . We listen (with our eyes) to addresses in our own well understood language."[16]

Rider himself knew well how this drive for companionship compelled many deaf people to travel enormous lengths to come to convention events. He lived in Malone, New York, an isolated town near the Canadian border. He painted the lives of the deaf in such communities as being filled with "tedious monotony."[17] Annual conventions and association meetings offered a welcome break from this monotony. For instance, an annual event in 1869 for the deaf of the greater Boston area attracted about two hundred deaf people and many more would have attended, a Deaf reporter asserted, but for the terrible snow storm that struck that day. The party went on in spite of the weather. The rented hall in Boston was kept open all night, and "the assembly did not disperse till eight o' clock the next morning."[18]

Soon, such increasing communal awareness would lead to the idea of a national convention of the deaf. Deaf leaders like Thomas Brown and Henry C. Rider argued strongly in favor of a national organization. A correspondent to the *Deaf Mutes' Friend*, H.C.R.—a thinly disguised Henry C. Rider— explained the need for such a convention in June 1869.

> The time has come when we should prepare to secure the general advancement of our own interests as a class. Such can only be the outgrowth of thorough organization. Perhaps an union can be formed at the meeting on the principle of absolute nationality. Such an one, ably and judiciously conducted on a sound social basis and amply supported by strong combination and unity of action, would be one of the most potent instruments for the good of our whole community. Its scope would be wider and its operation more extended than ever known before. It would elevate our national character, encourage an universal interchange of sentiment and educate the taste, so that the better and more pleasing traits of our national character may be developed. Why should we not let mind keep pace with mind in the onward march toward a higher development, both socially and intellectually? Let all deaf-mutes strive to attain that standard of equality which can be achieved by competent and well organized effort.[19]

The author suggested an organization similar to the National Association of the Deaf, which would not be founded until 1880. An organization with a national scope, he argued, could work more effectively for the goals of the community. In fact, he asserted that the deaf community constituted "a class" with a "national character." Even scattered across the country, deaf people, Rider believed, were all members of one community. They therefore needed one national organization that might represent their collective interests.

They also needed a national organization so that deaf people from across the country might meet one another and work together, as he phrased it, to "elevate our national character, encourage an universal interchange of sentiment, and educate the taste, so that the better and more pleasing traits of our national character may be developed." Deaf people, by Rider's lights, should conceive of themselves as a national community with a national character sharing a national culture. A sense of deaf nationalism was beginning to emerge.

Though a national organization, to complement the many local organizations of the Deaf community, was not established at this time, the fact that it was seriously proposed in 1869 is important. It suggests that by 1869 many deaf people recognized that they were not simply a loosely connected group of individuals all of whom had experienced some degree of physical hearing loss; rather, they knew that they were Deaf people, people who formed a community with a common culture. Rider proposed his idea assuming that a responsive audience existed. He believed that he was addressing a community that, to some extent, shared his assumptions about Deafness. By 1869, Martineau's fraternity was quite real.

Deaf Nationalism

Bernard Mottez famously called deaf people "a people without a homeland."[20] He cited the growth of a tradition of holding banquets in France to celebrate the birth of the Abbé de l'Epée as an indication of the way nineteenth-century Deaf people began to claim and honor their collective heritage. A people must know their history in order to honor it. The fact that the Parisian Deaf ritually gathered to celebrate their past offers a proof to Mottez that Deaf people felt themselves to be a people, a people with a common heritage they were charged to remember and pass on to younger generations. We have already seen the way that this heritage was handed down to the deaf students in the American School. They were taught their history, which allowed them in turn to claim their place in the larger community of the Deaf. In this way, they became a people, possessing at least a common heritage, even if they lacked a common homeland.

Modern theorists in the field of Deaf Studies, like Lennard Davis and Harlan Lane, have referred to deaf nationalism and ethnicity, even if the nineteenth-century Deaf community did not use those terms. But, Davis writes, "If an ethos is defined as a culturally similar group sharing a common language, then the Deaf conceivably fit that category."[21] Evidence for this kind of nationalistic thinking is difficult to come by in the nineteenth-century sources. But Edmund Booth, at the time a young student at the American School, made the case in 1831 in the form of an invented dialogue between a Deaf man and a Greek patriot.

The Deaf man begins by saying, "I ought to be thankful for these blessings so freely bestowed on my country, but there is something that makes me often unhappy in the midst of pleasure." The Greek patriot replies, "I suppose it is your feeling yourself different from your companions in being deprived of hearing, which makes you so." He is obviously hearing; Booth has him express a typical belief of hearing people. "It is not that which I meant," corrects the Deaf man. "It is the deplorable condition of my unfortunate uneducated deaf and dumb brethren." To emphasize his point, Booth makes the Greek patriot deliberately misunderstand the Deaf man. "I did not know that you had brothers and sisters deaf and dumb," he says in wonder. "Pray how many have you under that calamity?" And now the Deaf man can clarify, announcing, "By my deaf and dumb brethren I mean all the deaf and dumb in the world. They are as dear to me as your country was to you."[22]

But there is additional evidence to suggest that Deaf people had begun to think of themselves as an ethnic group even in the nineteenth century. It is the Deaf State movement. As Lennard Davis argues, "The fact that some Deaf people wanted to found a separate state is a strong enough argument for seeing them as a nationality or an ethnic group."[23] So too would be the fact that the originator of this idea specifically wrote that, in the state of the deaf, the hearing man was to be regarded as a foreigner.[24] Characterizing the hearing as "foreigners" leaves the deaf as "natives," a group with an identity of their own that the hearing cannot, and do not, share. Being natives speaks almost inevitably of possessing a nationality, a sense of commonness, of being Deaf together—and, accordingly, of desiring a homeland.

The idea of the Deaf State, of this homeland for the Deaf, was the brainchild of John J. Flournoy (1800-1879), one of the great eccentrics of the Deaf community and, indeed, of the entire nineteenth century. As historians John Vickrey Van Cleve and Barry Crouch note, "Flournoy rarely cut his hair or his beard. He wore a rubber raincoat in all seasons, and he rode about on a small donkey." Yet he had studied at the American School for the Deaf and briefly attended the University of Georgia. He was influential in establishing a school for the deaf in Georgia. He had, in other words, seen some schemes through to fruition. And in 1855, inspired at least in part by the Mormon example, he proposed another, the founding of an all-deaf state in the West.[25]

He sent a letter outlining the idea to William Turner, then the principal of the American School. Turner, in response, replied to the letter publicly, having Flournoy's letter and his own published in the *Annals*. In so doing, he touched off a wave of public debate on the topic that drew in more participants as the letters flew back and forth, in a heated printed conversation that lasted until 1858.[26]

As he told Turner, he wanted to create a deaf state in order specifically to free deaf people from the tyranny of hearing prejudice. Deaf people, he claimed, unfairly suffer "rejections and consignments to inferior places" by hearing people.[27] In making this charge, John Flournoy touched off one of the earliest debates about the nature of disability in American history. He asked his readers to consider whether or not the so-called handicap of deafness was physically created or socially constructed.

Flournoy was clearly a believer in social construction. Physical deafness did not naturally mean anything; the meanings assigned to it, like inferiority or inability, were created by people, and largely by hearing people at that. Hearing people projected their ideas onto deafness and resisted Deaf attempts to define deafness differently and positively. Even though he believed in social construction, Flournoy was increasingly pessimistic about the chances of changing the minds of hearing people, as long as the deaf and the hearing continued to live side by side. He asked, why continue to struggle against this irrational prejudice? Rather, let the deaf prove their capabilities to hearing people by creating a model all-deaf society.

Flournoy did not limit his ideas about social construction to deafness alone. He asserted that disability generally was a socially constructed phenomenon. As Flournoy put it in an 1856 letter to Turner, "The old cry about the incapacity of men's minds from physical disabilities, I think it were time, now in this intelligent age, to *explode!*"[28] Using deaf people again as an example, he allowed that perhaps deaf people could not literally do everything that hearing people could do. "But we do attest," Flournoy insisted, "that we are capable of many of which the prejudice, and sometimes even malignance of our hearing brethren deprive us!!"[29]

Going beyond the idea of the social construction of disability, in 1856, Flournoy even anticipated a theory of audism, a late-twentieth-century theoretical apparatus that attempts to capture the ways in which deafness has been unfairly constructed solely as a medical rather than a cultural condition. Consider this passage: "The auricular are not satisfied with hearing, nor with the usual mutual sympathies of their own class, but are banded and combined together in associations, open, and societies, secret, until they form a compact moral mechanism, that fairly by their majority, puts us in the shade."[30] And here is theorist Harlan Lane in 1992: "Audism is the corporate institution for dealing with deaf people, dealing with them by making statements about them, authorizing views of them, describing them, teaching about them, governing where they go to school and, in some cases, where they live; in short, audism is the hearing way of dominating, restructuring, and exercising authority over the deaf community."[31]

Lane's audists and Flournoy's auriculars would seem to share much in common, both operating through their own societies and institutions to dominate deaf lives to their own advantage. As is the case in much of his writing, though, Flournoy failed to follow up on his own ideas. It is scarcely a wonder that his nineteenth-century critics did not know what to make of such notions; he was writing more than a century ahead of his time.

Responses to Flournoy's proposal, and his analysis, generally fell into two camps. One we might call practical objections. William Turner, for one, asked how the Deaf State would remain deaf, since most deaf people have hearing children. Flournoy's response— "If our children hear, let them go to other states"—was not exactly sympathetic. Turner also questioned how many deaf people would honestly be willing to leave their settled lives for this scheme. Their friends? Their relatives? Their homes? Their livelihoods? Turner did not believe that deaf people were as dissatisfied with their lives as Flournoy made them out to be. Others, like Edmund Booth, raised concerns about expenses and population. Where would the money for the land come from? Would enough deaf people choose to live in this state to make the project viable?

But Turner and others also expressed what might be called theoretical differences with Flournoy. Turner, for one, would not concede that Flournoy's depiction of hearing prejudice was accurate nor did he believe that prejudice was largely responsible for limiting deaf options in life. Deafness itself limited those options, he said. "You would not send a deaf and dumb man to Congress or to the Legislature of a State; not for the reason that he was deficient in intelligence and education, but because his want of hearing and speech unfits him for the place."[32] Turner, in other words, refused to accept that deafness might be socially constructed, as Flournoy contended. He insisted that deafness imposed some "natural" limitations. Flournoy's quest to supersede them was therefore doomed to fail. One could not exceed the limits of one's nature.

But this was exactly the point to which Flournoy most strenuously objected. He continued to insist that many of the so-called handicaps of deafness were socially constructed. He himself was a frustrated politician; he ran unsuccessfully for political office several times. Flournoy argued that hearing prejudice, and not deafness, stood in his way. Hearing people, just like Turner, believed a deaf man would not be able to function as a legislator. What a limited view, Flournoy announced. "Place *me* for an example in any Capitol, . . . and I will move for an *aid* [sic] . . . to reveal to me what is said, what is to be done, what to do, and to read my speeches. And in this way I can get along supremely well, as Legislator. The gist . . . being that my intelligence and judgment may prove better and superior to the hearing majority."[33] Flournoy asserted that his deafness could be easily and reasonably accommodated by an interpreter. What prevented this from happening were erroneous hearing ideas, ideas even Turner as principal of the American School sometimes expressed, about deafness.

It was not only hearing people, however, who expressed ideas about deafness that Flournoy found objectionable. Deaf people also were divided about the meaning of deafness. The Deaf journalist Edmund Booth (1810-1905) actively participated in this debate.[34] In 1858, he wrote that he believed it better for the deaf "to remain as they are—scattered and in one sense lost—among their hearing associates. In such situations they are compelled to read and write, and thus keep their minds under the educational process through life."[35] Flournoy objected that many deaf people struggled with English and were not good readers. They might benefit by the example of more educated mute readers around them and also be able to pursue their education lyceum-style by attending lectures and tutorials given in American Sign Language instead.[36]

The two men took up a debate that marked two great fault lines in the nineteenth-century American deaf community, first, the difference between educated and uneducated deaf people, and second, the difference between those fluent in English and those more comfortable in ASL. Booth believed that, in the North at least, the masses of people, including the educated deaf, were readers.[37] Even if the deaf sometimes struggled with English, Booth believed that ground could be made up with better education. If deaf people were better educated, the gap between them and the hearing would close. In such a widely educated society, the deaf could never truly be lost, Booth believed. They would always have educated hearing companions with whom to communicate in written English. Expanding educational opportunities among both the hearing and the deaf would ensure inclusion. If the hearing were not also educated well, Booth conceded, "among such a population, an educated deaf-mute must necessarily be almost literally lost."[38]

In addition, Booth charged that this was a sectional problem. Flournoy was a southerner, and the South, Booth observed, lagged behind educationally. In the North, educated deaf people took their place in a largely educated society, and more educated deaf people joined them daily as the schools reached more and more northern students. Once the South caught up in such things, Booth assured Flournoy, he would feel better about the future for deaf people even in predominantly hearing states.[39]

But, Flournoy argued, Booth seemed to focus only on English as the primary language of communication, as when he stressed reading. His argument seemed to neglect entirely those deaf people who preferred to communicate primarily by using ASL. What about those deaf people, Flournoy wanted to know? Did they benefit by being scattered in a population that did not understand their language at all? Booth perhaps forgot that all deaf people were not like him. He was a newspaper editor, married to a deaf woman, living in a hearing community. He was equally comfortable in both English and ASL and moved easily between the hearing and deaf worlds. While this was indeed the ideal outcome for an educated deaf person, it remained an ideal that not all deaf people attained. Flournoy wanted to address the lives of those who had fallen short of this ideal. How could life improve for them in a world of hearing prejudice, when deaf elites like Booth refused to even acknowledge such prejudice?

Flournoy finally got some support for his ideas in April of 1858, when the *Annals* published a letter from William Chamberlain, another Deaf journalist. Like Flournoy, he attacked Booth's depiction of deaf readers, saying, "I have always found deaf-mutes to be greater readers, better informed and more intelligent, where there are a number of them in the same place, than when scattered, as many, if not most of them are among the hearing. . . . A deaf-mute, generally speaking, is not apt to understand what he reads, by himself, so well as when he has access to some individuals of the same class. What one does not understand another can explain, and thus they promote each other's improvement."[40] A state might be too much to start with, and Chamberlain recommended that a township might serve the purpose. For "when all things are considered," he concluded, "I think the benefits to be derived . . . are enough to render such a community desirable."[41]

Chamberlain was not alone in offering encouragement to Flournoy. The most poignant letter of support came from P. H. Confer, about whom almost nothing is known. He was a deaf man living in Indiana, unconnected with the elites who had to date participated in this debate. As such, he perhaps presents us with the best view of opinion from the deaf street.

> The deaf-mutes would all be happy, as they can not now be, because they have nobody that can or will converse with them, and many people look on a deaf-mute as if he were a fool, because he can not talk, and because to them deaf-mutes look so foolish, just because they can not understand them. If they were by themselves, they could be happy; but as they are separated, they are in many cases despised by hearing men. That I have found

out myself, because the hearing man says to the mute, You are a fool. . . . Therefore I say, I am for a place where all my deaf-mute brethren could live and be happy; and I would say to J. J. Flournoy, that I like his enterprise, and if it should come so far as to buy the land, I would say, that I would give $5,000 to it in cash.[42]

Here the weaknesses in elite thinking became most painfully clear. While Booth assumed that being scattered among the hearing improved deaf lives, Confer indicated that such a life was merely lonely and isolating. Hearing people did not want to take the time to communicate in writing with deaf people. They seemed instead to resent that deaf people could not simply speak to communicate. Some even mocked the use of sign language on the part of the deaf. Confer charged that hearing people "despise" deaf people.

Booth and Turner both expressed dismay and disbelief at Confer's appraisal of the feelings of nineteenth-century hearing people, but it would come as no surprise to twenty-first-century disability scholars. As Lennard Davis writes,

> In our culture, it is permissible to "pity" or even "resent" people with disabilities. It is sometimes loosely permitted to make fun of some disabilities (stutters, mental retardation, age-associated deafness, myopia, and the like) but one is generally not supposed to "hate" disabled people. . . . But the "hate" against people with disabilities is a much more subtle and ingrained hatred. It is a hatred of difference, of the fact that someone cannot see a clearly posted sign, cannot walk up unblocked stairs, needs special assistance above what other "normal" citizens need. This kind of hatred is one that abhors the possibility that all bodies are not configured the same.[43]

This was the kind of hatred that Confer and Flournoy believed they knew all too well in the mid-nineteenth century. After all, Confer said, the hearing man calls the mute a fool. Flournoy pointed to the secret hearing heart of darkness as he observed, "When we would claim equality, it offends."[44] It is no wonder that Flournoy's peers had difficulty in accepting his views. They came in an admittedly underdeveloped form and, more importantly, lacked a political or cultural context within which they could be understood. It would take the development of the disability rights movement, and its corresponding outpouring of scholarship, to truly make Flournoy's positions comprehensible. But even in their nascent form there were some, like Chamberlain and Confer, who recognized the strength of his arguments.

The epitaph for this movement came in the fall of 1858. Members of the New England Gallaudet Association took up this discussion of the Deaf State at their third convention meeting in Worcester, Massachusetts, in September 1858. William Turner, Rev. Thomas Gallaudet, and Laurent Clerc all spoke out against Flournoy's plan. The association reported, "Mr. Clerc asked the Convention whether the members were despised or maltreated at home. Receiving a general *no!* for answer, he asked, then why emigrate? He also asked them whether they would prefer to form a community of deaf and dumb, and the general answer was that they had rather live mixed among those who hear and speak."[45] Having been brought before the only major organization of deaf people in the country and rejected, Flournoy's dream finally died. The idea faded into historical oblivion.

But it did not do so before sowing some significant theoretical seeds that would lie dormant until disability scholars and activists began to cultivate them in the twentieth century. More important, the conversation about the Deaf State powerfully demonstrated the existence of a growing sense of Deaf nationalism among the American Deaf community in the nineteenth century. "Flournoy's call for a Deaf colony tapped into the dreams of Deaf people worldwide," historian Hannah Joyner writes enthusiastically. "Deaf people fantasized about what their connections could build. . . . And that connection transcended the regional identities that hearing Americans were feeling so profoundly by the late 1850s."[46] While hearing Americans at this time increasingly felt fragmented into camps, northern or southern, deaf Americans were asserting their growing sense of national identity as Deaf Americans.

And, as Flournoy's ideas for a state indicate, they were claiming their deafness, that common physical experience, as the basis of their culture. The ability to sign was not enough, in Flournoy's view, to claim a space in the Deaf State. The Deaf State, and more broadly the Deaf experience, was not merely about using a minority language. One had to be deaf, physically, biologically, audiologically deaf, to be welcome in a Deaf state. Flournoy's proposed state would have sought to turn a stigmatized condition in the mainstream community into a point of pride in a self-directed Deaf world.[47]

With the failure of the Deaf State to materialize, that transformation would have to proceed not in building a deaf homeland but rather in a series of deafcentric institutions that came into existence in the nineteenth century.

Radical Experiments in Education

Given the growing rise in what Harlan Lane has called "the ethnic conscious-ness" of the Deaf in the 1850s, as evidenced by the Deaf State movement and other cultural events discussed below, it comes as no surprise that one of the most provocative educational experiments in the Deaf world would also take place in the 1850s.

In 1852, David Bartlett, a hearing man with twenty years of teaching expe-rience in the field of deaf education, opened a new school for the deaf in New York City. He called it "Mr. Bartlett's Family School for Young Deaf Mute Children"—"young," because it would serve children between the ages of four and a half and seven, students usually considered too young to attend residential schools; and "family" because hearing siblings were encouraged to attend with their deaf siblings.

This was an unprecedented educational experiment. Deaf and hearing students attended school together. The language of instruction was manual, apparently a form of signed English. Bartlett assumed that hearing siblings would need signed language skills in order to be able to communicate with their deaf family member and also to interpret for other hearing family members, even parents. Bartlett also assumed that, for the deaf and hearing to blend in a classroom on equal footing, a visual, not oral, language was required. This was a very different way of accommodating the difference of deafness. "Bartlett suggested that hearing families could adapt to their deaf children," historian John Vickrey Van Cleve writes, "rather than vice versa, and he placed deaf and hearing pupils on a truly equal footing."[48] Bartlett was a pioneer, one John Flournoy would have appreciated, as he insisted that hearing people could, and should, do more to accommodate the deaf in daily life, even going so far as to learn their language.

The school, like many small educational endeavors, was a financial fail-ure. It moved at least four times in its brief existence, struggling to find a workable financial arrangement to secure its future. It finally closed its doors for good in 1861 and Bartlett resumed his teaching career at the American School. But pedagogically it must be judged a success. The school's graduates include Henry Syle, the first deaf man to be ordained an Episcopal priest, and Gideon Moore, the first deaf American to earn a doctoral degree.

Its brief life also points to a road left untaken after its closure.[49] There were other similarly integrated schools by the late nineteenth century, such as Alexander Graham Bell's school in Washington, DC, and F. Knapp's Insti-tute in Baltimore. Both small, private schools, much like Bartlett's, they brought deaf and hearing children together as students. Unlike Bartlett's, they brought the deaf into hearing classrooms on hearing terms. Speech and lipreading were required; gestures of any sort were forbidden.[50] The idea that accommodating deaf people into the mainstream would require the embrace, rather than the rejection, of deaf language was by then completely abandoned. Likewise, the notion that the two groups could achieve equality best on deaf linguistic terms was rejected out of hand. By the late nineteenth century, only hearing terms would do. Bartlett's experiment was therefore an idea whose time perhaps could only have come in the 1850s, together with the birth of Deaf culture. Given the oralist assault on Deaf culture that was still to come, it was not an idea that could easily have survived, finances or no.

The second major educational experiment of these years proved one of more lasting success. It was the founding of Gallaudet College, now Gallaudet University, in 1864.[51] The Deaf community had for years been clamoring for a college of its own, in order to prove itself intellectually to the wider hearing world. John Carlin had called for the establishment of a college for the deaf in 1854. But it was Amos Kendall, a prominent hearing Washingtonian, who set in motion the events that would make that vision a reality.

Kendall was a wealthy man who had made a fortune investing in the telegraph, the invention of his good friend, Samuel F. B. Morse. He was a well-connected man, an early political advisor to Andrew Jackson, later rewarded for his efforts with the position of postmaster general of the United States. And in the 1850s, he became the legal guardian of five orphaned deaf children. Accordingly, as a man with his wealth, position, and influence, he sought to open a school for the deaf in the District of Columbia. In 1857, he wrote to Harvey Prindle Peet, at the New York School, for his advice. Peet suggested contacting Edward Miner Gallaudet, Thomas's son.

Gallaudet had not planned to follow in his father's footsteps. He had taught briefly at the American School, but was dissatisfied there. In 1857, in fact, he was about to move to Chicago to accept a position at a bank. He was wary of the idea of getting back into deaf education. But he sought out his friend, Jared Ayres, a fellow teacher at the American School, to discuss this new opportunity. Ayres suggested that this might be the moment to do more than merely head a new residential school. Might Kendall be persuaded to support a plan to open a deaf college? The two friends had supported the idea immediately, when it had been proposed, but both believed it impossible to realize without sufficient capital to bankroll it. A wealthy philanthropist like Kendall could certainly fit the bill.

Gallaudet agreed to meet with Kendall. He explained that he would take the position as superintendent of Kendall's proposed school on one condition, namely, that Kendall back his plans to open a college as well. Kendall readily agreed, delighted with the idea that his initially small project would turn into one with national reach and scope. The two embarked upon a campaign to raise both funds and awareness. Congress passed legislation to allow Kendall's Columbia Institution for the Deaf and Dumb and Blind to grant collegiate degrees. President Abraham Lincoln signed it in April 1864. In June 1864, an inaugural ceremony was held for the new college. Laurent Clerc and John Carlin both attended and made speeches. Clerc expressed his pride at seeing the seeds planted by the American School bear the fruit of a college for deaf people. Carlin called the day, June 28, the marker of "a bright epoch in deaf-mute history. The birth of this infant college, the first of its kind in the world, will bring joy to the mute community." Carlin was awarded an honorary master of arts degree by the fledgling institution. In the fall of 1864, the college opened its doors to students. In its first year, it had five students and three full-time faculty members.

It is clear that the power of Gallaudet College in those early years lay more in its symbolism of deaf capability than its educational reach. That is, very few students attended Gallaudet in its earliest years. As late as 1950, the incoming first-year class had but seventy members, including six foreign students. Nonetheless, the image of a college for Deaf people was undeniably significant. This was the first college for deaf people in the world. Its very existence seemed to indicate that the Deaf had arrived on the American scene, and that Deaf Americans would draw the rest of the Deaf world to them.

The college's foundation also seemed to prefigure an expansive future for Deaf Americans. It is deeply ironic that the precise opposite turned out to be the case. "The triumph that the college represented for deaf Americans turned out, in retrospect," as Douglas Baynton, Jack Gannon, and Jean Lindquist Bergey conclude, "to be the high point of deaf education in the nineteenth century."[52] For as the Civil War ended, the field's turn toward oralism became ever clearer.

Deaf Churches

There were several churches for the deaf in the nineteenth century. Given that the manual schools were founded at least in part out of evangelical fervor, it is perhaps unsurprising that their alumni wanted to continue their practice of Christian worship after graduation. The students had been accustomed to attending Protestant worship services together in school. A student at the American Asylum described one such service in 1822, reporting that both the sign language and English were used to great effect. The preacher would begin by signing a short prayer. Then he would write several verses from Psalms on a large slate, positioned at the front of the chapel. These verses he would then explain "to their eyes." After another short signed prayer, the preacher would begin a sermon. Again, he would utilize the slate. He would select a passage from the Bible, writing down the chapter and verse and perhaps a line or two. Then on two other slates, he would outline the sermon in English before finally preaching it in the sign language. After the sermon, he would offer one more signed prayer and the service would conclude.[53]

The ready use of both English and Sign indicate a deaf population that was comfortable with both languages. As churches with deaf congregations began to emerge as more graduates entered into communities throughout the Northeast, bilingual worship would emerge as a normative practice. In Willimantic, Connecticut, beginning in 1840, a group of deaf people, numbering about fifteen, gathered regularly to worship together in a Sunday-school room at a local Protestant church. In 1851, similar situations were reported in Boston, Massachusetts, and in Nashua, New Hampshire; both churches drew about twenty deaf people together weekly.[54]

The best-known church of the antebellum period was St. Ann's Church for Deaf-Mutes, in New York City, founded and pastored in 1852 by Rev. Thomas Gallaudet, the son of Thomas Hopkins Gallaudet. Gallaudet, as son of one of the cofounders of the American School for the Deaf, had long been committed to deaf issues and, after his ordination as an Episcopal priest in 1851, put that commitment into practice by founding St. Ann's. St. Ann's served a mixed congregation, with deaf and hearing parishioners worshipping together. Gallaudet's sense of inclusiveness made the church a welcoming space for other people with disabilities, including blind parishioners, and people of all races as well.

Gallaudet took it as his mission to serve not only his deaf parishioners' spiritual needs but their secular ones as well. He would meet with hesitant employers to reassure them that the deaf of New York City would make worthy employees. He passed along communication tips to employers, encouraging them to use writing and fingerspelling in the workplace. Hearing members of the parish were also encouraged to learn fingerspelling and even the sign language, in order to communicate with their deaf fellow worshippers or with deaf co-workers. The church also conducted outreach to the deaf unemployed, organizing gatherings where information about open-minded employers and prospective job opportunities could be exchanged.

St. Ann's embodied the self-help ethos of the nineteenth-century Deaf community. Choosing not to organize to demand an end to discrimination in the workplace, a move probably not politically viable in the mid-nineteenth century anyway, the Deaf community pursued the more limited strategy of self-help. The community sought to prove its employability by performing well on the job, and honest brokers, like Thomas Gallaudet, tried to make that strategy pay off. As a hearing person, Gallaudet could talk with hearing employers directly and attempt to assuage their concerns, especially about communication, over deaf employees. He could also reach out to hearing people in his parish and enlist them to proselytize on this topic in their own workplaces. Hard work, good examples, and the cooperation of the hearing with the deaf were the lynchpins of St. Ann's, and the Deaf community's, accommodationist strategy in the middle of the nineteenth century.[55]

Deaf churches were crucial organizations therefore in promoting this strategy, as well as providing accommodating places of worship for Deaf people, places that used their own vernacular, the sign language, in every Sunday service. The Grace Episcopal Church in Baltimore, Maryland, encouraged by a visit from Rev. Thomas Gallaudet, organized the All Angels' Mission to the Deaf in 1859.[56] More churches for the deaf appeared by the turn of the century. These services were largely organized in a very Deaf way, with liturgical changes made by the hearing ministers in order to best facilitate worship by a bilingual deaf congregation.

The Deaf Press: Newspapers and Journals

Newspapers devoted entirely to Deaf issues were creations of the 1850s. But one New York newspaper, the *Canajoharie Radii*, had been acquired by Levi S. Backus, a graduate of the American Asylum, in 1837. As the first deaf editor of a newspaper in the country, Backus had the masthead of the *Radii* printed in fingerspelling. In addition to the newspaper's regular features and articles, Backus added a column consisting of news of special interest to the Deaf community. The New York School for the Deaf called the paper "a living testimony to the expediency and sound policy of educating the deaf and dumb."[57] In 1844 he succeeded in convincing the New York State legislature to give him funds to mail the *Radii* to "educated deaf people" across the state. Backus's printing office burned down in 1846. Undaunted, he moved his operation to Fort Plain, New York, and renamed the paper the *Radii and Phoenix*.

By the 1850s, many Deaf people had graduated from schools for the deaf. These alumni began to clamor for a truly Deaf newspaper. The *American Annals of the Deaf* had been in publication since 1847, but it was beginning to be seen as unsatisfactory. In 1859, William M. Chamberlain (1833-1895) explained why. "It seems that the *Annals* are better suited to the use and benefit of the teachers. I doubt not that the publishers think so too," he wrote. "There is a loud call for a paper of our own."[58] The *Annals* had become the sounding board for the opinions and suggestions of hearing educators. Deaf people contributed articles as well, but the focus was nearly always on education. In other words, the *Annals* was a journal, not a newspaper. A newspaper, with more information about the Deaf community, was lacking.

The Gallaudet Guide and Deaf-Mute's Companion would try to fill this need. The paper was sponsored by the New England Gallaudet Association of the Deaf and was edited by Chamberlain. It first appeared in January 1860 and was published monthly for five years. It was the country's first Deaf paper, founded and published by Deaf people to serve the interests of the Deaf reading public exclusively. As Van Cleve and Crouch have noted, the *Companion's* appearance signaled both "a recognition of a growing deaf self-awareness" and a "realization that deaf Americans were different from hearing Americans, that they had interests that could best be met through their own efforts."[59]

Other papers soon followed. The *Deaf Mutes' Friend*, edited by two Deaf men, William B. Swett (1824-1884) and William M. Chamberlain, was published in Henniker, New Hampshire, for one year: 1869. The paper included stories from Swett's colorful life as a guide in New Hampshire's White Mountains.[60] The stories were interesting, not only because they commented extensively on life in the hearing world but also because they were told to Chamberlain in the sign language by Swett and then translated into English. "How well or ill this is done," Chamberlain wrote, "is not for us to say; we will simply observe that, deaf ourself, and educated at an Institution for the deaf and dumb, we can use and understand signs as well as we can the English language."[61] The paper was therefore very Deaf in tone, full of translated signed stories and tidbits about the Deaf community in New England. It is, of course, not surprising that such a paper came out of Henniker, as it was a Deaf enclave in New England. William B. Swett was a member of the leading Deaf family in Henniker; his mother was Persis Brown Swett and he was Thomas Brown's nephew.

While independent newspapers and journals of the silent press started and folded at a dizzying pace, the papers most consistently available to alumni throughout the nineteenth century were the school papers of the residential schools. Collectively, these school papers have become known as the "Little Paper Family" or the "Little Papers." These papers were published at various intervals, some monthly, some weekly. At least one school, the Rochester School for the Deaf, in Rochester, New York, published a daily newsletter. By the late nineteenth century, nearly fifty schools contributed to the Little Paper Family. Titles included *The Deaf Mute* (begun in 1849, North Carolina), *The Mute* (begun in 1868, Ohio), the *Deaf Mute Advance* (begun in 1870, Illinois), and the *Deaf Mute Pelican* (begun in 1870, Louisiana).[62]

Many of the Little Papers were founded for practical reasons. They were written, edited, and printed on campus and so provided vocational training for deaf boys. Printing was, during the years of the linotype machine, a solid occupation for deaf men. It paid a good wage and the industry proved willing to hire deaf and hearing men alike. For a few deaf men, like Levi Backus, who started the *Canajoharie Radii* (New York) in 1837, and Edmund Booth, who founded the *Anamosa Eureka* (Iowa) in 1856, a knowledge of printing provided the skills they needed to run newspapers of their own.

The Little Papers provided much more than job training, however important that was for the students. They also provided a way for deaf people to stay connected to one another after graduation. They helped to weave the Deaf community together. The independent papers and the Little Papers, taken together, helped to build a self-aware and national Deaf community.[63]

Through the papers, Deaf people were able to stay informed about events at their old schools, about their old school friends, and about important events and services. Often, papers listed the names of deaf-owned businesses, so that other deaf people could patronize them. They listed businesses and shops that hired deaf people, so that deaf people might know where to find willing employers. They listed the times and places of interpreted religious services, so that deaf people might attend a worship service they could understand and actively participate in.

The papers of the silent press also ran "personals" columns. These columns were made up of contributions from Deaf readers. Readers submitted updates about their own lives, news of marriages, births, and deaths, travel plans, changes of address, and the like. The *Silent World* urged its readers to take advantage of this opportunity to stay in touch with old friends.

> We would remind our readers that we are wholly dependent upon their good nature and courtesy for the matter contained in the Personal Department. It does not take long to write and send a short item for this department, yet the shortest item about an old schoolmate or friend may be of

more value than all the rest of the paper to any one of our readers. We ask, therefore, that each and every one of our readers will consider himself or herself one of the editors of the Personal Column, and send anything, no matter how little, which may be of interest.[64]

By offering readers this chance to keep abreast of one another, the papers helped to form a national Deaf community. The papers were an early social network that bound them together. Reading them and subscribing to them signaled a personal choice to be a part of a wider Deaf community. The papers provided a solution to the twin problems of being a scattered community and a minority culture in a hearing world.[65]

The papers not only served to strengthen the Deaf community; they also gave advice on how to succeed in a hearing world. That advice did not include becoming culturally hearing or learning to speak. Some articles simply suggested "How to Be Happy" or "How to Keep Your Friends" or recommended "Steadiness of Purpose." Others focused on behavior. They reminded readers that, in any encounter with hearing people, a deaf person signed not just for himself; he represented the deaf community to that hearing person. Hearing people had so little experience with the deaf that it was incumbent on all deaf people to try to manage to best effect the impressions they made upon the hearing world. In this way, deaf people were like so many other ethnic minorities, trying to make headway against discrimination in the mainstream.[66] The papers regularly advised against smoking and drinking. Avoiding vices, the papers argued, would make deaf people more employable, and in a world where deafness itself could be an obstacle to employment, deaf people needed to make the best possible impression on a potential employer.

This was, perhaps, a conservative approach to dealing with the problem of hearing prejudice. Rather than attack that prejudice directly, by calling attention to it and denouncing it, the nineteenth-century Deaf community largely chose to try to work around it. They would focus on their own behavior, not on hearing behavior, and tried their best to fit into the mold of the model employee that hearing people demanded. As the *Silent Worker* reminded its readers, "many [hearing] people do not want to hire a deaf person."[67] Once hired, a deaf worker must remain aware that he might be opening a door for others to walk through. As Henry C. Rider put it in 1875, "Live so that you will command the respect and approbation of your employers and you will have won a great triumph not for yourself alone, but also for the deaf of the land."[68]

This strategy, developed in the nineteenth century, survived into the early twentieth, when Deaf people would work to combat hearing prejudice, not by attacking hearing ideas as discriminatory or audist, but rather by presenting themselves as normal, able workers, in need of no special accommodations to do their jobs well. The community reasoned that if its members were perceived as needing special accommodations to integrate them into the hearing workforce, they would be even less likely to be hired, as employers would probably not be willing to take additional steps to hire deaf employees. This was a strategy common to minority groups in the American workforce at that time. As historians Robert Buchanan and Susan Burch have each noted, the approach, in its reliance on self-help and individual initiative, resembles the one advocated within the African American community at the turn of the century. "Self-control and self-reliance," as Buchanan notes, were the watchwords of the day.[69]

Deaf at Work

As the silent press suggested, Deaf people would come to share the experience of hearing prejudice as they left the Deaf world of the residential school behind to enter the workforce. The educators and administrators of the schools were not unaware of this prejudice of the hearing world, and they tried to prepare their students for it. Some schools organized what was called "a High Class," a select group of deaf students performing college preparatory work. For instance, the American School organized its first High Class in 1852. The High Class represented the brightest deaf students a school had to offer. Yet upon graduation, very few of these students were able to find work at the level for which they were qualified. One school official admitted that, even among graduates of the High Class,

> few of them . . . can obtain situations as clerks or bookkeepers. There is always a press of applications for such places and employers naturally prefer those with whom they can readily converse orally. . . . I would earnestly appeal to business men in want of copying clerks or bookkeepers to give a trial to well recommended deaf mutes. But in the mean time, the trade of printing seems the best resource we could offer to the more gifted of our pupils.[70]

Not all Deaf people, however, subscribed to the notion that hearing people acted out of any understandable or "natural" preferences. John Carlin, much like the disability rights activists who would come after him, questioned the so-called naturalness of hearing behavior. He instead insisted that it was simply discriminatory.

What is the true obstruction in their way? Prejudice? I am sorry to say that it is. The spirit is common among even the most intelligent—the most benevolent men of business, who so blindly believe that the want of hearing and speech must necessarily incapacitate a deaf-mute applicant from fulfilling his functions at the desk—an opinion as illogical as it is cruel.[71]

Hearing employers were afraid to take on deaf employees, according to Carlin. They feared being unable to communicate with them or doubted their ability to do the required work. This prejudice, he theorized, was the result of ignorance. Once educated about deafness, Carlin believed, hearing employers would be more likely to hire deaf workers. Carlin recommended that hearing school officials from residential schools should work with potential employers, explaining to them the skills and capabilities of their former students.[72]

But until such a time as enlightenment came to hearing employers, Carlin believed that deaf applicants for such white-collar jobs would have to "patiently bide their time and wait for better luck, knowing that when it comes to them, they will be in clover."[73] Unlike the deaf and disability activists who would follow him in the twentieth century, he did not recommend a more activist strategy. In the mid-nineteenth century, he could not conceive of directly protesting, even against what he recognized as discriminatory treatment. Carlin very much stands out as a deaf man of his times here.[74]

Deaf encounters with hearing prejudice were not limited to difficulties in obtaining a position. Deaf people continued to battle prejudice even once on the job. William B. Swett provides an example. In New Hampshire, he worked out of a lodging house, performing guide work as well as odd jobs, and he had a reputation as an excellent guide to the mountain trails. On one occasion, a hearing visitor from New Jersey arrived, asking for a guide to lead him up to a particular mountaintop. The house enthusiastically recommended Swett. But Swett reported, "On learning that I was deaf and dumb, he flatly refused to take me, adding some very uncomplimentary remarks, which were reported to me, of which I took no apparent notice, although I made a memorandum of them in my mind."[75] The man decided that he would be better off going up the mountain alone.

As the day went on, however, the man failed to return; it quickly became apparent that he was lost. Now Swett got his chance. "I was requested to go in search of him, and at once consented, glad of the chance to show him that his estimation of the deaf and dumb was wrong, and I started off alone." Soon, Swett found the man, who was positively overjoyed to see him in that instance; "he danced and capered about in fullness of joy," according to

Swett. The incident quickly changed the man's ideas about the capabilities of deaf people, as Swett had hoped. "For the rest of his stay," Swett recalled, "he employed me as his guide, paying me liberally, besides stating, at the close of my engagement that, although he had travelled much, both in the Old World and the New, he had never had a better guide."[76] Swett's encounter with hearing prejudice came to a happy ending because he got a second chance to prove himself. Many deaf people never received that opportunity.

Hearing prejudice may have limited or interfered with the employment aspirations of many deaf job candidates. What the community would have preferred were ways to introduce more hearing people to the Deaf. The arts were one possible venue by which to introduce Deaf culture to a hearing audience, while providing a living for Deaf artists. John Brewster Jr. worked as a portrait painter in New England in the late eighteenth and early nineteenth centuries. Brewster enrolled in the first class at the American School in 1817 at the age of fifty-one, the oldest pupil in the school. He left the school in 1820, to return to his painting career. Today, he is considered one of the greatest American folk painters of his generation. His biographer, Harlan Lane, has pointed to his deafness as a factor in the power of his art, citing it as the source of Brewster's great success in managing the gaze of his subjects. Fixing on the eyes of his sitters much as deaf signers maintain eye contact in a signed conversation, Lane argues, Brewster brought out the character of his subjects more deeply than his contemporaries. He had, Lane writes, "an uncanny ability to capture facial expressions." Lane believes this marks his work as that of a Deaf artist, even if Brewster himself never identified as Deaf.[77]

Other Deaf people believed the stage offered possibilities. On at least one occasion a group of New York School graduates organized as a sign language troupe, called the "Epsilon Sigma Society." They performed at a benefit for the Library of the Fanwood Literary Association, in New York City, raising over one hundred dollars by the sale of roughly five hundred tickets. They had apparently organized only for this purpose; a career on the stage had not been their intent.[78]

But the *Deaf Mutes' Friend* reported that other Deaf people believed that acting would be a possible career for others. An article cited a report out of New York.

Since some enthusiastic mutes have started the idea of a national convention, the New York Mutes, determined not to be outdone, have hit upon an entirely new idea which, to some persons, may appear ludicrous. It is well known that mutes have a natural genius for Pantomime, and some are very skillful in arranging the signs so as to suit hearing persons, giving them a large, if not complete, understanding of what is going on. Well, some of the most skillful in this art have got it in their heads to assemble when they leave school and try their fortune on the stage. The idea has been in existence for some time. . . . Should they still entertain the idea when they graduate, and assemble as proposed, it is not at all impossible that some day we will have "A Great Travelling Pantomimic Troupe" . . . to brighten up the name of the Deaf and Dumb.[79]

While the paper did note that "the life of a strolling player is not often conducive to good morals," there was clearly some excitement surrounding the notion of "A Great Travelling Pantomimic Troupe." The troupe would allow students to utilize their particularly Deaf talents and bring Deaf art to a wider public. By attending Deaf theater, hearing audiences would have an opportunity to see Deaf people as creative and energetic, contributing to the common cultural life of the community. They would also see the fruits of Deaf culture in an approachable and accessible way.

The idea for a pantomimic troupe highlighted the most visible symbol of the students' deafness, the sign language. Their eagerness to perform in their own way, to express themselves creatively in their own vernacular, also indicated the extent of their Deafness. Their willingness to modify their delivery, to use more gesture and pantomime to make their performances more accessible to a mixed deaf-hearing audience, indicates as well how ready they were to share their culture with hearing people. The pantomimic troupe did not emerge at this time; evidently the students' passion for the scheme had cooled by graduation. But similar thinking eventually fueled the creation of the National Theatre of the Deaf, roughly one hundred years later.[80]

But if hearing prejudice limited job options and the arts did not provide many with lucrative careers, how did most nineteenth-century deaf people make a living? Deaf education provided one career option. Robert Buchanan reports, "In the first half of the nineteenth century, deaf people assisted in the establishment of two schools; between 1850 and 1875, they founded seven; between 1875 and 1900, they established an additional thirteen."[81] Schools founded by Deaf people include the American School for the Deaf (1817), the Indiana School for the Deaf (1843), the Kansas School for the Deaf (1861), the Arkansas School for the Deaf (1868), the Oregon School for the Deaf (1870), and the New York School for the Deaf at Rome (1875).[82] By the 1850s, roughly

250 of the 550 teachers and administrators of the residential schools were themselves deaf, a figure representing a high-water mark for deaf people in the profession.[83]

Even in a period of nearly equal employment within the profession, there was still a glaring discrepancy. Deaf teachers were typically paid much less than their hearing counterparts. Many complained bitterly about this injustice. Schools tried to justify the policy, at least in part, by claiming that since deaf teachers were so readily available, the supply drove down wages. But, once again, simple discrimination would seem the more likely explanation. Nonetheless, the profession was welcoming to deaf teachers and hired them in numbers that have yet to be matched in the field. As Susan Burch explains, Deaf teachers returned again and again to the classroom because "teaching represented more than a traditional and well-respected profession for educated Deaf people. It also presented the most obvious means of intergenerational cultural transmission."[84] Deaf teachers knew that they were role models of Deafness to their deaf students. The impact of their presence in the residential schools was invaluable to their students.

A closer look at the graduates of the American School reveals that teaching attracted both men and women. Of the approximately 2,100 students who attended the school between 1817 and 1877, twenty-five men (out of about 1,175; roughly 2.1 percent of male graduates) and sixteen women (out of about 925; roughly 1.7 percent of female graduates) became teachers of the deaf. The profession held nearly as much attraction for deaf women as for deaf men.

The men include some of the most prominent figures of the field in the nineteenth century.[85] Job Turner, for instance, became the first teacher hired at the new Virginia School for the Deaf, where he would spend the rest of his career. Four graduates, Melville Ballard, Amos Draper, James Denison, and John Hotchkiss, taught on the Gallaudet College campus, two at the collegiate level and two at the campus's primary school, the Kendall School. Ballard would also go on to become the first student to enroll at Gallaudet College and the first to receive a B.S. from the college in 1866.

Some graduates stayed on at the American School as faculty members, but others spread across the country and beyond. Male graduates found employment in Ohio, Virginia, Tennessee, Oregon, Minnesota, and Indiana. Samuel Greene moved to Canada and became the first deaf teacher at the school for the deaf in Belleville, Ontario.[86] Josephus Edwards, from Lexington, Georgia, returned there after graduating to open his own private school for the deaf. (Georgia did not have a state school of its own until 1846.) George Loring, Fisher Spofford, Wilson Whiton, and Levi Backus become the first male graduates to enter the profession.

Loring and Spofford are usually singled out in historical accounts as the first deaf Americans to become teachers of the deaf; in truth, that distinction belongs to two female graduates, Abigail Dillingham and Mary Rose. One assumes they are not widely remembered as the first deaf teachers of the deaf in the United States because they were women and because the men had longer careers. Still, these women ought to be given their due as the first deaf Americans to teach their fellow deaf.

Abigail Dillingham was thirty-one years old when she entered the American School in 1817, a member of the inaugural class of seven students. Upon finishing her studies in 1821, she was immediately hired at the Pennsylvania School for the Deaf, where she taught until health reasons forced her to retire in 1824. She was teaching there when Laurent Clerc took over as principal, and he wrote of her, "She has a vigor of constitution and a decision of character which admirably qualify her to take charge of the uncultivated scholars on their entrance into the Asylum."[87]

Mary Rose (1808-1897) was the seventeenth student to enroll at the American School when she was just nine years old, making her the youngest student there, but, as she was from New York City, when the New York School opened in 1818, her family transferred her there, giving her the distinction of being the only deaf student to attend two schools for the deaf in the first year of their existence. When she finished her studies at the age of fourteen, the New York School promptly hired her, together with a male classmate, John Gazley. The pair became the first New York School graduates hired back as teachers. Even at fourteen, the school hired her for her "maturity, intelligence, and academic skills." She left teaching when she married in 1826.[88]

Other women followed in their footsteps. Starting in the 1850s, the American School began to hire women to teach the younger students. Until 1842, the American School admitted pupils between the ages of ten and thirty. In 1843, the policy was changed; the school would accept pupils between the ages of eight and twenty-five. They hired their first female teacher, Catharine Brooks, an American School graduate, in 1850, and she worked there until 1855.

When Brooks retired, she was replaced by Mary Mann and Sarah Storrs, both of whom had attended the American School; Mann completed her studies in 1847 and Storrs graduated as a member of the High Class in 1854. The two women worked with students under the age of eleven. It would seem that, as the school welcomed younger pupils, officials increasingly hired female graduates to teach those classes. Women were viewed, in accordance with the gender stereotypes of the day, as being particularly suited to teaching young children. Nevertheless, these women held the same job titles as their male counterparts. They were welcomed alongside their male colleagues at the school's faculty meetings; their attendance and participation is duly noted in the meeting minutes.

It is unclear where the other female teachers ended up. One, Martha Cunningham, who was from Greenville, South Carolina, returned there after she graduated in 1851 to take a position as an assistant teacher at the South Carolina School for the Deaf. The American School would hire several others, including Elmina Clapp, Elizabeth Weston, and Clara Seaverns. They also hired hearing women, to be sure, just as they hired hearing men. Elizabeth Clerc Beers taught there from 1859 to 1864; she was the daughter of Laurent and Eliza Clerc, and she was the only one of their children to follow in their famous father's footsteps. Other graduates described themselves as teachers, but I have been unable to find out where they taught or for how long.[89] More research is needed on the place of female teachers in the field during the years of the manualist control of deaf education. Historians have looked closely at the place of hearing women in the profession, during the rise of oralism. But little is known about the role female teachers, both deaf and hearing, played in manualist schools; here they only begin to emerge from the shadows.[90]

Still, as historian Phyllis Valentine has noted, "Graduates of the American Asylum who became teachers established high standards for their developing profession and were in constant demand to fill instructorships and administrative posts in numerous new satellite schools."[91] This conclusion would seem equally true for male and female graduates. Teaching was an attractive profession to both genders and, on a percentage basis, they sought it out in nearly equal numbers.

Of course, the deaf people who became teachers represent a tiny percentage of the American School's graduates. The majority of graduates sought work in other areas. Most learned a trade at school, as residential schools provided vocational training. Cabinet making, shoe making, and tailoring were all taught to boys in the early years of the American School by local artisans. For girls, the most frequently offered vocational classes were dressmaking and sewing, followed by training for domestic service.[92]

In the postbellum period, printing emerged as the most dominant industrial employer of deaf men, and nearly every residential school in the United States would teach printing to its male students.[93] Printing was popular within the Deaf community for a variety of reasons. First, given the prestige of the deaf press in the community, the occupation seemed like a deeply respectable career. Many deaf men who studied printing in school, like Henry Rider, went on to serve as printer, writers, editors, or owners of their own newspapers. The Little Family Paper was well respected in the community at large and these were printed at the residential school. The printing teacher, usually the editor of the school paper, occupied a place of pride in the community. Second, printing paid a good wage. By 1880, deaf printers could earn as much as thirty dollars a week, whereas carpenters received only half that amount.[94]

But the turn toward industrial employment for the deaf community would largely wait for the twentieth century. During the nineteenth century, the most commonly reported occupation for deaf men was that of farmer. Even the 1890 and 1900 censuses "indicated that the largest number of employed deaf American men were still in agricultural jobs, and most deaf women were either housewives or servants."[95] William Breg spoke for many of his fellow students when he declared in 1847, "I will leave this school room. I will go home and work in a cabinet shop or meadow or corn field or dig potatoes."[96]

After farming, the next most frequently reported occupations for deaf men were shoemaker and carpenter, respectively. Skilled craftsmen turned up in smaller numbers; at midcentury, deaf men could be found working as glass-cutters, bookbinders, coopers, tailors, and lithographers. As more and more deaf men and women moved to Massachusetts, both sexes reported finding work as mechanics, spinners, and weavers at the textile mills of Lowell.[97] Lovey Mayhew described how, by working at Lowell, she "has laid up a good deal of money," money she apparently used to move herself to Nantucket.[98]

While deaf men were far more likely to be employed in the nineteenth century than deaf women, a few deaf women also worked outside the home. I have identified twenty-eight such women, employed between 1817 and 1877, in addition to those who were working as teachers. The majority of these women, eleven in all, reported working as a "tailoress." Others could be found in the following occupations: dressmaker, seamstress, weaver, matron, carpet weaver, shoe binder, and housekeeper. One woman, Laura Merriman, was engaged in skilled labor as a clock face painter.[99] But it was far more common for female graduates to be reported simply as "married."

Deafness and Gender: The Lives of Deaf Women

"Married" was a common description for the American School's female graduates, sometimes modified by the addition of "married a deaf mute." Eliza Boardman is described as having "Married Laurent Clerc," while Sophia Fowler is described as having "Married Rev. T. H. Gallaudet." It seems terribly antiquated to see these women discussed solely in terms of their marriages to famous men. But these two women in particular should be seen as trailblazers for all deaf women of their times.

Eliza Boardman (1792-1880) arrived at the school in 1817, when she was twenty-three years old. She had lost her hearing at the age of two and a half, due to a childhood illness, but had retained some hearing as well as a speaking voice.[100] However, once she married Laurent Clerc in 1818, it was clear that she would live her life as a Deaf woman. Her husband, neither a speaker nor a lipreader, used the sign language to communicate, and so would she. Rising in local prominence, the couple had their portraits painted by Charles Wilson Peale in 1822.

Eliza posed with her daughter, Elizabeth, and, with her right hand, signed /E/. Whether this is Eliza's name sign or Elizabeth's is unclear. But the point of the portrait could not be clearer. The use of the manual alphabet here marked Eliza as a deaf woman. Though she had an invisible disability and could have chosen to pass as a hearing woman in her portrait, she made her deafness visible. By signing, she revealed herself. By signing, she indicated that her deafness was nothing to hide. By signing, she showed that she wanted viewers of the portrait to know that they gazed upon a Deaf woman, one who was also a wife and a mother. She claimed for herself, as a deaf woman, a right to become a republican mother.[101]

While espousing motherhood as a path to public respect and approbation may seem quite conservative, for disabled women like Eliza Boardman, it was deeply radical. Boardman claimed the right to behave exactly like an able-bodied woman, to marry and to mother. This was radical in her time, and remains so even today. Hers was a time when the right of the disabled to marry was continually challenged, a time when even her husband's good friend would question her right to assume both roles. (This pressure on the disabled to remain single, and in particular not to procreate, would increase as the century wore on and the eugenics movement emerged, with its attendant concerns about ensuring individuals' "fitness" to marry and warnings of the threat that "unfit" babies posed to the nation.)[102] In this way, Eliza Boardman, precisely as a wife and a mother, was a true trailblazer.

Her place as one half of the country's most famous deaf-deaf marriage helped to broker increasing acceptance of deaf people, at least in the greater Hartford area. The *Hartford Courant*, the local paper of record, regularly covered in its pages news of the asylum and of the larger Deaf community. It referred to the Grand Reunion of 1850 (more on it below), for instance, as the "Jubilee of the Deaf and Dumb," and told its readers that the general public was welcome to attend, alongside "the deaf and dumb of New England."[103] In 1850, state legislator Henry C. Deming became closely attached to the Deaf community of Hartford; he married Sarah Clerc and found himself the son-in-law of Laurent and Eliza Clerc, marrying into the very heart of the nineteenth-century Deaf world. This was therefore a community he knew well when he came to serve them, and their hearing neighbors, as mayor of Hartford in 1854.

His constituents knew it well, too. In 1855, the *Courant* complained that the *Edinburgh Review* had impugned the reputation of Hartford's Laurent Clerc by declaring that "when compared with other educated men," Clerc would have to fall short, due both to his deafness and to his lack of speech. Recall that England was still in the hands of the oralists, opposed to the use of the sign language and to the creation of signing communities. But the *Courant* was having none of it and defended its famous resident in no uncertain terms. It blasted back, "The fact is, the deaf mute schools of Great Britain are old-fogy affairs" and added that "we could show [the author], in five minutes here in Hartford, many things that would be novelties to him, although they are as familiar as the A.B.C. to a large portion of our citizens."[104]

It is this last line of defense that leaps out. Deaf ways were, by the *Courant's* lights, "as familiar as the A.B.C." to many of Hartford's hearing citizens. The paper's judgment raises the question of how well the deaf and hearing communities of Hartford knew each other and how much interaction they enjoyed. For the hearing mayor to attach himself to this family makes it clear at least that the Deafness of his in-laws did not strike him as a political liability. He would go on to serve two terms as mayor and two terms as a Republican representative to Congress, so he was proven correct.

It was simply by assuming a traditional place in Hartford society, as a wife and a mother, that Eliza Boardman Clerc was able to wield her influence. She was able to demonstrate, just by raising her family, that deaf people would lead lives similar to those of hearing people, and that deaf women were just as capable of raising good, civic-minded offspring who would be a blessing to the republic.

And so of course was her classmate Sophia Fowler (1798-1877), who soon followed in her footsteps. Fowler was nineteen years old when she arrived at the American School in 1817, and only twenty-three when she married Gallaudet in 1821. The couple understood and honored their place in the larger Deaf community, even in the naming of their children. They choose to name one of their daughters Alice Cogswell.

Upon her death, Amos Draper eulogized Sophia Gallaudet in this way:

> The home which they built soon attracted a society of its own. It drew many visitors, among them men and women famous in art and science, in letters and politics, and indeed in almost every walk of life. Who can tell how much of the liberal spirit always manifested by the American public and its legislators towards the deaf and dumb is owing to the spectacle thus early presented of a beautiful woman from that class entering society and presiding over her own household with equal sweetness and tact?[105]

The example of both of these marriages, and their presence over the years in Hartford, served both to educate the larger hearing community about Deaf lives and to remind the young hearing men who came to teach at the school that their deaf students would become deaf adults who would pursue lives and loves just like hearing people.

The other young female graduates who are listed simply as "married" also serve to offer that same quiet but powerful testimony. They married, not viewing deafness as an impediment to that life choice, and they had children, proclaiming that their deafness was not an obstacle to raising a child, even a hearing child. They married, too, with some sense of what the duties of a wife were, by the standards of their day. Maria Guile commented, "Her duty as a wife is . . . to make her husband comfortable, and to keep her house in order and pleasant. . . . Her husband feels refreshed and pleased to see the smiling face of his wife and tidy and well arranged room, with plenty of books and newspapers."[106] Or, as another young woman described them in 1831,

> A good wife should occupy the house where she should still keep it, and happily live with her husband. She should be always neat, clean, and careful of her furniture, and the articles of clothes, and arrange them well. She must know well how to attend to domestic concerns. She should be industrious, diligent, and punctual. . . . She should dress with simplicity and plainness. . . . When her husband . . . commands, she should be obedient to him, and be also respectful to him. . . . She should well bring up her children with care and earnestness.[107]

Even by pursuing the ordinary course of most female lives in the nineteenth century, they are extraordinary examples, reframing the meaning of disability in the majority culture of their times. Most able-bodied Americans took for granted that disability would mean difference, both in ability but also in life course. A disabled life was assumed to be one that would not resemble an able-bodied life. Deaf women, by becoming wives and mothers, insisted on finding common ground, cultivating the space where a disabled life would follow the same trajectory as an able-bodied life, and insisting in this way on their right to lead that life.[108]

Teachers of the deaf, by accepting that their students would have lives much like their own, also helped to shape the larger cultural arguments about deafness, in directions often in sharp contrast to the discussions that swirled around other disabilities. Take the example of the blind, for instance. Samuel Gridley Howe, as director of the Perkins Institution for the Blind, articulated a quite different vision of the future for his students. When he began his work with the blind, Howe had believed that they were the equals of the sighted. "But in the mid-1840s," historian Ernest Freeberg notes, "he had decided that the blind were different, that their sensory deprivation had serious physical, intellectual, and moral consequences." These consequences were understood as overwhelmingly negative. By 1848, Howe had come to believe that the blind were not only physically but also mentally inferior to the sighted.[109]

At the same time, Howe came to the conclusion that blind adults should never marry or procreate. Literary scholar Mary Klages argues that "the interpretation of blindness and other forms of physical disability as incontrovertibly signifying suffering barred disabled people from reproductive sexuality. Only the most hardhearted could insist on engaging in even the most sanctioned forms of sexuality when those acts might result in the creation of a disabled—that is, a suffering and miserable—child." In order to dissuade the students in his care from even desiring to marry, he moved to segregate the sexes at Perkins.[110] This antipathy toward blind marriage continued in some professional circles into the early twentieth century; the American Association of Workers for the Blind, for example, continued to recommend chastity to blind women.[111]

A look at the history of other disabled groups reveals that professionals largely held similar sets of assumptions about the future of their charges. Interest in educating the developmentally disabled, commonly referred to as "idiots" in this period, also began in the United States in the 1840s, with Samuel Gridley Howe once more playing a part in New England. In 1851, Howe became the director of the first institution of its kind, the Massachusetts School for Idiotic and Feeble Minded Children. While the possibility of educating this population was beginning to be explored, it was not believed that these "idiots" would either marry or have children. As one reformer put it, "They are powerless to resist the physical temptations of adult life, and should be protected from their own weakness. . . . Especially should they be protected from marriage and the reproduction of their kind."[112] To ensure that protection, the trend among professionals devoted to the education of the feeble-minded was to recommend that these children be segregated from the general population. A policy of permanent institutionalization of the so-called feeble-minded emerged accordingly and prevailed deep into the twentieth century.[113]

"Married" as a descriptor of deaf women is now revealed as even more radical than it first seemed. Those first two much-heralded deaf marriages, of Eliza Boardman and Sophia Fowler, coming so soon after the establishment of deaf education in the United States, allowed the deaf community to quickly establish both the expectation and the practice of marriage as a normative experience for all deaf people.

Deaf students assumed that marriage was in their future. At the New York School, in January 1869, the Fanwood Literary Association debated the question, "Which is the best condition for deaf-mutes, celibacy or marriage?" After both sides presented their cases, the student audience was asked to vote. Among the boys, seventeen voted for celibacy while seventy-three voted for matrimony. "Many girls," a reporter noted, "declined to vote, but of those who did so, only four voted for single-blessedness, while twenty-three honestly and boldly stood up for the cares and responsibilities, as well as the pleasures, of wedded life."[114] A midcentury snapshot of the graduates of the American, New York, and Ohio schools revealed that, while seventy-five deaf men and fifty-eight deaf women reported hearing spouses, 188 deaf men and 187 deaf women reported deaf spouses.[115] While resistance to deaf marriage, as to all disabled marriages, would increase with the rise of eugenics in the late nineteenth century, by then, the practice of deaf marriage, at least, was well established. Eugenic leaders, most notably Alexander Graham Bell, who argued in 1883 that deaf-deaf marriages would lead inexorably to a "deaf variety of the human race" and should therefore be outlawed, would struggle, mostly unsuccessfully, to undo a deeply rooted tradition of deaf-deaf marriage.[116]

Deaf Events

As more Deaf people graduated from school and settled into lives full of work and family, many began to search for ways to give back to the schools that had made those lives possible. They also sought to honor the people who had helped to build the American Deaf community.

The first major public event sponsored by and for Deaf people was the so-called Grand Reunion of 1850, held on the grounds of the American School for the Deaf on September 26, 1850. The reunion gathered 208 alumni, as well as the school's student population of another two hundred, together with the American School's teachers and staff, principals and teachers of other deaf schools, the invited guests, and the governor of Connecticut. The event, as historian Phyllis Valentine puts it,

> had the flavor of a family reunion as much as an alumni event. Most married couples who returned had met their spouses at the school. These marriages between students—knitting together families of origin, spouses, and mutual friends into a large deaf community—had created an interlocking social network that was centered in New England but extended outward across the United States and upward into Canada.[117]

As a New England–centered community, all New England states were represented on the guest list, with the vast majority of the alumni coming from Connecticut and Massachusetts. New York sent around thirty-five attendees. Five Virginians came, as did one South Carolinian. Two people, both graduates of the New York School for the Deaf, made the trip from Canada.[118]

The guest list for the 1850 event reads like a *Who's Who* of the Deaf community. There was a young Henry C. Rider, only eighteen years old. Levi Backus was there, proudly identifying himself in the register as the editor of the *Radii*. His wife, Anna Ormsby Backus, must have been delighted to see Mary Wayland Carlin, who was there together with her husband, John Carlin, the painter. The women had been classmates together at the New York School.[119] William and Margaret (Harrington) Swett were there. Wilson Whiton attended. Nancy Dillingham, working as an assistant matron at the American School, was there. Several Chandlers came down from northern New York. The Curtis-Rowe clan, from Maine, was well represented, too. But the guest list is also full of the names of ordinary deaf people, not simply leaders of the community but proudly self-identified members. Here one spots Maria Bailey Lamb, of Norwich, Connecticut, who traveled to the event with her husband George Lamb, a fellow graduate of the American School. Joseph O. Sanger, who found work as a shoemaker, came. Harriet Knapp, employed as a dressmaker in Northfield, Vermont, returned to Hartford for the reunion.

They all came at the urging of Thomas Brown, a member of the class of 1827, who had organized the event to honor Laurent Clerc and Thomas Hopkins Gallaudet. Brown had written of his idea to his fellow alumni, and they had responded with both good wishes and cash, contributing over six hundred dollars to the proposed event. Eventually, it was decided that the money would be used to purchase two sets of silver trays and pitchers to present to the school's cofounders during the reunion, as the inscriptions on the pitchers put it, as "a token of grateful respect" from "the deaf mutes of New England."

As Christopher Krentz argues,

> The event demonstrated just how much deaf Americans had come together as a community and culture. The ceremony was in their language, the natural language of signs. It celebrated their common history and values. In Clerc and Gallaudet, they had tangible heroes responsible for bringing them together. . . . [The 1850 reunion] officially marked the emergence of deaf Americans' collective consciousness.[120]

But the reunion was only the beginning, as far as the Deaf community was concerned. The decade of the 1850s was also marked by the emergence of Deaf nationalism, as seen in the debate over a deaf state. The independent silent press gained journals of both note and longevity in this crucial decade. A critical mass of educated Deaf people, graduates of institutions around the country, had at last been reached by this point, enough to sustain a common cultural life even outside of school walls. The story of the 1850s, as Harlan Lane puts it, is "the story of a growing ethnic consciousness."[121]

At last, the cultural moment to mount a public celebration of Deaf history, values, and heroes had arrived, and the Grand Reunion was full of speeches that did just that. The speeches of Fisher Spofford and George Loring were filled with references to the historical events that had made the reunion possible. Spofford and Loring were two prominent members of the nineteenth-century Deaf community. Spofford (1808-1877) was the featured orator of the day; a graduate of the American School, he was known as an especially gifted signer.[122] Loring (1807-1852) was from an economically and socially prominent Boston family and was seen as "the 'acknowledged head' of the Boston deaf community."[123] His father, the wealthy Boston merchant Elijah Loring, had contributed generously to the fledgling school for the deaf, and he had quickly enrolled his son there. George was the second student to officially enroll in the American School. He would become one of the first American Deaf teachers in the country. He started teaching there in 1825, together with fellow graduate Wilson Whiton. He worked in Hartford until 1834, when he returned to Boston, his home for the remainder of his life.[124]

Spofford dwelled at length on the French contribution to the education of Gallaudet, specifically mentioning the Parisian school and the generosity of the Abbé Sicard, before he turned to praise Gallaudet and Clerc for the efforts in Hartford. "We all feel the most ardent love to these gentlemen who founded this Asylum, and to these our earliest instructors," Spofford announced. "This gratitude will be a chain to bind all the future pupils together. Those who succeed us as pupils will be told of the debt of gratitude they owe to the founders of the American Asylum."[125] Spofford pictured the reunion as an event that would tie past and future Deaf generations together. Their knowledge of their history would bind all the generations of the Deaf community together.

Loring echoed Spofford's sentiments of gratitude. He addressed Gallaudet and Clerc directly. "It is fortunate and it was also by a kind dispensation of Divine Providence," he told Gallaudet, "that you adopted the best method of instruction of the deaf and dumb. By this method we have been instructed in the principles of language, morality and religion, and this education has qualified us to be useful members of society."[126] Even this celebratory event turned political here. Loring offered a not very veiled comment on oral education to his audience, calling manualism the "best method of instruction," the one that enabled the deaf to become "useful members of society." Loring himself did not speak, and he would never have ceded ground to those who believed a lack of speech hindered the deaf in any quest to become useful members of their communities.

The best example of the power of the manual method was Laurent Clerc himself, significantly another mute, like Loring. To Clerc, Loring added directly, "[Y]ou did not hesitate to leave your beautiful country. You accompanied Mr. Gallaudet in his travels to raise funds for the benefit of the deaf and dumb, and interested the public, by your intelligence and conversation, in favor of that unfortunate and neglected portion of this country."[127] By Loring's lights, it was Clerc's example that transformed public thinking about deaf people in the United States. By impressing audiences with his "intelligence," Clerc, in Loring's account, single-handedly changed the future for all deaf Americans. Together, Loring suggested, these two men changed history, and the Deaf community wanted them to know that they both knew and appreciated it.

The Deaf community would gather again only four years later, in 1854, once more on the grounds of the American School. This time they met to raise a memorial. Thomas Hopkins Gallaudet had died only one year after the reunion, in September 1851. Immediately, Thomas Brown was back in action, organizing an association to raise a monument to Gallaudet. Laurent Clerc was tapped as the association's president and state agents were appointed to solicit funds from the Deaf community. The necessary funds were raised over the course of two years. A Deaf artist, Albert Newsam, a graduate of the Pennsylvania School for the Deaf, was hired to prepare the plan for the monument, and he tapped his classmate, Deaf sculptor John Carlin, to make additional contributions to the design.[128]

The Gallaudet monument was dedicated in a ceremony in Hartford, held at the American School, on September 6, 1854. Three hundred and eighty-two deaf people signed the guest registry; there were 402 signatures altogether. Many of the same people returned, including the Browns, the Carlins, and the Backuses. But there were newcomers too. Mary Rose made an appearance. William Breg attended. P. H. Skinner, a hearing man who would later open a school for African American deaf and blind children in Niagara Falls, was there with his deaf wife and fellow teacher, Jerusha Hills, a graduate of the New York School.[129]

This time, the single largest contingent of Deaf people came from Massachusetts, about 125 people in all. This number included a strong showing of Deaf people from Martha's Vineyard. By 1854, thirteen deaf students had come to Hartford from Martha's Vineyard. The Mayhew family, who through the years had sent three children to Hartford by this time and who would send three more, was well represented, with Sally Smith Mayhew, Lovey Mayhew, and Ruby Mayhew in attendance. Zeno Tilton and his wife, Harriet Closson, also an American School graduate, originally from Lyme, Connecticut, were there as well. Mary Smith, who was from the island but was living in Henniker, New Hampshire, with her husband Thomas Brown, would surely have welcomed the chance to visit with her fellow Vineyarders.

Their presence would seem to indicate that the Vineyard Deaf were better connected to the mainland Deaf community than has been previously understood. It also suggests that there was more of a Deaf consciousness among the Vineyard Deaf than historians have previously thought. Harlan Lane has pointed to "an absence of events and structures that set Deaf people apart from hearing people" on Martha's Vineyard. Accounts of island life, he argues, "do not reveal any leader, any organization, any gathering place, any banquet or other ceremony, any monuments—indeed anything at all that suggests that Deaf people on the Vineyard saw themselves as a distinct people, with their own language and culture." While not foreclosing the possibility that something new could come to light, he nonetheless concludes that "it seems unlikely that the difference in degree of ethnic consciousness between the mainland and the island will be eliminated by future discoveries."[130]

Lane is correct that the island itself shows no sign of Deaf life; no monuments were raised there, no organizations founded there. But perhaps we have been looking for evidence in the wrong places. Perhaps the Vineyard Deaf wanted their integrated life on the island and their Deaf life as well. Their intermarriages with Deaf off-islanders, their participation in the seminal Deaf events of their lifetimes—these would seem to be the signs of "ethnic consciousness" that Lane has been looking for. Another would be the fact that nine Deaf people from Martha's Vineyard were listed as members of the New England Gallaudet Association in 1857, when the organization had 154 members altogether.[131] It would seem that the Vineyard Deaf did think of themselves as Deaf, as members of a larger Deaf community. It may be that while they thought of the Deaf world as vital to them, they also regarded it as separate from the world of the Vineyard. In any event, we need to revisit the question of the relationship of Martha's Vineyard to the mainland Deaf community.

Besides the emergence of the Vineyard Deaf into the mainland community life, the guest list reveals some other equally significant attendees. Henry Simons attended the Grand Reunion in 1850 and he came back to Hartford again in 1854; by then, he had already settled into the maritime industry where he would spend his working years. George Boardwin and his sister Susan Boardwin also attend in 1854. They had only recently completed their studies at the American School, graduating in 1851. Both were quite young, seventeen and eighteen, respectively. George reported that he was working as a barber, while Susan was a dressmaker. The fact that these three free black graduates attended these important Deaf events suggests that they felt welcome within the larger, and largely white, Deaf community. Presumably, none of them would have made the trip to Hartford if they had felt unwelcome or if they had had terrible memories of their time at school there.

But more than a monument was raised here. The New England Gallaudet Association of the Deaf came into existence as part of this effort to remember Gallaudet. This event proved a springboard from which the Deaf community launched organizations and institutions that would sustain it for the rest of the nineteenth century.[132]

That organization, the New England Gallaudet Association of the Deaf, would itself meet twice in Hartford for its annual convention, once in 1860 and again in 1866. The 1866 meeting was held in Hartford, as the guest registry put it, "to celebrate the 50th anniversary of the landing of Gallaudet and Clerc, August 1816." About 231 deaf people attended in 1860, and nearly 400 came in 1866.

The two Boardwin siblings came again. By the 1866 event, Susan Boardwin and Henry Simons were a couple. They had married in 1862 and were living in Bridgeport, Connecticut, where he worked on the steamboats that ran between Hartford and New York City. They were joined at both events by Adam H. Metrash, who brought his wife Elizabeth Pepinger Metrash, a graduate of the New York School for the Deaf, in 1866. The couple had married in 1861. The guest registry indicates that the couple had settled in Norwalk, Connecticut, where he worked as a fisherman. Ten African American students had attended the American School by 1866, and four of them came back to campus, in various combinations, for these important Deaf events. Their numbers may be tiny, but as a percentage of the entire African American deaf alumni available, their presence is huge.

The Vineyard deaf community was even better represented at the events of the 1860s. Alfred Mayhew, Lovey Mayhew, Ruby Mayhew, Sally Smith Mayhew, and Hannah Smith Mayhew all attended, in various combinations, both conventions. Prudence Lambert, from Chilmark, attended in 1860. Zeno and Harriet Tilton came in 1860 and again in 1866, as did Zeno's sister, Deidamia Tilton West, together with her husband, a hearing man named George West. Their brother, Franklin, and his wife, Sarah Foster Tilton, also a graduate of the American School, an off-islander from Seekonk, Massachusetts, came in 1860. In marrying Sarah, Franklin made new ties to the off-island Deaf community. Sarah's sister, Sophia, was also at the convention in 1860. She was there with her husband, American School alumnus Charles Steere. There are tantalizing glimpses here of the way in which the Vineyard Deaf found themselves increasingly woven into the lives of the larger Deaf community.

More research into the question is needed, but it is perhaps unsurprising that the Vineyard Deaf began reaching out to their mainland brethren increasingly in the 1860s. The first headline in an off-island press source about the population of deaf people on the Vineyard came in 1860, when a newspaper in Maine published an article about the Vineyard as a resort destination. It added that the Vineyard was afflicted with "calamities," including "an almost incredible number of deaf and dumb persons." Vineyarders responded angrily to this negative characterization of its population, but this was a sign of things to come. More negative coverage would appear over the later course of the nineteenth century. Such coverage would draw the eugenicist Alexander Graham Bell to the island in the 1880s to study these "defectives" for himself. It could be that the Vineyard Deaf sought to solidify their ties to a larger, allied community in response.[133]

The Deaf events of the 1850s and 1860s also point to the ways in which Deaf families contained both hearing and deaf individuals. Accommodating family members from across the audiological spectrum was a daily issue for many Deaf spouses and parents. Some seemed to reach accommodation by having the hearing person stay home, while the Deaf person claimed his or her own place in the Deaf world. The guest registries for all events include entries like that for Edwin Lager, from Allentown, Pennsylvania, who noted at the 1854 event that he had "married a hearing lady," a lady who did not accompany him to Hartford. Likewise, Laurette Warriner, of New Britain, Connecticut, attended in 1854 without her hearing husband. It is not that it was unheard of for mixed couples to come together. The Grants, Wentworth (deaf) and Sarah (hearing), did so in 1854. But they seem to have been in the minority. Of most mixed deaf-hearing marriages, the deaf partner was likely to attend such Deaf events alone.

But there are glimpses of families trying to include hearing members in the life of the Deaf community. For instance, Martha Atkins, the hearing sister of Lauretta Cook, accompanied her sister to Hartford in 1854. And Deaf parents began bringing their hearing children to such events as well. Helen Webster, the eleven-year-old hearing daughter of the Deaf couple George and Caroline Webster, came along with her parents in 1854. Similarly, the Deaf couple Artemas and Ruth Smith brought their ten-year-old hearing son, Augustus, with them in 1860. Minerva Smith, who had married a hearing man, brought her four-year-old hearing daughter, also named Minerva, with her to Hartford in 1860. Little Minerva's hearing father, however, did not attend. It seems clear that Deaf parents wanted their hearing children to meet and know the important people in their lives, the other Deaf people they went to school with and befriended. The various events in Hartford helped Deaf people not only to solidify their ties with one another but also to share this crucial aspect of their lives with hearing family members. In particular there was an effort to include in the Deaf world the hearing children of deaf adults.

What is not clear is how many of these hearing people signed. Would a hearing sister know her deaf sister's language? Did all children of deaf adults sign fluently? Unfortunately, it is impossible to say. At least for the public speeches and other presentations at these events, the hearing attendees would not have needed to worry about their language skills. As the *Hartford Courant* noted in both 1860 and 1866, there were interpreters provided for these events. In 1860, the *Courant* reassured its readers that all were welcome to attend, as interpreters would be "rendering the sign address orally and vice-versa." And again in 1866, it reiterated that speeches "will be interpreted for the benefit of any auditors who may be present."[134]

The *Hartford Courant* provided extensive coverage of these deaf events in the local, largely hearing, press. The paper noted that these events were of extraordinary benefit to the Deaf people of New England. "Such gatherings," the *Courant* editorialized, "must be productive of great good to these our brethren whom God had indeed made a peculiar people."[135]

During the 1860 event, the *Courant* described the ways in which the event made Deaf history visible in the Hartford landscape. The members of the New England Gallaudet Association took a walking tour of Hartford with Laurent Clerc, in which "he pointed out to them the different localities associated with the early history of the Asylum; the City Hotel as the building in which it was founded; the residence of Mr. Robert Watkinson, as the home of Alice Cogswell when he arrived here . . . from France; the residence of Mrs. Thomas Day, in the upper story of which the class-rooms were arranged for a while."[136]

Moving through downtown, the procession made not just Deaf people but also Deaf history visible on the city landscape. This was no longer Robert Watkinson's house; it was Alice Cogswell's home. So often, lacking monuments or markers, the history of subaltern groups is lost to view, rendered absent in the culture through a corresponding lack of place in the landscape. Here in 1860, the gathered Deaf community, as the hearing paper noticed, made visible its presence on and history in the local Hartford cityscape.

In 1866, the paper noted that some four hundred graduates were returning to Hartford "from all parts of the country." They "represent various trades and employments, a large number being farmers. Upon inquiry we were told that probably more than one half of the whole number are married."[137] The paper reflected positively that this would not remain the case for long, as Cupid was at the convention, "fully armed." Many singles will meet a partner here, the *Courant* predicted confidently. "If this shall prove true, who shall say that the fiftieth anniversary of the Asylum was not a splendid success in more ways than one? And so mote it be."[138]

Again, it is the public approval of burgeoning deaf romances that grabs attention. The paper applauded the very idea of deaf-deaf marriages, and hoped to see more of them. This sort of easy acceptance of the most commonplace experience of able-bodied adult life as an equally reasonable expectation for a deaf life marks a significant point of departure between the deaf and other disabled communities in the nineteenth century. Again, at the Perkins School, Samuel Gridley Howe opposed holding reunions for the school's blind graduates and refused to organize them, precisely because he feared that such social events would encourage graduates to marry one another.[139]

Here, the deaf are described and understood as being very similar to, rather than quite different from, the hearing majority around them. And yet, crucially, their difference is not denied. The *Courant* also remarked of the conference attendees that "communication by sign is probably as dear to them as our own wordy pronunciations."[140] The paper reminded readers that the communication preference of the Deaf was sign language, and not spoken English. There was no indication that the newspaper reporter expected any different, no discussion that perhaps it would be better if the deaf would learn to speak like the hearing, rather than sign. Their similarity to hearing people may have been stressed, but their Deafness was equally acknowledged. This would seem reflective of the Deaf attitude of the nineteenth century generally. The Deaf community largely sought both Deafness and inclusion for itself. Their reception in the local press in Hartford would seem to suggest that these goals were understood and approved.

Deafness and Race: The Lives of Deaf African Americans

As suggested above, black deaf Americans were included in the life of the larger Deaf community in the antebellum period. Even if the full picture of interracial relations has yet to come into sharp focus, we can at least see already that the Deaf world was both black and white in the years before the Civil War.

Black and white deaf students attended school together. They graduated side by side. They also attended, as we have seen, larger Deaf community events together. They married within the deaf community. Adam Metrash married Elizabeth Pepinger. Four of their children survived to adulthood; the oldest, Robert, was deaf while the other three, Mary, Caroline, and Lucy, were hearing. Henry Simons married Susan Boardwin; they had two children. George Boardwin married his classmate, Sarah Taylor, listed in the American School's registry as "a mulatto native of Halifax, Nova Scotia." Their sister, Delia Boardwin, also married, inside one community and outside another. Delia married within the Deaf community when she married fellow American School student Oliver Badger. But she had married outside of the African American community; Badger was a hard-of-hearing white man. The school had brought them, as deaf people, together. Boardwin attended from 1845 to 1851, Badger from 1848 to 1854.[141]

These graduates found a variety of employments. The maritime industry welcomed several graduates, including Henry Simons. George Boardwin worked as a barber, while his sister Susan was a dressmaker. The 1880 census uncovers Susan Cisco working as a servant in the house of Robert and Delia Benham in New Haven, Connecticut, still single; Horace Crawford, married, working as a laborer, and living in Alabama; and John Anthony, also married, still in New York City and working as a porter. The occupations of their peers remain to be uncovered. We need to know more about the various social worlds these people occupied after leaving the confines of school.

We know the most about the Connecticut couple Adam Metrash (1837-1884) and Elizabeth Pepinger (1838-189?). As it happens, the Metrash family had made their home in the coastal town of Norwalk since the 1790s. Adam's parents, Adam and Ruannah Metrash, owned both land and a house in Norwalk, where the elder Metrash worked as a boatman. After the younger Adam graduated from the American School for the Deaf in 1857, he returned to Norwalk. He and Elizabeth married in 1861. It is not entirely clear how the couple met. Family lore has it that "they met at the school for the deaf"; however, since they did not attend the same school, this seems unlikely. Furthermore, the free black students of the New York School do not appear to have been deeply connected to the wider Deaf community. None of them, for instance, attended the various events held at the American School in the 1850s and 1860s. The American School graduates, as we have seen, were well represented at such events, by contrast. It was Adam, in fact, who brought Elizabeth into that social circle.

However they were introduced, their match seemed a happy one. Adam reported, from the early years of their marriage, "We are perfectly well as usual and our living are very comfortable and happy since our marriage." They had already welcomed their first child, a daughter named Julia, by 1863. Adam described her as a young toddler as "very well and healthy. She can speak or spell the words, Papa, Mamma. She sits on the floor to play with everything as she is pleased to choose. She has got two white teeth in the upper jaw."

With their domestic life well settled, Adam turned to develop his professional life. In 1862, Adam obtained rights to oyster beds from the town of Norwalk. The oystering business suited Adam. In a February 1863 letter to a cousin in nearby Stamford, Connecticut, Adam reported that he was ready "to plant the seeds in my two acres of the ground in the sea which I bought lately" and that he anticipated that the oysters "will grow to good size in three to four years." He harvested them from his boat, *The Silence*. In addition, he supplemented his income by captaining the yacht of a wealthy New York family around Long Island Sound in the summer of 1862, a job for which he was paid twenty-five dollars a month. He worked for the family again the following summer. By 1868, the couple had built a house of their own on Metrash land in Norwalk. Adam was joined in the oystering business by his brother-in-law, John Hawley Hubbard, in 1870. Angelina Metrash Hubbard,

Adam's sister, and her husband had two sons who also went to work at sea, one as a sailor and the other as a cook on a boat.[142]

Adam Metrash was a fortunate individual. He was very lucky in his deafness, for it allowed him access to a better education than was generally available to most free blacks in Connecticut in the antebellum period. He was also lucky in his lineage. His extended family's longevity and stability as citizens of Norwalk gave him a solid base on which to build his own maritime career after he returned home from Hartford.

It is because the Metrash family had such deep roots in Norwalk that we know as much as we do today about Adam. His descendants, who still live in Connecticut, have kept his memory alive. One family member, Dorothy Harper, recounts the following story of Adam's children. The couple's only deaf child, Robert, like his father, attended the American School, from 1872 to 1880. His siblings, however, were hearing. Regardless of their auditory status, the Metrash siblings all signed in order to communicate with their deaf parents and with each other. As two of the hearing sisters grew old together, they continued to sign with each other, even as they became the only family members who remembered the language. Harper can even remember them engaging in what linguists call code switching when they would start a conversation in spoken English and finish it in sign, especially, she adds, if the pair decided that they did not want other hearing relatives, like small, spying children, to know what they were talking about. The reverberation down into the twentieth century of the nineteenth-century sign language used at the American School for the Deaf offers a remarkable testimony to the power of Deafness in one African American family.

The Metrash family story offers an exceedingly rare glimpse into the lives of Deaf free black families. There is much we need to do to recover more such stories. We also need to know more about the racial attitudes of the nineteenth-century Deaf world. The attendance of African American alumni, like the Metrashes themselves, at deaf events is suggestive, to be sure, of a more tolerant attitude toward race among the deaf. Even more so is the fact that Charles Hiller, a deaf man of mixed race from Nantucket, was reported as a member of the New England Gallaudet Association of the Deaf in 1856. The records of the association were reportedly lost in a fire, but the published membership list that appeared in the *Annals* in 1857 clearly indicated that Charles Hiller was a member. The organization's constitution makes no mention of race.

This is in clear distinction to later deaf organizations. The National Association of the Deaf, founded in 1880, at first admitted both black and white deaf people as members. In 1925, the NAD moved to bar blacks from the organization; racial barriers to membership were not lifted until 1953. Historian Susan Burch concludes, "White Deaf community members resembled their hearing peers in their discrimination against African American Deaf persons."[143] Undoubtedly, this is true. However, if the antebellum period was more inclusive, and the Deaf world became less inclusive over time, this might suggest that the Deaf community was adopting a more mainstream set of racial values, in a bid for greater acceptance by the hearing world. This move would parallel those made by ethnic immigrants, who, whiteness studies scholars have noted, espoused more racist beliefs after living in the United States for years, as they realized what attitudes and behaviors were required of them to win native-born white acceptance and become white themselves.[144]

A similar transformation within the Deaf community would make some historical sense, as Burch describes the 1920s as a period when the Deaf community, under siege by dual forces of oralism and eugenics, made other culturally conservative moves, like distancing themselves from, rather than allying with, other disabled Americans, in order to appear as "capable" and "normal" as possible.[145] Obviously, further research is needed to tell a more complete story of the history of race in the Deaf community.

Material Culture

Living a Deaf life sometimes meant living with objects that marked one as deaf. Physical deafness frequently required creative thinking to overcome certain of its obstacles, especially obstacles created by a material world structured around the assumption that everyone can hear. For instance, how was one to know that a visitor was knocking at the door? Thomas Widd was happy to tell readers of the *Deaf Mutes' Friend* that this problem had been "Conquered at Last."

> We were all "dummies," as our neighbors were pleased to call us, and we had to devise a plan by which we might know when the post-man, the milk-woman, or other visitors, came to the door. A bell was out of the question, and as for knocker we had none, even if that would have done us any good. A happy idea occurred to us, for "necessity is the mother of invention," and we discovered a means of overcoming the door difficulty. We cut the bell away, attached a spring to the wire, and to this another piece of wire, which had a block of wood fastened to one end, and the whole was so contrived that the least pull of the bell-handle at the door would send the block of wood, with a dull, heavy thud, to the floor of

the room, and the noise, or vibration, it caused never failed to attract our attention. The loud thumps, which followed every pull of our bell-handle, alarmed the people and somewhat annoyed our neighbors; but on learning the nature of the invention and its importance to us, they laughed and said it was capital. We were often annoyed by people who loved a joke at the expense of others and who thought it capital fun to pull our "bell" as they passed.[146]

The problem of how to arise at an appointed time without the benefit of a chime of a clock was similarly solved.

There is also an alarm continuance which can be attached to clocks and will awaken a sleeping deaf mute at any time desired. We had one in our house, made by ourself, from a hint given us by a deaf mute friend, for a long time and it always worked perfectly. It can be attached to any clock. . . . The simplest is a cord attached to the alarm wheel of a clock, passing from the drum to a point in the ceiling over the head of the bed, where a small spring or trap is fixed with a little wire, upon which a pillow or cushion can be hung. The alarm being set at the desired hour, when it strikes, the drum winds up the cord and the pillow or cushion drops upon the sleeper, who is aroused thereby. We must observe, however, that one must arise when first awakened or it will, in time, fail to be of any use. . . . It is rather startling, at first, to have a pillow drop suddenly in one's face while sound asleep, but one gets used to it and finds it really useful, especially on dark winter mornings.[147]

Physical deafness introduced some aspects of material culture into Deaf lives that were radically outside the everyday experience of hearing people. Certainly few hearing people were ever awakened by a falling pillow! The perceptions both sides brought to their shared encounters also differed vastly. The small size of the deaf population in any given state, with the exception of the large population on Martha's Vineyard, ensured that most hearing people would be unfamiliar with deaf people. Deaf people, on the other hand, encountered hearing people on a daily basis and necessarily confronted the sometimes edgy border that separated the two cultures. They therefore had to develop strategies to promote smooth interaction and accurate communication.

Most Deaf people assumed that communication with hearing people would be complicated. They knew that they would have to rely upon pencil and paper, not unfamiliar items in the lexicon of material culture, to communicate with hearing friends and acquaintances. Deaf people did not expect hearing people to know the sign language. Some did advocate the teaching of the manual alphabet in the common schools. In 1850, at the first convention of American instructors of the deaf, a resolution was passed.

> Resolved, that in the view of this Convention, the general introduction of the manual alphabet into our common schools would both furnish the best means of giving practice in orthography and produce great advantages to educated deaf-mutes, in facilitating their necessary communications with strangers and greatly increasing their social enjoyments.[148]

The teaching of the manual alphabet was never introduced into the common schools, but the resolution indicates the state of mind in the profession in 1850. Hearing and deaf teachers alike believed that hearing people needed to make some efforts to help to integrate deaf people into American society. Deaf people had to learn English well, for efficient communication by fingerspelling required a strong grasp of English, but they did not have to do all of the accommodating. In 1850, the profession believed that hearing people had to make adjustments as well. Even as late as 1869, the director of the New York Institution optimistically wrote, "And I trust that the time will come, when the ready use of the manual alphabet will be regarded as a necessary accomplishment by all persons of intelligence and benevolence."[149] An integrated hearing-deaf society required effort on both sides. The advocates of oral education succeeded in placing the entire burden for integration and accommodation on deaf people. The time in which all hearing persons would regard the manual alphabet as a necessary accomplishment for learned people never arrived.

To facilitate communication, some deaf people took to carrying a small slate, not nearly as common a material item, with them wherever they went. Such an arrangement was fairly unusual. At least once, it resulted in a very peculiar reaction from a hearing observer. William B. Swett recalled the incident.

> The next day I was able to go to work and was much amused by the whisperings and pointings of my fellow workmen. They regarded me, for some time, as a strange person and seemed to be much afraid of my slate and pencil. One of them, who stood near me one day when I pulled out my slate for some purpose, ran away as fast as possible, showing fear on his

face; but whether in fun or in earnest I did not know, nor did I care, so long as there was nothing offensive in the manner. In course of time they got over this and treated me as one of themselves.[150]

Presumably, Swett was the first Deaf individual these men had ever met. They found him a "strange person," obviously very different from themselves. The slate did not serve its intended purpose of promoting communication, instead provoking stares. One man reacted with particular emotion, running away in dread from the sight of the slate. Maybe he feared confronting his illiteracy. Or perhaps, as Christopher Krentz suggests, "early-nineteenth-century hearing people may have sometimes felt afraid of deaf individuals who did not speak, seeing them as both familiar and foreign, as otherworldly reminders of the danger of isolation or even as a kind of living death."[151]

Whatever the reasons, Swett chose to believe that these hearing people simply had very little experience with Deaf people and did not know how to react appropriately to them. But appropriate or not, they did have a reaction: they whispered, stared, and pointed. As literary critic Rosemarie Garland Thomson has argued, this behavior is in fact highly ritualized. She reminds us, "The dynamic of staring registers the perception of difference by the viewer and enforces the acceptance of difference by the viewed."[152]

How could Deaf people respond to such behaviors? How did they survive in a hearing world that stared and pointed at them? Swett's weapon was humor. He faced each new awkward encounter with grace and humor as he waited for the hearing people to adjust to his deafness and treat him "as one of themselves" instead of as "a strange person." He refused to accept any stranger's judgment of him as different, and therefore inferior.

Still, these types of confused or tentative encounters were common for Deaf people. They had to make them repeatedly, with each new hearing person they met. Swett was no exception. After he had won over these hearing companions, a stranger arrived on the scene. A new exchange occurred.

My signs and gestures and my little slate, of which I made free use in talking with my companions, soon attracted the attention of the company, to most of whom a deaf mute was evidently a new thing. One man in particular, an Irishman, who was seated in a corner, smoking a pipe, after eyeing me intently for some time, approached me, laid a hand on my shoulder, looked me in the face, and then, making a sign of the cross, he nodded, went back to his seat and resumed his pipe, apparently satisfied that it was all right. I could not help smiling at his behavior and did not know what to think of it, but have since concluded that it was his way either of getting acquainted or of expressing sympathy.[153]

Swett not only maintained his sense of humor; he managed to retain a sense of wonder as well. He was surprised that these men had never met a deaf person before. And even when the Irishman expressed his sympathy for Swett, Swett retained his composure. He rationalized away the Irishman's behavior. Maybe he was merely "getting acquainted."

In recounting Swett's story, Christopher Krentz suggests that it calls attention to what we he terms "the hearing line, that invisible boundary that separates deaf and hearing human beings." Swett offers a "perspective from the deaf side of the hearing line, where visual communication is the norm."[154] Comfortable on his side of the line, a Deaf man from a Deaf family, Swett did not feel the need to hide his Deafness. Instead he seems to say that when "confronting the formidable hearing line that so often separates the deaf and hearing . . . the best way to try to achieve connection is with empathy and laughter."[155]

Worlds Collide

A certain degree of cross-cultural misunderstanding was probably inevitable. Deaf and hearing people faced each other across a line that marked a physical, cultural, and linguistic divide. The gap between them displayed itself most obviously in the opinions that both groups held about deaf education. Deaf people passionately supported manual education and the use of the sign language. Manualist educators had similar opinions. Together, in residential schools, students and educators, deaf and hearing, had witnessed the creation of a Deaf community. When those students reached adulthood, they made their lives in this new Deaf world, a world that continued to have strong ties to residential schools, especially to the American School for the Deaf, as the seminal Deaf events of the nineteenth century make clear.

But a new generation of educators favored the oral method, over the objections of the very people they sought to educate. With Deaf culture a reality, the debate over the future of deaf education only intensified. Oralist educators believed that the best way to put an end to cross-cultural misunderstandings was to eliminate the oppositional culture in question, namely, Deaf culture. And the best strategy for eliminating Deaf culture was to dismantle manual education.

Horace Mann and
Samuel Gridley Howe

The First American Oralists

It is a great blessing to a deaf mute to be able to converse in the language of signs. But it is obvious that, as soon as he passes out of the circle of those who understand that language, he is as helpless and hopeless as ever. The power of uttering articulate sounds, of speaking as others speak, alone restores him to society.

—Horace Mann, 1844

The years prior to the 1840s saw the emergence of a solid pedagogical consensus among educators of the deaf. The New York School had led the way and American Sign Language had become the preferred language of instruction. Hearing teachers had to learn this natural language of signs and become fluent in it. Other schools had quickly followed suit. A remarkable consensus emerged around the merits of this new pedagogical course.

If educators and administrators were so confident in their bilingual-bicultural method, why didn't it survive the century? Just as the field coalesced around the New York School's method, it was attacked by outsiders, led by Horace Mann (1796-1859) and Samuel Gridley Howe (1801-1876), beginning in the 1840s. How are we to understand their dissatisfaction with the state of deaf education? What are we to make of their strenuous objections to this manual method, a method with which professionals working in the field were evidently more than satisfied? Why should they have advocated so stridently a switch to the oral method?

As previously noted, Mann showed little interest in deaf education prior to 1844, when he issued his *Seventh Annual Report of the Massachusetts State Board of Education*, and after 1844 he never wrote on the subject again. Indeed, it has been suggested by several historians that nothing happened in the 1840s, that Mann was simply ignored at the time; his claims for the effectiveness of the oral method were proven to be exaggerated and so disregarded.[1]

Yet, there are reasons to think that this was not the case. First, the Clarke School itself understands its institutional history quite differently. The celebratory history of the Clarke School, written by a long-time teacher, entitled *My Words Fell on Deaf Ears: An Account of the First Hundred Years of the Clarke School for the Deaf*, points to the important roles of both Mann and Howe in its establishment. And, historian of special education Margret Winzer has similarly posited that the Massachusetts legislature supported oralism due to the power of "the voice of Horace Mann" in the state, especially when combined with that of so respected a reformer as Samuel Gridley Howe.[2]

Second, the 1840s and 1850s saw the emergence of a tremendous debate within the field of deaf education about the relative value of methodical signs as a tool for teaching English. The debate raises an obvious question: why then? The time to debate the merits of methodical signs would seem to have passed by 1844; they had been out of use in most schools since the middle of the 1830s. Any debate would seem to have been needed then, but the decision to drop them was in fact made with no widespread debate at all. A consensus about their limitations was widely established across the field; apparently, no debate had been needed.

Mann's call for change touched off a wave of professional soul-searching among those working in the field of deaf education. Old ideas were resurrected and reconsidered; new ideas were pondered and debated. The decades of the middle of the century, the 1840s and 1850s, were pivotal, for it was then that the future course of deaf education, and with it the place of the deaf community in American society, would be plotted. The question still remains, then: why Mann? Why did he involve himself, and his influence, in a field about which he had never before taken an interest? What did he hope to accomplish by addressing the issue of deaf education? Why did he consider the oral method superior to the manual method?

Why Horace Mann?

A couple of theories have been advanced to explain Mann's involvement. From one point of view, Mann has been considered the instrument of Samuel Gridley Howe, the prominent nineteenth-century social reformer and principal of the Perkins Institute for the Blind. Howe wanted Perkins to become responsible for the education of deaf, as well as blind, children in Massachusetts. Howe was a personal friend of Mann's, and this explanation holds that Howe persuaded Mann to address the topic of deaf education on this one occasion in order to support his bid to educate deaf children. The *Seventh Annual Report of the Board of Education* of 1844 is seen as having been written by Mann in order to offer public support for his friend Howe.[3]

The theory does have some merit. It explains Mann's motive for getting involved in a field about which he was nearly entirely ignorant, as well as why he never wrote on the subject again. This theory does not, however, attempt to demonstrate how Mann's views on deaf education may have been tied to his views on common school education. Making Mann's participation in the first public debate over the merits of oral education rest solely on his personal friendship with Howe prevents exploration of the possible connections with his wider views on education for the nation as a whole. This interpretation fails to consider that the two men were not just friends and casts Mann in the role of offering purely personal help to Howe. They were also professional colleagues and collaborators, as we shall see below. Howe would not have had to use Mann; Mann's support for Howe's work was quite genuine.

The other common view of Mann's involvement in the oral versus manual debates of the midcentury is that they had no bearing whatsoever on the triumph of oralism at the end of the century.[4] From this perspective, Mann and his contemporaries had little influence on the oralist movement. They are seen as proposing an idea whose time had not yet come. The wider culture was not yet willing to accept oral education for deaf students. It was not until the rise of anti-immigrant and nativist feeling at the end of the century that oralist arguments would gain currency. A more nativist culture could be persuaded to see native-born Deaf people as foreigners in their own land. Hearing parents would, from this perspective, then see deafness as an even more stigmatizing condition and seek to make their children as much like them as possible. If their deaf children could not hear, they could at least be taught to act like hearing people and speak. Oralist arguments would suddenly make cultural sense.

Again, this argument is convincing as far as it goes. Certainly oralists did have the upper hand in the cultural environment at the end of the nineteenth century. Nativist feeling persuaded the oralists to define deafness as foreignness and, in a xenophobic culture, this argument was indeed compelling. However, it only explains the timing of the oralist victory; it explains why the oralists succeeded in capturing the wider public's imagination when they did. But it ignores the fact that they had been trying to win the field for years before victory finally came and leaves unexplored the development of oralist thought throughout the century. It overlooks the internal conflicts in the manualist camp that oralists had been exploiting since the middle of the century. In short, to divide the end-of-century victors from their midcentury forebears is to ignore the historical development of the logic of oralism. These two groups cannot and should not be so neatly separated.

Mann's Educational Philosophy

The 1844 report, after all, gave Howe the necessary fuel to press the Massachusetts state legislature to establish a separate oral school in Massachusetts, after his own bid for Perkins to take over deaf education in Massachusetts failed. The state legislature finally agreed and, in 1867, Clarke School opened. It followed the method of pure oralism. The success of Clarke School led to the founding of other oral schools across the country. By the end of the century, schools previously using the manual method had switched to the oral method. Edward Miner Gallaudet, the son of Thomas Hopkins Gallaudet and president of Gallaudet College (now University) was left to ask pitifully, "Must the sign language go?"[5]

The involvement of Horace Mann and his contemporaries would seem more necessary to the eventual victory of the cause they espoused than has been previously understood. Still, perhaps the best place to begin to try to unravel the meaning of Mann's role in the rise of oralism is with Jonathan Messerli's authoritative biography of Horace Mann. Messerli offers two clues to understanding Mann's actions in 1844. First, as he views it, Mann intended for the *Seventh Annual Report* to awaken Americans to the fact that they were falling behind the Prussians in education.[6] It was a tour of Prussian schools in 1843, undertaken during his European honeymoon upon which he was accompanied not only by his bride, his second wife, Mary Peabody, but also by Samuel Gridley Howe and his bride, Julia Ward, that inspired Mann's report. The tour included numerous visits to Prussia's schools for the deaf, which followed the method of pure oralism.[7]

Mann everywhere praised the Prussian system as a model of practicality and efficiency. He was not supportive of the political ends that he perceived the Prussian educational system was designed to promote, but he argued that an American system modeled along Prussian lines could use those means while aiming toward a very different end, namely, the development of good republican citizens.[8] Thus, when Mann complained that American schools lagged behind the Prussian schools in everything from teacher training to pedagogy, he had both deaf and hearing schools in mind. And American schools for the deaf were laboring under the additional handicap of their outdated methodology; the Prussian oralism was perceived as the more modern method by Mann.[9]

Second, Messerli suggests that Mann thought of children not as individuals but instead as a mass, as a whole generation in need of education. "There was in this man's mind," Messerli comments, "both the power and compulsion towards an invincible abstractness."[10] It was as young humanity in America that children needed to be educated. Accordingly, Mann's educational thinking was directed toward the establishment of a program for all of young America. In Messerli's phrase, this was a "vision of an entire nation going to school" and thereby gaining for itself a common set of values and mores.[11] Sharing a common culture, republican citizens could work together to rid the nation of poverty, crime, disease, and ignorance. Education was the cure for all that ailed America.

Deaf people, it seemed, could not be left out of this vision. Mann could not afford to leave them out of the project of building a common culture. By educating deaf people in separate schools with a separate language, other hearing educators were, by Mann's lights, failing to include deaf people in the wider common culture. It was not enough that deaf people were taught to read and write English. They had to learn to speak it as well. They had to share in the same oral culture as hearing people.

It is not readily apparent why spoken English should have been considered so much superior to written English. One could easily imagine that reading books enabled people to readily access a common, wider culture. Perhaps only by investigating Mann's conception of the nature of language itself can we begin to understand his position on deaf education. Mann's *Second Annual Report of the Secretary of the Board* dwelled in some detail on the nature of language, abstractly considered. He considered language training an essential part of a child's education because "language is not merely a necessary instrument of civilization, past or prospective, but it is an indispensable condition of our existence as rational beings." As rational beings, Mann argued, we would find that "for all social purposes, thought and expression are dependent each upon the other."[12] Just as the New York School had done, Mann explored the perceived link between thought and language, but he reached an entirely different conclusion.

Mann elaborated on this point.

> An unscientific language . . . will keep a people unscientific forever. So the knowledge of a people on any subject cannot far exceed the compass of the language which they fully comprehend . . . language reacts upon the mind

which uses it. It is like the garment in which some nations clothe themselves, which shape the very limbs that draw them on. Men are generally very willing to modify or change their opinions and views while they exist in thought merely, but when once formally expressed, the language chosen often becomes the mould of the opinion. The opinion fills the mould but cannot break it and assume a new form. Thus errors of thought and of life originate in impotence of language.[13]

Following this line of reasoning, one can begin to see how deaf people would fit into this vision. The use of the sign language would clearly pose a problem for Mann. The sign language, like any language, would "react upon the mind that uses it" and shape a "mould of opinion" that the mind would be unable to break. By using this signed language, so different in both grammar and form from that of the majority's spoken language, for daily conversation, the deaf would be inclined to think in that language and therefore would not truly be living in the same culture as hearing people. The sign language, not English, would become the garment that their minds would wear.

The *Seventh Annual Report* provides more reasons for preferring an oral language to a signed language. Mann argued that very few hearing people "have the time, means, or inclination to hold written communication" with the deaf. But if the deaf could speak and read lips, hearing people would "converse with them willingly." Mann acknowledged that some deaf people would have to abandon speaking "on account of being unintelligible," but stressed that if they mastered lipreading, they could at least follow the conversation of hearing people well enough to participate in society.[14]

While proponents of the manual method saw reading and writing English as a way of establishing social equality between hearing and deaf people, Mann completely disagreed. "The power of uttering articulate sounds," Mann wrote, "of speaking as others speak, alone restores him to society."[15] By his lights, it was not enough that the two groups shared a common language; they also had to share a common mode of expression. The majority not only read and wrote English; they also spoke it. To truly become the equals of hearing people, deaf people had to speak English as well. In the social vision of the manualists, both groups made adjustments to interact with one another; in the oralist vision, deaf people had to do all the accommodating.

Mann believed that the use of the sign language did nothing to help deaf people accommodate themselves to life in a hearing society. In fact, he argued that, while "it is a great blessing to a deaf-mute to be able to converse in the language of signs," it is "obvious that as soon as he passes out of the circle of those who understand that language, he is as helpless and hopeless as ever."[16] Deaf people argued that they would use written English with those who knew no sign language. But we have already seen why Mann would reject this solution. Besides, he believed that deaf people could be taught to articulate "substantially in all cases."[17]

If articulate speech had the power to restore deaf people to society, Mann believed it also possessed another remarkable power. Speech, Mann wrote, "has an extraordinary humanizing power, the remark having been often made, and with truth, that all the deaf and dumb which have learned to speak have a far more human expression of the eye and countenance than those who have only been taught to write."[18] Speech made deaf people more human, in a way that writing and, one can imagine, signing, did not.

Here Mann's beliefs about language become especially relevant. Recall that he believed that language was part of our existence as "rational beings" and, since "thought and expression are dependent each upon the other," the kind of language we use makes us the people that we are because "language reacts upon the mind that uses it" and "moulds our opinions." People who spoke English thought in English; thus their thought and expression were linked together. Presumably, this union honed the language to act upon the mind more forcefully, and the result was a more rational and human being. Deaf people who were taught English by signs would forever experience a bifurcation of thought and expression. If they were taught English alone, in all its guises, they would essentially become more human.

Mann may not have succeeded in establishing an oral school himself and, since he died in 1859, he did not live to see oralism replace manualism in classrooms for the deaf in the United States. Yet his writings were influential, even crucial, in making the eventual oralist victory possible. His belief about the humanizing power of speech became a cliché in oralist circles. His insistence that speech alone, not signing, not writing, not even literacy itself, restored a deaf person to society likewise became a favorite oralist argument.[19] Mann earnestly believed that speech alone would restore deaf people to the human family and enable them to participate in the common culture he was trying to create via the common school. His arguments in 1844 set the oralist agenda for the rest of the century.

Samuel Gridley Howe, for one, took care to remind his audience that Horace Mann was owed a debt by the oralists who followed him. For instance, at the 1867 hearings in front of the Massachusetts state legislature that resulted in the state's decision to support the Clarke School for the Deaf, one of the first pure oral schools in the United States, Howe directed the legislators to fund the school to honor the memory of Horace Mann, reminding them that it was Mann who wanted to bring oralism to deaf children and announcing dramatically that "up to the day of his death he cherished this idea, and in his last letter to me he made mention of his wish."[20]

Why Samuel Gridley Howe?

Howe was not simply a personal friend of Mann's. The two men were also professional partners in reform. They worked together at Perkins, Howe as director, Mann as the school's attorney and a founding member of its board of trustees. Later, when Mann served in the Massachusetts state legislature, he was able to use his connections to put Howe's annual reports into the hands of key legislators.[21]

Mann was very interested when Howe accepted Laura Bridgman, a deaf-blind girl, to Perkins to try to educate her. This became one of the most famous pedagogical experiments of the nineteenth century. The details of the efforts to educate her need not be investigated here. Rather, I would like to draw readers' attention to the ways in which Howe's work with Bridgman, and with the other blind students in his care, shaped his thinking about disability more generally.

When Howe began his work at Perkins in 1833, he did so with certain beliefs about blindness in mind. Howe posited that the blind, if treated as individuals and not as members of a class, could be educated according to their talents and could take an independent place in society, not yoked to charity, but as self-sufficient citizens.[22] But he went even further than demonstrating a faith in the power of education. Howe also assumed, as literary scholar Mary Klages has written, that "there were no significant differences between blind and sighted people that education could not correct."[23] Like other New England reformers of his generation, Howe believed that "public institutions . . . could transform unfortunates of any sort into useful and productive members of society."[24]

Productivity would be an important measure of the school's success. If Howe was correct and the blind were in essence no different from the sighted, then the role of the school could rightly be to educate them to take a role in society and a place in the American economy. There should be no need of conceiving of the blind as a burden on the state or as charity cases for private philanthropists. Equal access to education would change all of that.[25]

Yet, as Howe began his work, he did so with limited experience with the blind, either in schools or out. After he had taught for several years, he began to modify his beliefs about what it was possible for the blind to achieve. First, he emerged from the classroom with new linguistic theories of disability. As Klages argues, Howe posited that the blind could never fully master the nuances of spoken English precisely because of their sightlessness. How could they comprehend the full meaning of words when those words were linked to objects the blind could not see? Klages concludes, "Linking the capacity for language comprehension to physical sensation, Howe defined the body that was lacking a sense as incapable of full linguistic competence."[26] Howe drew this conclusion about the capabilities of the disabled body from his work with the blind, but the connections to his later work with the deaf are readily apparent.

The differences with the manualist reformers of his generation are also clear. While Howe was reaching the conclusion that the blind could never achieve full linguistic competence, Gallaudet was learning the precise opposite. Once more, the importance of the presence of Laurent Clerc is thrown into sharp relief. His very presence, and his multilingualism, prevented Gallaudet from theorizing about the linguistic capacities of the deaf in the ways that Howe did with the blind. Working with a multilingual Deaf adult was a necessary corrective to theorizing, from a hearing and sighted point of view, about the capabilities of the deaf. Howe had no such useful adult blind partner at Perkins.

Further, after ten years in the field, Howe had reached the conclusion that the blind would not be able to support themselves. After witnessing firsthand the trouble his graduates had getting jobs, and keeping them, after leaving Perkins, Howe, even though he did admit that his graduates faced discrimination and prejudice, nonetheless concluded that he had overestimated the abilities of the blind all along.[27] Years of experience, he admitted in the Perkins annual report of 1848, had forced him to reverse the opinion with which he had entered the field. It turns out, he was wrong. Capitalizing his words for dramatic effect, he announced, "THE BLIND, AS A CLASS, ARE INFERIOR TO OTHER PERSONS IN MENTAL POWER AND ABILITY."[28]

This was especially true of those born blind, who suffered from a "defective physical organization" that must, by its nature, affect their entire being. But Klages points out that Howe did not limit his pessimism to the congenitally blind. Those who went blind later in life due to accident or illness, for instance, were also, by Howe's lights, now limited in their potential, for blindness would prevent physical exercise, which would interfere with the healthy development of their bodies, and without a healthy body, the health of the mind would soon suffer in turn.[29]

Significantly, Howe's work with Laura Bridgman fueled his reassessment of the disabled generally. The year 1841 was "the high-water mark of his optimism" for Bridgman's future, reports historian Ernest Freeberg.[30] But by the mid-1840s, Laura's adult personality had started to emerge. "For a decade," Freeberg concludes, "Howe had been inspired by a vision of who Laura *could* become, and now this ideal was contradicted by who she actually was."[31] To put it bluntly, as Howe concluded that this reality did not match his vision, he responded by rejecting both Lauras, the project and the person. Whereas she had once been the pride of Perkins, Howe now abandoned her. And he did so quite publicly, writing of his shift in opinion in the annual reports of the Perkins Institution. Freeberg writes, "Howe decided that her physical handicaps did have mental and moral consequences. Laura's mind and soul . . . had been fundamentally damaged when she lost the use of her eyes and ears."[32]

Thus, as Howe literally wrote Laura off, he found that his work with his star pupil had forced him to rethink his entire project at Perkins.[33] He revised his expectations for all his blind students, and for blind people generally. Their inferiority to the sighted could no longer be denied and, indeed, had to be explained to a wider public. No longer simply promoting the cause of education for the blind, Howe had turned to interpreting the meaning of blindness for the largely able-bodied public. His new opinion of blindness made it clear that the sighted public could rest easy in its superiority.

Perhaps not surprisingly, Howe also began to reimagine the role of institutions like Perkins. New England reformers in the antebellum period were largely driven by an optimistic faith in progress.[34] But what is a reformer to do when he no longer believes in progress—or, going further, when he determines that the group of people he serves is not biologically capable of making progress? This was the crossroads Howe had reached. He determined to paint a picture of the blind as incapable yet worthy of charitable and benevolent able-bodied support.

In discarding his earlier ideals, Howe no longer challenged able-bodied ideas about the meaning of blindness, ideas that invariably placed the sighted in a privileged, superior position while consigning the blind to perpetual inferiority. In fact, Howe confirmed that the blind were inferior on all levels: physical, moral, intellectual.[35] Suddenly, Perkins promoted, rather than challenged, the sighted prejudices of the day.

Having gathered the blind together in the residential school, Howe even began to have second thoughts about the worthiness of that project. According to Freeberg, "Howe decided that, in the long run, institutionalization harmed the blind, encouraging their sense of isolation from the rest of society and amplifying their worst characteristics. Because Perkins's residents spent most of their time interacting only with other blind people, Howe noticed, they became more 'clannish.'"[36] This is a significant charge; in fact, it is precisely the same one that Howe would later make against residential schools for the deaf. They, too, he would come to believe, promoted "clannishness."

It is clear that Deaf culture was promoted by the living arrangements of the schools. As Christopher Krentz writes, "[By] segregating deaf people who otherwise might not have found each other, the schools contributed to the rise of a distinct and subversive group identity."[37] But this distinctive identity was claimed in the presence of and with the support of hearing people. The schools for the deaf were, as we have seen, to use Krentz's phrase, "established through a symbiotic deaf-hearing collaboration."[38] That made all the difference. As partners in the institutional endeavor, the deaf collaborated with the hearing to build not only their educational system but also a community and, with it, a language. Working together, deaf and hearing adults side by side, taught both groups much about the other. The result was that the ideas that hearing people held about deafness were challenged and reshaped.

Howe, working with other sighted adults, interacting with blind children, working from the position of a superior and sighted adult over a subordinate and blind child, saw the prejudices of his day affirmed, rather than abandoned. What Howe perceived as the clannishness of the blind was a threat that had to be dealt with. Steps had to be taken to prevent such clannishness from developing further. In part for this reason, Howe decided that the blind would be better off living among the sighted. He proposed that older Perkins students should room off-campus, in the homes of sighted, "normal" families in the surrounding neighborhood.[39] By doing so, the blind students would be exposed to the normalizing influences of the able-bodied.

Eventually, Mann's theories about language and Howe's theories about disability would combine to arrive at a potent theory of oralism. With Mann's death, it would eventually be left to Howe to argue oralism's case, as we shall see. But first, Gallaudet tried to respond to Mann directly to persuade him that his vision of the deaf was ill-founded.

Measuring Mann's Impact: Thomas Hopkins Gallaudet Responds

Even in 1844, manualists recognized the seriousness of Mann's criticisms of their method. This antebellum challenge to manualism prompted a swift response from a long-since-retired Thomas Hopkins Gallaudet. He had retired from his position at the American School in 1830, but Mann's spirited attack on manualism forced Gallaudet to take up his pen once more in defense of the system he had helped to found. He wrote to Mann directly and privately to express his concerns, in a letter dated May 13, 1844.

Gallaudet's response to Mann made clear the distance between the two men. Mann focused on articulation to the exclusion of nearly everything else, believing that speech was a kind of magic bullet to cure the isolation of deafness. If deaf people could only speak, then they would be entirely restored to society. But Gallaudet took issue with this conception of deaf education. He quite pointedly corrected Mann, and argued that truly educating deaf people meant far more than simply teaching them how to talk. Here is Gallaudet's description of deaf education.

> The teaching of the deaf-mutes to articulate and to understand what is said to them is but *one part* of their education. The development of the intellectual and moral faculties of deaf mutes; their intellectual and moral training; their government, by moral influence; the imparting to them moral, religious, and other knowledge; their participating, understandingly, in the social and public devotional exercises of the Institution; the furnishing of their minds with the ideas, the facts, and that amount of knowledge, which are necessary to prepare them to understand a vast number of the *words* which must be taught them; their becoming acquainted with our social and civil institutions; with arithmetic, grammar, geography, and history; with the history, simple doctrines, and the precepts of the Bible; with their duties to God, to their fellow-men, and themselves; and their acquiring a trade, or some means of gaining a livelihood; and especially their being taught to *write* the English language correctly and to *read books intelligently*, (one of the highest solaces and means of constantly progressive self-culture, which deaf mutes can enjoy,) all these are essential parts of their education. They may have them without being able to articulate, and to understand what is said to them.[40]

Gallaudet here sounded very much like the Whig reformer that he was. He emphasized the need of deaf students to learn to control their passions and exercise their moral faculties. He wanted them to discover, embrace, and fulfill their duties to God, their country, and themselves. He assumed, in other words, that education would enable the deaf to become contributing Christian citizens, able to support themselves and to participate in the civil and social institutions of their communities. He also assumed, of course, that deaf people were capable of doing all of these things. There is not a hint of the hopeless, biological inferiority of the deaf asserted here. Gallaudet posited that the deaf would take up their "duties . . . to their fellow-men," just as if they could and should do so. By 1844, Howe was already hurtling toward the conclusion that the blind were capable of none of this, and Mann, toward the conclusion that only speech would serve the deaf. The two sides were light years apart already in 1844.

For Gallaudet placed not speech, but literacy, above all. The most important thing that educators could do was to teach the deaf to write and read, "especially" and "intelligently," and again for Whiggish reasons, as the best means to promote a "constantly progressive self-culture." Articulation, Gallaudet noted firmly, was not necessary to any of this. Indeed, only "the beautiful language of *natural signs*" could make this education possible.[41]

Gallaudet went so far as to charge that the pursuit of articulation would undermine the chances of achieving this fuller education he sought for deaf students, warning:

> How far the essential parts of a complete education, which I have above specified must be retarded, sacrificed, or neglected . . . in order to go through with the long, laborious, and to them, certainly, in many cases, as experience has abundantly shown, very tedious and irksome process of learning to articulate, and to understand what is said to them.[42]

With this warning, Gallaudet also suggested that educators risked alienating deaf students from their own education. How invested could students be in an irksome education full of nothing but labor and tedium? Learning English was, as Gallaudet knew well, a difficult enough task. Deaf students needed to be partners in this educational process; they had to be active in pursuing their own education, and not passive. The sign language alone, Gallaudet concluded, enabled deaf students to raise with a teacher "*the questions they may wish to propose to him . . . a most essential part of the proper instruction of the child.*"[43] Only manual education, Gallaudet implied to Mann, would ever be embraced by deaf people themselves, the objects of all this educational attention and controversy.

The Meaning of Disability and Reform

Gallaudet and Howe have rightly been connected as two of nineteenth-century reforms greatest lights. Ronald Walters argues,

There were . . . lesser-known varieties of asylums in the antebellum period, some of them remarkable for their accomplishments and decency. Particularly impressive were the endeavors of Thomas Gallaudet with deaf-mutes and of Samuel Gridley Howe with the blind. . . . Their work . . . gave ample evidence that human sympathy toward disadvantaged "others" was very much a part of asylum building.[44]

But leaving disability theory out of an interpretation of reform efforts, it should be clear, has led to a misapprehension of reform history, as it intersects with disabled lives.

This investigation of both men, together with Howe's collaborator, Mann, reveals that their relationship toward the so-called other was hardly a straightforward story of sympathy. The two branches of reform efforts might have been the same in that both took as the object of their efforts the disabled child, but there their similarity ends. Howe, through his work with the blind, later came to his work with the deaf with an entirely different set of principles than those that guided Thomas Hopkins Gallaudet and the other manualists of the antebellum period.

Viewing these men together makes it clear that they emerged as the first reform leaders of their generation to engage in a large-scale public debate about the meaning and place of the disabled body in American life. The nature of disability was explored and debated, and the educational policies these men advanced were largely influenced by the ideas of disability each held to be true.

As we have seen, Gallaudet had learned that some of his ideas about deafness were wrong, and he learned this from the source directly, from deaf adults, especially Laurent Clerc. It is important here that French Deaf culture was already strongly developed by the time the French influence reached American shores.[45] Clerc already took the transformation of deafness to Deafness for granted as a Frenchman. Witnessing a similar transformation within American schools would have come as no shock to him, and, eventually, not for the hearing Americans he tutored, either.

This meant that, within the field of deaf education, hearing ideas about deafness alone did not predominate. Deaf ideas about deafness also had power in the field. Whereas some scholars considering asylum building in the nineteenth century have invoked a colonial metaphor to describe the unbalanced power relations in such institutions, Christopher Krentz reminds us of the limits of this metaphor. "Unlike native groups who had lived independently before colonization," he writes, "deaf Americans never lived apart from hearing people, and had indeed come together because of hearing involvement."[46]

We can go further. It is not just the case that such institutions brought the deaf together in great numbers for the first time. They also brought the hearing into intimate contact with the deaf for the first time. Most hearing people had never lived or worked with deaf people in such close proximity. Deaf identity may have been formed with "an abiding double consciousness," asserting both a commonality with hearing people as well as their basic difference as deaf people.[47] But these Deaf ideas of identity and Deafness also had an influence on hearing educators in the antebellum period. This truly was "a symbiotic deaf-hearing collaboration," and that means that its ideas moved in both directions, from the hearing to the deaf and from the deaf to the hearing. The guiding principles in the field of manual deaf education were shaped collaboratively by both hearing and Deaf people.

This is why the initial educational system was so visual in orientation. There was no effort to make speech training, or even lipreading, a part of the curriculum. Laurent Clerc was firmly against it. One only realizes how countercultural this stance truly is when one stops to consider the ways in which Western culture has always privileged speech over sign. "Since ancient times, people believed that the ability to speak vocally is what makes one human," Christopher Krentz writes.[48] Or, put another way, as Lennard Davis notes, "Since it is assumed that the dominant sign production will be oral and sign reception will be aural, then the deaf are seen as bereft of language, hence humanity."[49] These are exactly the beliefs that American manual education would reject, especially since it refused to train its students to speak. Manualists would challenge these cultural norms and argue instead that literacy and speech be regarded as equal forms of communication. Then, the hearing world could be redefined as the literate world, a world the hearing and the deaf could occupy harmoniously together.[50]

It was Clerc who led here, as he consistently argued throughout his career that writing was a viable substitute for speech.[51] To the extent that the manualist establishment followed his lead, it embraced Deaf ideas of education and citizenship. Deaf people would not have to be remade in a hearing image to gain an education or to participate in the life of the wider society around them. This was an understanding of disability as located more in the society than in the body. The deaf body may not hear, but it need not be made over to approximate hearing norms. Rather, social norms may be adjusted to accommodate the deaf body. Hearing people would learn to communicate with the deaf through writing, as both groups broadened the base of literacy in American society. And yet there was not a denial of deafness either. It was assumed instead that it was as natural for the deaf body to sign as it was natural for the hearing body to speak. Deafness was in some ways accepted on deaf terms in the manualist vision. In this way, the manualist education offered a complex recognition of the physical and social natures of disability, and realized that the two were deeply entwined.

Yet, the guiding manualist assumption that the disabled body could be accommodated into the mainstream of American life on disabled terms was a vision that the oralists, led by Howe and Mann, would not accept. Both men vigorously reasserted the primacy of speech, threatened so by this manualist conception of writing and signing as ample substitutes. Only speech and speech alone was humanizing, let alone communicative. There was no need to respect Deaf ideas about education because deafness, like other physical disabilities, invariably corrupted the mind and the spirit of the disabled, making them hopelessly inferior.

The most that could be done would be to mask this inferiority by making it possible for the deaf to pass as hearing and so to reify the norm of the able-bodied. The way for a society to deal with disability, in this oralist vision, was to make it invisible. This erasure of the disabled from public view, in order to preserve the body politic as uniformly able-bodied, accounts for the impulse to train the deaf to pass as hearing, as well as the impulse toward permanent institutionalization of the developmentally disabled, an impulse that also emerged in the nineteenth century and was not reversed until the late twentieth century.

The visual presence of disability, as Lennard Davis reminds us, challenges "the hegemony of normalcy." In many cases, "disability . . . is a disruption in the visual, auditory, or perceptual field as it relates to the power of the gaze. As such, the disruption, the rebellion of the visual, must be regulated, rationalized, contained."[52] The oral training of the deaf, as Mann and Howe conceived of it, was one way to accomplish this cultural project of containment. The presence of the deaf, as deaf, was to be erased from the social scene, because the visual marker of deafness is signing. Deafness is an invisible disability, but deaf behavior, signing, makes a bodily difference visible. With oral training, that visual mark of difference would be eliminated. The deaf would be like the hearing. They would pass.

Passing only serves to reinforce the hegemony of normalcy; because hearing is the privileged, superior status, any attempt of the deaf to pass as hearing only serves to confirm this categorization. Howe, we have already seen, wanted the superiority of the able body confirmed; he had concluded that the blind, as a class, were inferior to sighted people, because their disability rendered them inferior. So too the deaf not only had to be inferior to the hearing by their nature; they had to be recognized as such. Given his beliefs about disability generally, Howe could only possibly support an educational theory that would confirm, rather than challenge, the assumption of deaf inferiority. Oralism would be premised on the belief that the disabled body is inherently inferior to the able body. Under oral deaf education, deaf people would be reminded of their inferiority to hearing people daily, while they would simultaneously be encouraged to approximate that norm and become as hearing as possible.[53]

Manualism and oralism therefore stand not only as two different educational philosophies but as two different responses to the disabled body in our midst. Manualism destabilized the hegemony of hearing by challenging the great symbol of the superiority of hearingness, namely, speech. It urged the acceptance of Deaf difference in American life. Oralism reacted by reasserting the power of normalcy, and sought to use the coercive power of education to police the deaf body and force it to conform with the norms of hearingness.[54] These nineteenth-century pedagogical efforts suggest the very different paths that reform movements could take in grappling with the question of disability in American life.

6

Languages of Signs

Methodical versus Natural

The use of signs, in their improved condition, accustoms the pupil to the free and familiar use of a real language, embracing terms general and figurative; and thus . . . forms an excellent preparation for the ready apprehension of the language of words.

—*American Whig Review*, 1846

It is proper to remark that deaf-mutes' colloquial signs are often accompanied by grimaces and laryngean creakings, extremely disagreeable to the ears, but in the exercise of systematic signs, these accompaniments are impossibilities, for a systemized mind regulates all things.

—John Carlin, 1859

Mann's forceful condemnation of the American system of deaf education set off a heated discussion about the future of deaf education among professionals in the field, a conversation that lasted well into the 1850s. Few voices spoke up on behalf of pure oralism, Mann's actual recommendation to the field, as most educators continued to see a wholesale switch to oralism as an impossibility. But the mission of deaf education did suddenly seem up for grabs to these educators. In the years immediately following Mann's report, a debate about the nature of the sign language and its role in deaf education engulfed the profession

In the 1840s and 1850s, the defenders of the natural language of signs remained both abundant and vocal. They detailed with renewed vigor the nature and usefulness of the natural language of signs, determined to head off the oralist challenge by promoting the benefits of both bilingual education and the sign language itself. But there was a difference in the field now. These were no longer the only educators who called themselves manualists. Some from within the manualist camp wanted to reconsider the use of methodical signs within the field.

In part, this was a tactical move, a way to compromise with Mann's oralist demands for pure English. The methodical signs, after all, followed English word order and would introduce an English-only atmosphere back into the schools, and on this, manualists and oralists might find some common ground.

But this was not simply a shrewd tactic to ward off the threat of pure oralism. These supporters of methodical signs in fact shared some common ground of their own with the oralists. They too wanted their students to be English monolinguals; they just wanted to use the methodical signs, rather than the oral method, to assure that outcome. Like the oralists, they too wanted their deaf students to be culturally hearing. As the linguistic debate played itself out within the manualist camp, it became increasingly clear that the real target of debate was Deaf culture itself.

It is not altogether surprising that this debate should have emerged with renewed passion in the 1850s. As Lennard Davis reminds us, the words to discuss such concepts as "normality," "normalcy," and "normal" had only recent arrived in the English language. "The word 'normal' as 'constituting, conforming to, not deviating or differing from, the common type or standard, regular, usual,'" Davis notes, "only enters the English language around 1840. (Previously the word had meant 'perpendicular'; the carpenter's square, called a 'norm,' provided the root meaning.) Likewise, the word 'norm,' in the modern sense, has only been in use since around 1855, and 'normality' and 'normalcy' appeared in 1849 and 1857, respectively."[1]

The arrival and use of these new terms provides an indication of new social thinking, especially about the body. Davis continues,

> The concept of the norm . . . implies that the majority of the population must or should somehow be part of the norm. . . . So, with the concept of the norm comes the concept of deviations or extremes. When we think of bodies, in a society where the concept of the norm is operative, then people with disabilities will be thought of as deviants.[2]

Davis goes on to explore the link between the rise of the concept of the norm and the emergence of statistical sciences and the eugenics movement, movements that would grow to dominate the last quarter of the nineteenth century, surely not coincidently a time when oralism would secure its grip on deaf education.

But here, at this earlier historical moment, the internal debates of the field provide a window into the ways in which those later battles would proceed. In the 1850s, deaf education became a battleground. The arguments offered here shed light on the ways in which normalcy and disability, hearingness and deafness, biology and culture, were being culturally constructed and deconstructed. These mid-nineteenth-century actors entered into a debate where others, especially eugenicists, would later follow. Examining the terms of these debates closely therefore gives us a window not only into the world of deafness and the field of deaf education but into American disability history more broadly, and into the shifting nature of American beliefs about the disabled body.

Again, the timing of this conversation—the emergence of American oralism in the 1840s, followed by the debate of the 1850s—also comes as another consideration of the body is taking place. While it may be true that "bring[ing] into society the concept of a norm, particularly a normal body . . . in effect create[s] the concept of the disabled body," exploring the meaning of the body's senses contributes to the same cultural project.[3] Historians of aurality have begun to identify the antebellum period as a time when hearing people explored what it meant to be hearing, and to know themselves, self-consciously, as *hearing* people. Mark Smith focuses on this history of hearing in the antebellum period in order bring attention to "how important aurality, listening, and hearing were to the process of creating real and abiding notions of slavery and freedom, North and South, especially during the last three decades prior to the Civil War."[4] Growing sectional differences, Smith argues, were embodied in sound—in hearing sounds, making sounds, and interpreting sounds. If aurality increasingly shaped a sense of what it meant to be northern or southern, then it is no surprise that professionals working in the field of deaf education were increasingly drawn into a debate about their pedagogy and their mission in the decades before the Civil War.

For, on the one hand, as Smith makes clear, the growing attention to the history of aural soundscapes does not necessarily imply a recovery of the sense of hearing. Northerners and southerners were exposed to each other's soundscapes mostly imaginatively—in print. "Print itself provided a form of recording, as the use of aural metaphors, similes, and onomatopoeia, and even mundane descriptions, attests," Smith argues.[5] But in coming to the world in print, readers enter into a deafened moment, as Lennard Davis has pointed out. "Even if you are not Deaf," he writes, "you are deaf while you are reading. You are in a deafened modality or moment. All readers are deaf because they are defined by a process that does not require hearing or speaking."[6] Deaf readers in nineteenth-century northern institutions were not therefore unexposed to this growing sense of sectional difference, or even unfamiliar with its sonic quality as conveyed to them through print. Certainly, Deaf readers knew enough about hearing perceptions of deafness to begin to play to the aural expectations of the hearing when they claimed the label "silent" to describe deaf lives.[7] But even as Deaf people claimed this label, as Christopher Krentz reminds us, at the same time "they pointed to its inaccuracy" as a metaphor for the deaf experience. They adopted the term, but in an ironic way.[8] So the deaf, too, like the hearing, could participate in the process of constructing identity through aurality in this way. This shift did not necessarily have to imply that Deaf Americans would find their culture under attack.

On the other hand, Smith argues, "'Otherness' in different guises was also constructed aurally."[9] It is easy to imagine two distinct ways in which this body of thought intersected with the Deaf world. The first is their supposed silence; they neither hear nor speak, so their silence operates both orally and aurally. They are rendered "other" because they do not physically participate in this aurally constructed world. The second is the question of their speech. If the deaf were made to speak, as the oralists sought, would they be rendered more or less "other" in the process? Would their speech come close enough to that of the hearing to close the aural gap between them? Or would it merely accentuate their difference by its sonic quality (or lack thereof)? In either case, if, as Smith posits, American sectional identities are becoming more, and not less, defined through aurality and soundscapes, the ways in which deaf people do, or do not, participate in them would probably be of interest to educators of the deaf in the mid-nineteenth century. This was a key historical moment for them to reconsider orality.

Reconsidering orality would necessitate a rethinking of deafness, as well as a renewed consideration of the meaning of Deafness. If the normal body creates the concept of the disabled body, a renewed attention to the hearing and speaking body would fuel interest in the cultural meaning of a body that neither hears nor speaks. But by the 1850s, deaf people had begun to assign meanings to that body as well, deeming it Deaf. We can see the Deaf community engaging in this larger cultural trend that directs more attention for deaf and hearing people alike to aurality and attempting to shape it to their own purposes, by playing with hearing metaphors for deafness and trying to engage with the majority culture in a language it can understand. But we can also see that the freedom to assign a Deaf meaning to a deaf body, a freedom the deaf took advantage of during the antebellum period to form a community and culture of their own, would also be called into question at this time. For even as Deaf culture coalesced in the 1850s, the larger culture was moving to define culture increasingly along aural lines.

In part, the debate between the educators that arose in the 1850s reflected these new cultural concerns. Educators rethought their pedagogy for deaf students. But that pedagogy was so closely tied to the creation of Deaf culture that any educational conversation was necessarily a conversation about and a response to Deafness. For if Americans were moving to define their culture by its sounds, how were they to understand a culture that was grounded instead in sight? The Deaf may ironically have called themselves "silent," but they were seen as "deaf," as evidenced by their use of a gestural language.

Deaf culture emerged at a moment in American history just as aurality, orality, and normality were beginning to gain ground as important ways of defining the American experience. The freedom of the deaf to define their deafness and to claim their Deafness would be significantly challenged. Historically, disabled Americans have found that their ability to shape their own lives has been powerfully circumscribed by able-bodied people and their ideas about what is best for disabled people. That is, disabled people have been more likely in history to be acted upon than to act. That is now beginning to change, as disabled Americans, fighting for their civil rights in the disability rights movement of the late twentieth century, scored legal victories and raised public awareness of the cause of disability rights.[10]

Yet these are fairly recent victories, and this look at the Deaf community in the mid-nineteenth century demonstrates how rare the opportunities were, historically, for the disabled to build their own community and make their own choices. The Deaf experience of the antebellum period was an all-too-brief historical moment when disabled Americans exercised some degree of cultural autonomy on their community's behalf, and it was a moment made possible, in part, by the tacit support of key able-bodied allies. But that moment would soon end, as concerns about normality began to preoccupy Americans.

Indeed, in an ironic twist, the historical forces that had given rise to Deafness in the first place were now giving rise to attacks on that Deafness, as educators, writing both from inside and from outside of residential schools, debated the pedagogy of deafness. It was here that some oralists and manualists would find common ground, for while their arguments were, on the surface, about pedagogy, more deeply they were about deafness, normality, orality, and Deafness.

Revisiting Sign Language

The first indications of a growing difference of opinion in manualist circles can be seen in a renewed interest in exploring the nature of the sign language. Officials at the New York Institution once again in the late 1840s offered detailed linguistic descriptions of the sign language to readers of its annual reports. It may seem tedious to modern readers to come across these seemingly endless descriptions of the language of signs, but, for manualists committed to the colloquial language of signs, this was precisely the heart of the argument. If Mann's oralism would not work, then they needed to explain why they believed the sign language would. To some manualists, this meant not simply asserting that the use of the sign language was the use of a real language, but also proving it. If the sign language was a real language, theirs was a project of bilingual education. But if it was not a real language, the field was utterly misguided in its attachment to it. Linguistic discussions, manualists believed, would help to bolster the case for bilingual education and defeat the nascent oralist threat.

Building a Case

The New York Institution therefore dwelled in its annual reports once again on the linguistic nature of the sign language. They acknowledged that the construction of sentences in English was very different from the construction of similar sentences in the sign language.[11] Of course, this fact was already well known by this time. The New York School had written as early as 1838 of the syntactical differences between English and ASL.[12] In this earlier presentation of the sign language, the New York School had come to this important conclusion: "The signs are by no means to be considered the literal equivalents of words."[13] From all this, it is quite apparent that educators well understood the linguistic differences between English and ASL. They knew that they and their students were using a language, and quite a different language, not something that was simply a gestural code for English, when they signed with each other. Indeed, this understanding had of course been the foundation for the move to abandon methodical signs in the first place, as we have already seen.

It is striking that now, in 1845, a year after Mann's attack, it seemed necessary to revisit this information. The eagerness to go over this ground yet again would seem to suggest this linguistic information needed more exposure in order for manual education to survive. The New York School therefore explained once more that the language contained signs for "nouns, adjectives, verbs, adverbs, and interjection. There are few conjunctions, prepositions, and pronouns. The observer must fill up the blanks."[14] Still, these differences did not at all indicate to the school that the language of signs was somehow incomplete or inferior to any spoken language. "Much of our conversation, which has many words and few ideas, would quickly fail before the rapid elocution of the deaf mute," the *Twenty-Seventh Annual Report* asserted. "A hearty shake of the head, a shrug of the shoulders, a shiver, would soon finish many of our lengthened salutations. It is no wonder that they love to speak in their 'mother tongue.'"[15]

"Their Mother Tongue"

But here was the point of departure. Could the sign language be a "mother tongue"? Aside from the fact that it could not be a "mother tongue" literally, did that preclude it from being a mother tongue even metaphorically? Some manualist educators still thought of the sign language in that way. For the deaf, they argued, this would always be their mother tongue. The field took for granted that the sign language was the native language of deaf people. It was, by nature, in a decidedly mixed metaphor, the mother tongue of the deaf.

Now other manualists, not only oralists, increasingly challenged that assumption. Not all assumed that the sign language was, in fact, the native language of the deaf, nor did they agree that the sign language was a language worth privileging in some ways above English. While previous years had seen teachers encouraging hearing parents of deaf children to seek out deaf adults and to learn the sign language from them, in the 1840s, some educators began to abandon that advice. These educators were increasingly concerned about which language, English or the sign language, the deaf child would claim as "mother tongue."

J. A. Ayres, who made his career at the American School for the Deaf, teaching there for thirty-one years, advised parents to learn only the manual alphabet and urged them to spell while they spoke to their deaf child. In this way, the "language which the child acquires is his mother tongue; he thinks in it and he converses in it."[16] English, in other words, through the method Ayres outlined, would become a deaf child's mother tongue. Importantly for Ayres, and other manualists, English would become the deaf child's first language. Signs, as Ayres explained in 1849, were, "however highly cultivated . . . only a secondary language." As such, they could only ever be "a help or an aid in the acquisition of a more perfect channel of thought."[17]

Here a hierarchy of languages begins to emerge. Only a spoken language that had a written form of its own could ever occupy a place of primary importance; only English could ever appropriately be called a "mother tongue." Ayres went so far as to assert that the sign language was needed mostly by that "large class of deaf-mutes whose intellects, being slow, are never fully able to appreciate written language"; for them, the sign language, he admitted, was "a treasure beyond price."[18]

Suddenly, we see the roots of what the late nineteenth century would deem the "oral failure." An attachment to sign language became an indication of mental slowness. For those of quicker intellect, the point of their education should be to slowly wean them from the sign language, to guide them to the use of "a language in which the intellect may expand to the full extent of its capacity."[19] The assertion raised a host of questions. Why should parents waste their time learning a language that was so inferior to English? Why should they expose their child to it? Why should they teach their deaf child a language that would not allow him to "expand his intellect to the fullest capacity"? Besides, Ayres concluded, learning the language of signs was too hard. It "requires a practice and effort equal to that necessary to learn a foreign spoken language . . . it cannot be learned from books; it must in all cases be taught by the living teacher."[20] It was simply too much to expect hearing parents to make that kind of effort.

Sign Language Redefined

A very different picture of the language of signs emerged from this perspective. Ayres offered an elaborate, if contradictory, account of it.

> It is true that this language, so wonderful in itself, is yet imperfect and limited when compared with the excellences of speech. It has not all the convenience of oral communication. . . . It is also a language requiring more effort, more exertion. In extreme languor and debility, where even the gentle whispers of speech are wearisome to the exhausted body, gesture with its life-like expression and energy is an effort which requires a yet greater stimulus. It lacks also in many cases that clear and mathematical precision which is the highest recommendation of any language. Based as it is upon imitation and not upon any fixed and arbitrary standard, its precision depends in a great degree upon the skill of him who uses it. Yet with all these deficiencies and many more, it is a language capable of cultivating the understanding, refining and drawing out the

emotions of the soul and meeting to an extent scarcely realized by those unacquainted with it, all the wants and exigencies of life. It is withal a beautiful language.[21]

Here the sign language was compared, at various points, with a mode, namely speech, and not with another language. While this mistake would become more common as the century wore on, it was not an error common to the earliest educators of the deaf. They understood the sign language to be a language, and they compared its grammar and syntax to that of other languages.

Comparing the sign language with speech might appear to be a minor offense, but it had major repercussions. In this way, the sign language could slowly be reduced to simply "making signs," a description that implied simply waving the hands about in a vague attempt to communicate or punctuating speech with gestures in a parody of English. One makes signs in the same way that one makes sounds; perhaps they communicate something and perhaps they do not. What neither constitutes is a real language.

If the sign language was not a real language, it was not worthy of study or respect. Its users could also be held in contempt as "oral failures," those who had failed to learn to speak clearly and were reduced to making signs in order to communicate with people. Oral failures were clearly unintelligent people; intelligent people, including intelligent deaf people, used speech to communicate.

As Ayres described it, the sign language had no fixed order at all and apparently lacked a grammar entirely. Its intelligibility was said to rest entirely on the skill of the user, since it was based mostly on imitation, and yet it was as difficult to learn as any foreign language. It lacked "mathematical precision" and yet was capable of "cultivating the understanding" and communicating the deepest of emotions fluently. It was limited and imperfect, and yet a "beautiful language." A confused and contradictory understanding of the sign language had begun to emerge in some quarters of the manualist camp by the late 1840s, one that stood out in sharp distinction to the measured, linguistic understanding that manualist educators had previously articulated.

This confused understanding began to emerge around the same time that educators started to realize that the deafness of their students was turning into Deafness. While not calling their students culturally Deaf, for that term would not emerge until the twentieth century, nineteenth-century educators clearly understood that a cultural change was happening. They also recognized that it was intimately connected with the students' use of the sign language. By painting the sign language as less than a real language, these educators indicated their level of discomfort with this new and emerging culture.

"Grimaces" and "Creakings"

In reinterpreting the sign language as an imperfect and limited language based only on the principles of imitation, these observers also began to attack the students' use of facial expression. Manualist educators had previously recognized facial expression as an essential part of the grammar of the sign language, explaining that certain facial expressions necessarily accompanied certain signs and that even grimaces were necessary and appropriate. As Charles P. Turner explained in 1848, "Again, expression not only necessarily accompanies certain signs, but moreover with the same sign, a change of expression may essentially modify its signification. . . . Degrees of comparison also are appropriately illustrated by grimaces; slight or more strongly marked in proportion to the required quantity." Turner provided an example for his readers, the adjective "large." "The process is as follows," he wrote. "Positive, large. The sign, accompanied by a slight swelling of the cheeks and a dilation of the eyes. Comparative, larger. Cheeks and eyes still further distended. Superlative, largest. Cheeks fully inflated and eyes ready to start from their sockets."[22]

Facial expression was here acknowledged as a vital part of the grammar of the sign language. This was a linguistic imperative, not a matter of a signer's personal style. The meaning of an individual sign could be altered by an accompanying change of expression. Even "grimaces" were of grammatical necessity. Turner felt compelled to add, "Without wishing to detract from the merits of the noble language of signs, we may safely assert that it owes its main force and beauty to the accompanying power of expression."[23]

But increasingly, educators began to question this supposed need for facial expression in the sign language. Educators like Lucius Woodruff saved their most pointed comments precisely for these Deaf "grimaces."

There is a strong tendency to *grimace* in the natural language of the deaf and dumb; arising probably, at first, from the difficulty which the mute experiences in making himself fully understood, leading him to call in the aid of distorted features and uncouth expressions to help out his meaning. Thus, he overacts, and as teachers learn the language of signs, in a considerable degree, from the mutes themselves, they imbibe, almost unconsciously, their peculiar expressions and manner and thus permanency is given to much that is both unnecessary and ungraceful.[24]

The rejection of the manualist interpretation of facial expression in the sign language is striking. Here facial expressions were understood as arising purely out of a deaf person's frustration, and not as significant parts of the grammar of the sign language at all. They were not necessary, but were merely "uncouth expressions." They were literally not seen as carrying any grammatical significance whatsoever. Woodruff went even further. He blamed the rise of rude faces on hearing teachers, who made the mistake of learning the sign language from their students and unquestioningly adopting the Deaf use of these "peculiar expressions." Worse, they then turned around and taught something that was "both unnecessary and ungraceful."[25]

In casting the fault onto hearing teachers, Woodruff rejected the early practices of his field. As we have seen, new teachers had long been advised to learn the sign language from deaf students, precisely because it was a deaf language they, as hearing people, were trying to master. In fairness, some still argued that this should be the case. At the Fourth Annual Convention of American Educators of the Deaf and Dumb in 1856, for example, John R. Keep, an instructor at the American School, chastised his fellow teachers for not having an adequate fluency in the language of signs. He "argued that the first generation of American teachers were more distinguished for the clearness and elegance of their signs than the present for the reason that they considered the science of sign-making as of great difficulty and importance, and devoted themselves more zealously to the study of signs than teachers generally do now."[26]

Then another participant at the convention, Samuel Dunlap, a teacher at the Illinois School, replied that he "heartily approved of Mr. Keep's doctrines and thought that if teachers were left to learn signs from the uneducated children under their charge, the signs would become vulgar and awkward."[27] It is not clear that Keep meant to urge teachers to stop learning the sign language from their students. But it is arresting that Dunlap took this to be the point of his remarks. The emerging Deafness of their students had colored the way in which educators understood their past practices, for it is clear that the first generation of American educators of the deaf had advocated learning the language of signs from their deaf students. They had recommended that prospective teachers spend time in classrooms simply watching students sign to one another. They had written extensively on this point and believed that teachers were best off using signs as their students did and using no signs that were not found to be in wide use among the students themselves.

That Dunlop could suggest that teachers follow the opposite course, and refuse to learn the sign language from deaf students, suggests how much the perception of Deafness had influenced some American teachers of the deaf. Native Deaf signing was now viewed as "vulgar."[28] Past practices in the profession were being reinterpreted in light of this new understanding of Deafness. For if Deaf signing was somehow vulgar, only a hearing style of signing, for both Deaf and hearing people alike, could possibly be appropriate. Hearing cultural norms had to displace and replace Deaf ones.

Woodruff made the same argument. He insisted that instructors should no longer learn the sign language from their deaf students; rather, they should present "constantly to their pupils the model of appropriate expression and graceful action."[29] The "appropriate expression" was understood to be the hearing expression, rather than the Deaf expression of the pupils. Teachers were to impose their style upon the sign language instead of learning the language from those for whom it was a mother tongue. The Deaf style of signing was not only inappropriate; Woodruff went further and claimed it was patently offensive.

"It is very generally true of the deaf and dumb, if not of their instructors," he wrote, "that they greatly offend against good taste in these respects; and it may be said that point and vividness in making signs demand it; but why is it necessary to outrage good taste in order to give effect to signs, more than to add strength to speech?" Deaf schools, he argued, should "banish from the midst of them all that detracts from the pleasing impression which is, in general, made upon visitors; and [should] send forth our pupils into the world possessed of pleasing manners and as free as possible from disagreeable peculiarities."[30]

Here a significant cultural charge was made against both bilingual education and the Deaf community. The method promotes offensive physical behaviors, actions that, when adopted by the Deaf community, literally mark them as inferior to the hearing majority. This emerging Deaf community was a site of "disagreeable peculiarities." This was a heavy judgment to lay at the feet of manualism, as well as a condemnation of Deafness. Its methodology promoted these disagreeable peculiarities, and deaf people then became seen as peculiar by the hearing majority around them. Only signing in an appropriately hearing way could stop this.

By freeing himself from any indicators of cultural Deafness, from "offensive peculiarities of countenance and manner," Woodruff suggested that the deaf pupil would soon "respect himself the more" and would see "that he has awakened more regard in those around him."[31] Cultural conformity, that is, achieving normality, had crept in as a goal of deaf education. The deaf students should not only learn English and write and read it fluently but should also behave in public in a way that hearing people could approve. Even their signing style, a language largely meant for them alone, since not even their hearing parents would learn it, should not reveal any indications of cultural difference. Deaf people were to emerge from their schools as culturally hearing; anything else would offend good taste.

Others agreed. Luzerne Rae had embarked on his career at the American School shortly after his graduation from Yale in 1831. He similarly attacked the Deafness of manual students.

> And let me add here that if signs are to be used at all, it is very important that they should be made with distinctness, naturalness, gracefulness, and dignity. I would not have them employed as they now too often are, in such a manner as to reveal, most painfully, the monkey element in man. Those contortions of the countenance and of the body in which so many of our pupils indulge, should be prevented in every possible manner, as half ludicrous and half disgusting.[32]

Once again, the pupils' own conception of the correct way to sign, of the grammatical necessity of facial expression, was ignored. This Deaf use of the sign language was firmly rejected as "half ludicrous and half disgusting." Deaf behavior was even compared to the behavior of "monkeys," an accusation that would take on a darker meaning with the introduction of Darwin's theory of evolution.[33] However dimly, Rae did see a connection between the natural language of signs and the development of real cultural differences; he did not approve.

John Carlin, the deaf poet and artist, also pointed to the Deaf way of signing with disapproval. "It is proper to remark that deaf-mutes' colloquial signs are often accompanied by grimaces and laryngean creakings, extremely disagreeable to the ears," he wrote, "but in the exercise of systematic signs, these accompaniments are impossibilities for a systematized mind regulates all things."[34] Once more grimaces, and now the Deaf uses of the voice as well, came under attack. Carlin viewed these behaviors disparagingly, and he also judged them from a hearing point of view. After all, how would he, a deaf man, know that the Deaf use of the voice was "disagreeable"? Carlin accepted the hearing perspective on these Deaf behaviors here and stood with hearing people to condemn them.[35]

Oralists similarly attacked the deaf voice. Samuel Gridley Howe found deaf noises repellent. He tried to impose silence on Laura Bridgman, calling her tendency to use her voice "bad." She, however, resisted this kind of policing of her body. Howe was finally forced to compromise with her, agreeing that at set times of day she could shut herself off alone and make as much noise as she wanted.[36] It is striking that Howe found her deaf voice so disturbing. But he also found other markers of her disability to be equally so. He always made sure that Laura wore a green ribbon to conceal her unseeing eyes, for instance.

Howe's biographer, Elizabeth Gitter, makes it clear that Howe was attempting to normalize, as much as possible, Laura's appearance and behavior. "In painting his idealized portrait of Laura," she notes,

> Howe carefully addressed the fears of his able-bodied audience. He reassured his readers that she had none of the distasteful habits—real or imagined—of other deaf and blind people. He could say truthfully that after she learned finger spelling she had shown no indication to use the "primitive" sign language of the deaf. And he simply denied that her voice bothered him. In his reports, he transformed her noises—the "bad" ones he had tried so hard to suppress—into endearing and distinctive little sounds, intelligent noises that were nothing like the "meaningless" growling of other deaf people.[37]

Once more, it is clear that a significant part of the oralist agenda was the normalization of the deaf body. The same deaf people who growl meaninglessly are also users of that primitive sign language. Oral education would transform them into vocally appropriate, speaking people.

To be clear, these manualists, like Rae and Carlin, did not support a switch to pure oralism. But they did agree with the oralists' cultural assessment of Deaf identity, language, and behavior. Like Howe, they believed all such markers of cultural Deafness were undesirable in deaf students. They shared Howe's larger pedagogical ends, though not his means. These manualists offered a means of their own to achieve the same ends. They argued for the return of methodical signs. By using the sign language in a hearing way, by restoring the use of methodical signs in deaf education, they would solve the problem of Deafness.

The Return of Methodical Signs

A debate about methodical signs and, more broadly, about the nature of the relationship among words, ideas, and signs dominated the pages of *The American Annals of the Deaf* in the 1850s. As the journal of record for the profession, the *Annals* served as host for this debate within the field. Many authors offered contributions, including John Burnet, J. A. Jacobs, John Keep, Harvey Prindle Peet, John Carlin, Luzerne Rae, Collins Stone, Charles Talbot, and Lewis Weld. Nearly all of these men had connections to a residential school, as teachers, administrators, or former pupils, and all were writing to and for each other.

As one reads the *Annals* from this period, one is struck by how this really was a debate. Participants wrote directly for one another, responded to each other at length, and frequently changed their own positions as a result of encountering a well-argued article from a colleague. Participants had strong views, but they were not merely trying to win the argument for the sake of argument. They were trying to understand the state of the art in their field. As a result, while each man tried to convince others of the rightness of his point of view, sometimes he had to admit that someone else had it right, or even better than he did. This was a conversation in print, and people interacted with each other in this intellectual free-for-all.

There was a clear camp of people who believed that methodical signs were needed to stem the rise of Deafness. J. A. Jacobs was solidly in this camp. The superintendent at the Kentucky School for the Deaf, who had initially trained at the American School, Jacobs argued in 1854 for the "disuse of natural signs" and "the substitution of methodical signs" as the only rational course for teaching deaf students English.[38] He attacked the notion that natural signs represented ideas, not words, and suggested that if that were in fact the case, those signs should be all the more quickly abandoned. "[C]an there be any doubt," he challenged, "that a mute can read faster in significant signs associated with the words, than in arbitrary and numerous characters abstractly associated with the ideas, if that were possible?"[39] Jacobs clearly rejected the position that the sign language was a real language, capable of being translated into English and therefore an aid to students in the classroom. By his lights, the colloquial sign language of the students was a hindrance, and not a help, to learning English.

By 1857, he would go further, arguing that deaf students could only learn English by associating signs with words; anything else made "the acquisition of the arrangement and grammatical connection of written language difficult and almost impossible."[40] He suggested that all the signs that students were exposed to should be made strictly in the order of English words. Methodical signs, Jacobs argued, could be made to resemble colloquial signs more closely. "Signs in the order of the words," he wrote, "should and can be made, not in a dull, imitative, mechanical, or methodical manner; but with the spirit and significance of colloquial signs. Unless so made, they will fail to answer the purpose here assigned to them as a means of instruction."[41] Of course, if methodical signs could be made with the same spirit as colloquial signs, there would remain little incentive for hearing teachers to learn or use colloquial signs at all.

John Carlin quickly embraced Jacobs's position, declaring in 1859, "I agree perfectly with Mr. Jacobs . . . for I have always condemned and still condemn the excessive use of colloquial signs in the school-room."[42] A poor speaker himself, Carlin could not support a switch to the oral method, but he agreed that signs were overused in deaf education. His own bilingualism notwithstanding, Carlin, like Jacobs and Mann, believed that the use of the sign language interfered with the acquisition of English.

As early as 1851, Carlin had argued that the natural language of signs "by their beauty, grace, and impressiveness, have a tendency to encourage [a deaf person's] predilection for them, and excessive indulgence in their use . . . retard[s] his intellectual progress."[43] Carlin himself favored methodical signs. He saw these as "most necessary and appropriate" and "eminently qualified for defining all necessary abstract words and the principles of the English grammar."[44] Only methodical signs had Carlin's blessing, and even these he believed should be replaced by writing or the manual alphabet in the classroom once students were comfortable in English. Once a sign had given a student to understand the meaning of an English word, the sign itself should be barred, he thought, from the classroom forever.[45]

Not everyone was willing to accept the return of methodical signs. Collins Stone, for one, was unconvinced that methodical signs added anything of value to classroom learning. He laid out his case in 1851. Stone was a hearing teacher at the American School at this time; he would take over as principal of the Ohio School for the Deaf the following year, before returning to Hartford to head the American School in 1863. He "considered them of little use in giving the pupil a knowledge of language."[46] He did not want students to merely model the correct form of sentences, dutifully parroting back the correct combination of methodical signs. He wanted students to understand the language they were using and, to this task, he argued, methodical signs added nothing.

Others, like John Burnet, also doubted the value of methodical signs. A Deaf man, Burnet wished that his fellow deaf would make greater strides to improve their English. He admitted that he too felt that "[if] the pupils of our institutions could be induced to use *habitually* methodic signs among themselves, it can not be doubted that the advantage would be considerable." Like other educators, he believed "they would become familiarized with the syntax of our language, in the same way in which speaking children are, by daily use."

But he also recognized that such a wholesale adoption of methodical signs was never going to occur. "[S]ince the best masters of methodic signs have never been able to bring them into colloquial use among their pupils," he pointed out, "there must be some principle of repugnance, some antagonism in mental habits of the deaf and dumb and in the genius of their native language, which opposes this attempt to make a language of one set of elements conform in syntax to a language of a totally diverse set of elements."[47] This explained, in part, Burnet asserted, why methodical signs had fallen out of favor in the profession in the first place. Deaf people themselves, according to Burnet, resisted the attempt to remake their natural language in this way.

By 1859, Harvey Prindle Peet had clearly become exasperated with the entire topic of methodical signs. His school, the New York School, had after all led the effort to abandon them. In a January 1859 article, he categorically rejected the use of methodical signs. Methodical signs, Peet had come to believe, suggested that the sign language was incapable of expressing concepts that English apparently could. Peet did not believe that this was the case. The sign language simply expressed those concepts in ways that were different from English. One did not need to insult the integrity of the sign language in order to teach deaf students English.

Furthermore, Peet now argued, along with Burnet, that Deaf students were right to reject the twisting of their signs to fit English grammatical structures. Jacobs may have wanted his methodical signs to invoke the spirit of colloquial signs, but this was impossible, Peet retorted, because, however natural the signs in the order of words seemed for hearing teachers, the "arrangement of his signs in the order of English words must always seem unnatural to the deaf-mute."[48] Here, Peet, though hearing, demonstrated his willingness to privilege the Deaf view of a quintessentially Deaf language: note that the signs are the deaf student's, not the hearing teacher's, in Peet's view.

Once more, a manualist invoked the metaphor of naturalness to make his point. The syntax of signs may seem unnatural to a hearing person, but it is entirely natural to a deaf person. Putting signs in the order of English could not help but appear unnatural from a Deaf point of view. This Deaf point of view of things mattered, Peet argued, and it had to be taken into account by teachers as they worked to educate young deaf pupils. These pupils were going to graduate and enter the world of the adult Deaf community, and that community needed its newcomers to come equipped with appropriate language skills, both sign and English. Peet implicitly acknowledged the cultural role of the residential schools in the emerging Deaf community.

Beyond the offense of abusing the language of the Deaf, he argued, it was completely unnecessary, pedagogically. "Indeed," Peet declared, "it seems reasonable that it should be easier to remember the order of words than of methodical signs."[49] It was easier because the order of words was natural for words, while the order of signs had its own separate and different order, natural to it. The grammatical orderliness of each language seemed perfectly appropriate separately, but they could not help but appear ridiculous to all observers when combined. If teachers wanted deaf students to learn English, Peet argued, they should simply present them with English, via the written word. It was not necessary to confuse students by treating their sign language cavalierly.

Peet went further, attacking the cultural bias that had crept into both Jacobs's and Carlin's arguments. He addressed the underlying issue in both arguments, namely, that signing in English word order produced more "systematized minds"—minds, in other words, that resembled those of hearing people. Deaf people would be more like hearing people, the argument went, if they would sign in the way that hearing people speak. Peet vigorously attacked this line of thinking. "Let Mr. Jacobs make his signs in the order of words for the Lord's Prayer . . . to some intelligent man entirely unacquainted with signs," Peet challenged, "and he may recognize what he seems in danger of forgetting, that making signs is not exactly the same thing as conveying ideas."[50]

Peet here drew attention to the fact that the vast majority of hearing observers would not be able to tell the difference between methodical and natural signs. The methodical signs were not in and of themselves going to convey ideas to a hearing person unacquainted with the sign language. More importantly, such signs were not going to automatically demonstrate to a hearing person that the deaf person was signing in an Englishlike manner. The methodical signer would not look, Peet stressed, to an average hearing person, like a culturally hearing person. What the students needed in the end to engage the wider, hearing culture was written English. That alone would enable them to "convey ideas" with an increasingly literate public. The colloquial signs offered the best way of teaching students that important language.

J. A. Jacobs was quick to respond to Peet's comments. In April 1859, Jacobs characterized as ridiculous the argument that colloquial signs could be used effectively to teach English. He exclaimed incredulously,

> [You] wish to teach him to write English; can a greater "absurdity" be committed than to attempt to do it by "colloquial signs," his vernacular dialect, the very opposite in all its characteristics of the thing to be taught? You wish to teach him to write in the English arrangement; and do so by explaining the meaning of the written words by an arrangement of ideas and expressions the very reverse![51]

Where Peet had viewed methodical signs as a confusing way of introducing English to deaf students, Jacobs viewed colloquial signs as confusing. They would invariably lead students further and further away from proper English.

As for Peet's observation that methodical signs could not help but appear unnatural to the deaf, Jacobs conceded the point. But he recommended that deaf people needed to adjust, to "encounter and overcome this unnaturalness."[52] Educated deaf people, Jacobs continued, should strive to abandon their "reverse order of thought" and learn to think in words, together with their associated, methodical, signs.[53] Once more, just as Horace Mann had suggested, it was clear that it was not enough that deaf people learn English; they had to think in it as well. They were to become as hearing people trapped behind deaf ears. Then, not methodical signs but colloquial ones would appear unnatural to deaf viewers as well.

Peet felt obliged to respond to this before the year ran out. A scant three months later, he wrote an article for the July 1859 issue of the *Annals*. Here, we truly witness a battle of beliefs and leaders, two very different positions, two principals of prominent schools. The New York School had opened in 1818, the second school for the deaf to open in the country. And the Kentucky School, which opened in 1823, was the first school in the South and only the fourth such school in the nation. This was a clash of giants in the profession.

Again, Peet emphasized that making signs was not the same thing as conveying ideas, even with those signs directed toward a deaf audience. Deaf students, he reiterated, would not take any sense away from a sentence presented in methodical signs "unless he has previously been carefully practiced in this order of signs and words. To get the sense in his own vernacular he must make a mental paraphrase into colloquial signs; and he can learn to do this at least as well from the words themselves as from the methodical signs associated with them."[54] The deaf pupil could learn to read and write just as well by translating colloquial signs into English, and this method, Peet suggested, had less risk that the student would go over a lesson without understanding it at all. Asking the student to translate an English sentence into colloquial signs would allow the teacher to judge how well the student was mastering English. Hearing people, too, Peet chided his readers, manage to learn a second language without abandoning their first.[55]

Peet was certainly correct to believe that colloquial signs could be effectively translated into English and vice versa. However, as 1860 dawned, this was no longer the issue. The voices within the manualist camp were not arguing solely about which teaching method was most effective, as much as Peet might have wished that were the case. Hearing educators were reacting to the emergence of a Deaf culture, an unintended consequence of the manual system. If the first generation of teachers had been rather sanguine about this development, increasingly teachers raised objections to this cultural turn. Certain manualists, like Jacobs and Carlin, as well as oralists, objected to the "grimaces," the "laryngean creakings," and the "monkey behavior."

Over the course of the antebellum period, educated deaf people were in fact becoming Deaf. The response of educators to this cultural development was to reexamine their linguistic principles. Methodical signs were then not only a pedagogical response in this context but a cultural one as well. Methodical signs, their proponents believed, would make deaf students more hearing and less Deaf. For Peet, and other manualists who continued to support the natural signs, the only question was which method worked best. They believed the answer was colloquial signs; the cultural concerns of the others largely escaped them. Already manualists were talking past each other.

The fissures within the manualist camp were making themselves more and more apparent. But this was not merely an internal squabble. Manualists who supported the return of methodical signs were tacitly agreeing with the cultural concerns raised by the oralists. While, pedagogically, they could not support a switch to the oral method, they shared the oralists' concern that deaf people were becoming Deaf, different from hearing people. And, together with the oralists, they alleged that it was the use of the colloquial language of signs in the classroom that was causing deafness to transform into Deafness. In the end, that basic agreement would prove the undoing of both bilingual and manual education by the 1880s.[56]

Still, in the 1850s, many manualist educators remained confident that their bilingual-bicultural approach was sound. Professionals in the field widely agreed that manual education was doing an excellent job of preparing students for any future of their choosing. The manual method, the Virginia School assured readers of its annual report, has "proved by experience to be the most productive of practical good to the deaf and dumb."[57] They concluded proudly that "in no other country are deaf mutes better educated, better prepared to act well their parts as citizens, as parents, and as Christians."[58] How could such an effective method ever be abandoned? "[We] think it will be long before the intelligent teachers in American institutions," Collins Stone confidently predicted, "will adopt [articulation] as a medium of instruction."[59]

These expectations would be dashed in the following decade, when oralists began to open schools based on their method. Not everyone looked at deaf people or their sign language in the way that manualist educators largely did. Oralists would find supporters in the general public who valued speech above writing for deaf citizens. As an anonymous writer in *The Knickerbocker Magazine* opined, while

> it is true that the power of giving vent to their thoughts by writing is not denied them, yet how much inferior is this power, in its ordinary bestowal, to the noble gift of speech! Their substitute for conversation is but a dumb show; mere symbols of words, conveying only the outline of the thought they would express, not its depth of feeling.[60]

Oralists would use this argument over and over again, and, in doing so, they built on Horace Mann's belief that deaf signers, who wrote rather than spoke to communicate with hearing people, were somehow less than human. They needed the noble power of speech to rescue them from their inhuman state. Indeed, the idea that fellow human beings "should pass through life in complete silence" was something difficult to imagine and "indeed hard to think upon."[61] One senses the dual referentiality of the phrase "complete silence" here; the deaf were understood as those who neither heard sounds nor made them. Oralism might not change one, but it promised to change the other. The deaf could be made to speak, silent no longer.

Manualists who argued for the return of methodical signs inadvertently contributed to this project of making the deaf speak. For once both manualists and oralists agreed that Deafness was a problem in need of a solution, and that the colloquial language of signs was at the very root of the problem, there would be little reason left to support any kind of signing. Why, after all, risk allowing any gestures in the classroom? If all agreed that the ultimate goal was to make deaf people culturally hearing, then let them communicate as hearing people do. But first, oralists needed a school to demonstrate that their method would succeed in these goals where the manual method, of any sort, had only failed. They would get it in the 1860s, with the opening of the Clarke School in Northampton, Massachusetts, in 1867.

The Fight over the Clarke School

Manualists and Oralists Confront Deafness

> Certain effects grow out of these infirmities which are undesirable, and the main object in the education of these children, taken as a class, should be to counteract the effect of this infirmity, to prevent it having any influence on the character, to make them just as much as possible like other children.
> —Samuel Gridley Howe, 1867

> We regard these children just the same as other children. In fact, we do not regard them as unfortunate. We treat them all alike.
> —William Turner, 1867

As the 1850s drew to a close, deaf education, under pressure from oralist outsiders, as well as emerging ideas about disability, normality, and aurality, witnessed the fracturing of the once-solid manualist establishment, with advocates of the natural language of signs increasingly pitted against the methodical sign supporters. But, during this same decade, even as the unity of manualist educators crumbled, Deaf culture grew stronger. Graduates of residential schools demonstrated a growing awareness of themselves as Deaf Americans, and they increasingly acted on this understanding by establishing Deaf organizations and newspapers.

In fact, the rapid formation of Deaf culture only fueled the disintegration of the manualist establishment. Preferring methodical sign to the natural language of signs was hardly a neutral choice. The preference for methodical signs signaled a preference for hearing culture over and against Deaf culture. By making deaf people monolinguals, by making English the only acceptable language for all, methodical sign manualists clearly intended to make deaf people culturally hearing.

Another group of educators, the oralists, shared these same cultural concerns. But it was not enough for them that deaf people should be culturally hearing. Oralists wanted deaf people to pass as hearing and believed that oral education could enable them to do so. By eliminating the natural language of signs from schools, by teaching only in speech, and by providing training in lipreading and articulation, oralists sincerely believed that most deaf children could be successfully made over in the image of hearing people and that being hearing was far better than being either deaf or Deaf.

The surging pure oralists and the increasingly beleaguered bilingual / bicultural manualists confronted each other directly in 1866, in Massachusetts, as the state held hearings to determine whether or not it would open a school for the deaf within its borders. By engaging in a close reading of this encounter, we will get a clearer picture of how the two sides understood each other, and how they made sense of the growing conflict between them. Lennard Davis has argued that the debate between oralism and manualism is more than an argument between the hearing and the deaf; "the issue is sharpened," he suggests, "if we think of it as involving a political attempt to erase an ethnic group."[1] We can begin to see that here, in these conversations in 1866.

Both sides brought to the table the themes that had preoccupied them throughout the nineteenth century. Discussions revolved around education and pedagogical effectiveness, at least nominally. But on a deeper level, both sides argued repeatedly about the meaning of disability in American life. Favorite metaphors like "mother tongue" and "restored to society" were once more deployed as both sides tried to sway Massachusetts law makers to their side. Most of all, the place of Deafness in American life dominated the conversation.

Howe's Initial Efforts

Though Horace Mann, together with Samuel Gridley Howe, had begun to press for oral education in 1844, the early efforts of oralists bore no fruit before Mann's death in 1859. But Howe did not give up. Involved deeply in many reform causes in Massachusetts, including the education of the blind and the care of the insane, Howe continued to press for reform in the field of deaf education, especially in his home state of Massachusetts.

In 1863, Howe was appointed chairman of the Board of State Charities in Massachusetts. From this position, in 1866, he launched a campaign, signaled by the publication of the *Second Annual Report of the Board of State Charities,* to persuade the state legislature to charter a school for the deaf in Massachusetts. While he acknowledged his personal preference for oral education, Howe suggested that the methodology of this proposed school should remain an open question to be addressed once the school was approved.

This suggestion notwithstanding, Howe's opinion of deaf education was clear. He was committed to the oralist position. His pedagogical beliefs were directly influenced by his larger beliefs about disability. As Howe took up the cause of oral education in Massachusetts, he outlined his own interpretation of deafness, heavily influenced by his previous experience with the blind. But now, in the 1860s, Howe had sharpened his thinking about deafness, as a disability, and he offered those thoughts to the public for the first time.

Howe reasoned that physical disability could have a horrifying impact on the character of the afflicted child. "The lack of an important sense not only prevents the entire and harmonious development of the mind and character," Howe explained, "but it tends to give morbid growth in certain directions; as a plant checked in its direct upward growth grows askew."[2] These "morbid tendencies," Howe assured the reader, "are not strong, certainly not irresistible. . . . Certainly however they ought to be lessened, not strengthened, by education."[3]

This education, then, was to be directed toward one simple goal. Howe put it most succinctly. "The constant object," he wrote, "should be to fashion them to common social influences, and to check the tendency to isolation and to intensification of the peculiarities which grow out of their infirmity."[4] In order to ensure that deaf children would be fashioned accurately into the likeness of the hearing majority, Howe believed that there should be as little association as possible among deaf people. As he put it plainly, the residential school "tends to isolate them from common social influences, and to intensify their peculiarities, and this is bad."[5] The "morbid tendencies" of deafness would only be corrected if deaf persons associated with the hearing; they would only be "strengthened by associating closely and persistently with others having the like infirmity."[6]

Howe never elaborated on what he precisely meant by "morbid tendencies." He never described these tendencies in detail, nor did he enunciate exactly which "peculiarities" grew out of the "infirmity" of deafness. He simply used these phrases forcefully and repeatedly. He apparently took for granted that they would resonate with his readers. Of course, Deaf people, especially in New England, had organized newspapers, journals, alumni associations, and churches by the time Howe launched his critique of deafness. He would have seen that physical deafness was increasingly leading, under the guise of manual education, to cultural Deafness. By associating together, deaf people claimed their Deafness.

This was precisely the process that Howe wanted to interrupt. He understood the genesis of cultural Deafness, what he termed the "morbid effect" of "infirmity." He wanted to prevent it, to stop these "morbid tendencies" from bearing fruit. Howe wanted to end cultural Deafness. He sought "to educate [deaf children] for the society of those who hear . . . and the earlier we begin the better."[7] He understood that the best way to accomplish this goal was to prevent deaf children from associating together. In community, they discovered their Deafness. Perhaps apart they would remain merely deaf.

And once simply deaf, how best to fashion them into the likeness of "persons of sound and normal condition"?[8] Oral education offered the only answer. "Speech is essential for human development . . . there can be no effectual substitute for it," Howe pointedly asserted.[9] Howe, like other oralists, equated humanity, normality, and hearing. Howe forcefully argued, following the logic of Horace Mann, that deaf people could never become fully human without speaking. There was simply no substitute for speech. Similarly, the Deaf community was no substitute for the hearing community, either. Howe concluded that "to be mute, therefore, implies a tendency to isolation."[10] Deaf people had learned through the nineteenth century that their deafness had brought them into a larger community, in the residential school. Deaf narratives, as we have seen, refer to being brought out of a crushing isolation and into community by the process of manual education. But this Deaf understanding is here rejected. Deafness itself implies a tendency to isolation, that is, isolation from the hearing world. It is toward the hearing world, and only the hearing world, that all deaf lives should aim.

Howe condemned the manual system of education because, by his lights, it encouraged deaf people to build a world of their own. He attacked a religious society of deaf-mutes in Boston as an affront to "sound sociological principles."[11] Such an association clearly promoted "their segregation and thus their formation into a special class."[12] Howe put the blame for the apparent tendency of the deaf to associate exclusively together socially directly on the manualist philosophy of education. He declared,

> Moreover, the desire or the want of such a society proves not only a mistaken system of education, but suggests that there was a mistaken method of instruction. If our mutes, educated at Hartford, had been taught articulation, and taught as well as children taught in the German schools, they

might attend public worship in our churches; they all would partake of the common spirit of religious devotion (which public worship does so much to strengthen); most of them would seize the sense and meaning of the service and sermon and the intelligent ones would catch enough of the very words of the preacher to understand his discourse.[13]

Like Mann, Howe wanted the deaf to associate with the hearing community and to be part of the common life, so much so that the company of other deaf people would never be sought out. Whether many deaf people would appreciate a worship service where they would catch only "the sense and meaning" of the event was not considered. It would be better for the common life if they were there. Any desire to the contrary simply indicated the influence of "a mistaken method of instruction."

Even while deaf people were, by Howe's own admission, able to communicate with the sign language, they were still effectively isolated. Why? Because they were isolated from hearing people who did not know the sign language. Deafness meant lack of speech; therefore, deafness meant isolation. It was this definition of deafness that proved crucial to the development of oralist philosophy. To bring deaf people out of their isolation, it was necessary to teach them speech. This point, Howe believed, could not be stressed enough. He complained that

it has not been enough considered that, by teaching a mute to articulate, we bring him to closer association with us by using our vernacular in our way, than by teaching him the finger language, which can never become our vernacular. The special method tends more to segregate him and his fellows from ordinary society. In the first case one party adheres to the natural and ordinary method of speech, and the other party strives to imitate it; in the second, both use a purely arbitrary and conventional method.[14]

Here the underlying assumptions of the first generation of oralists were laid bare. Howe viewed the deaf as "them" and the hearing as "us." It was to be the point of deaf education to make "them" more like "us." Howe reasoned that, to be like us, the deaf had to use "our vernacular in our way." This, at last, was why methodical signs simply were not good enough. They might be our vernacular, but they were not our vernacular in our way. Only the way of the hearing was acceptable, as only it was natural. And if only hearing was natural, only speech was natural; deafness and sign could never be considered natural at all, even for Deaf people.

But this educational preference was not simply about affirming the superiority of normal, hearing lives. Howe also deeply believed that he was acting benevolently on behalf of deaf people. He took for granted that oralism would make the lives of deaf people, as he understood them, better. They would no longer be isolated from normal, ordinary society. They would be more like "us" and less subjected to the "morbid effects" of their "infirmity." Oralism would save deaf people from their Deafness. Howe, like the oralists who followed him, never stopped to consider whether Deaf people wanted to be so rescued.

Howe's theories of deaf education had been largely worked out by the example of his association with the blind. As we have seen, Howe's work with the blind prefigured his work with the deaf. As biographer Elizabeth Gitter puts it, "In his habitual certainty that he knew best, he assumed that the requirements of the blind and the deaf were virtually the same: both populations should be taught to function as 'normal' people in the larger society."[15] Normalization was the point of a Perkins education, and it would also become the point of a deaf education.

The American Asylum Responds: Enter Collins Stone

The administration of the American Asylum at Hartford, Connecticut, however, did not share Howe's definitions of deafness, nor his enthusiasm for an education devoted to normalization, for they did not look at physical deafness from the oralist perspective. They rightly perceived that Howe had launched an attack on manualism as well as on the asylum. Howe wanted Massachusetts to cease sending its deaf children to Hartford to be educated, and he wanted those children to stop learning the sign language. Collins Stone, the principal of the American Asylum, responded to Howe directly in the *Fiftieth Annual Report of the Directors and Officers of the American Asylum* (1866).

Stone began with an admission. "There is a certain charm connected with the idea of restoring a deaf mute to speech," he wrote, "which is not without its effect upon the popular mind, so that any effort in this direction which looks toward success meets with favor."[16] The difficulty, as Stone tried to make clear, was that oral education was not at all likely to meet with success. One was far more likely to find that the "results attained are unsatisfactory and transient in their character."[17] Oral training may have its place for some deaf students, but Stone stressed that the question of what system of deaf education should prevail was the question of which system would return the best results for the majority of deaf students. He was clear that, for most deaf students, manual education was simply more successful.[18] On this basis, Stone rejected oralism as a system of deaf education.

To replace manualism with oralism would be foolhardy. Oralism wasted a lot of valuable educational time for most deaf students. "All the labor required to enable the pupil to utter sounds, and this as will be seen is immense," Stone stressed, "imparts no knowledge whatever."[19] Stone believed that the time and effort of deaf students would be better used in the pursuit of knowledge. The ability to utter an intelligible sound was simply not worth the labor it required of the congenitally deaf student.

And that student was definitely the object of Stone's pedagogical attention. Another problem with oral education as a system of instruction, by Stone's lights, was that it left this large group of deaf students uneducated.[20] Worse still, Stone noted, those deaf students found incapable of learning to speak were subsequently deemed by oralists to be "deficient in intellect." To Stone, this attitude betrayed nothing less than the fact that oralists were hopelessly biased against congenitally deaf people, for Stone noted that "where pupils are taught by sign, not one in fifty is rejected for incapacity and cases are rare in which pupils do not obtain a fair education."[21]

Oral education even failed to deliver on the one promise that its supporters most valued, namely, that oral education would somehow "restore a deaf person to society." In truth, according to Stone,

the ability to converse in general society is not secured by this method of instruction. While many deaf mutes may be taught a few common-place phrases and to communicate with their teachers on familiar subjects upon which they have received special instruction, their articulation, except in rare instances, is of little use to them. Nothing is more fully established than the fact that only a very few deaf-mutes can make themselves understood upon miscellaneous subjects in general society by articulation.[22]

In part, Stone argued, it was of little use because it was so "disagreeable" to the ear of listeners. Stone invoked the argument made against oral education during the early nineteenth century, namely, that the deaf voice is not a hearing voice. The deaf voice is not a welcomed sound in the hearing ear. Being unable to hear their voices, deaf people could not modulate their voices or control their tone. Most hearing listeners would find the deaf voice incomprehensible at best and offensive at worst.[23] Stone went back to a conversation about nature once more. The implication was that a deaf person speaking was going against his nature.

Stone therefore concluded that oral education itself was an act of "working against nature."[24] It was only in the nature of hearing people to speak. To educate deaf people successfully, one had to work with their nature and not against it. Stone believed that it was the nature of deaf people to communicate by signs and only an educational system that honored that nature could possibly succeed.

The two men were entirely divided in their understanding of the nature of deafness. Both invoked the concept of nature to build his own argument but neither would have acceded to the other's understanding of the term. Similarly, they also disagreed about another term, "isolation." Stone, like Howe, believed that deaf children faced the problem of isolation.[25] But Howe considered them isolated because they lacked speech; to break them out of their isolation, one had to teach them to articulate.

Stone understood the isolation of the deaf quite differently. He explained,

> So the mind, if unexcited, sinks into imbecility and idiocy. The strongest intellect, shut out from any action or stimulus from other minds, will become demented. . . . The crowning element in the calamity of the uneducated deaf mute is that in the midst of society, his misfortune isolates him from it. He is shut up in the darkness of his own dark mind. Living in an atmosphere of light and intelligence, he does not perceive it.[26]

Stone's description here closely mirrored that of deaf students who reflected on their lives before they came to school, a frustrating time when they were shut out from participation even in the lives of their immediate families.

Stone clearly understood the problem of physical deafness as the problem of communication. Segregation, so feared by Howe, was the answer for Deaf people. Being in school together, they were surrounded by people who could communicate with them. They escaped from their former isolated state not through speech, for they had been surrounded by nothing but speech at home, but through the sign language.

Stone had come to embrace this essentially Deaf perspective. He could not truly grasp the point of Howe's complaint. By fearing their isolation and segregation, Howe did not fear the deafness of the children; he fretted instead over their Deafness. Their segregation in residential schools did not lead the students out of their isolation, from Howe's point of view; instead, it caused the growth of "morbid tendencies"—it resulted in Deafness.

Stone could not respond effectively to this charge because he had already embraced the Deaf understanding of deafness. He took cultural Deafness for granted even as he expected his deaf students to learn to make their way in a hearing world. Stone was predictably baffled by Howe's attack on the Deaf Mute Christian Association of Boston as the inevitable and undesirable outcome of segregating deaf pupils together. "This Association is composed of mutes who have been educated and are now respected and prosperous members of society," Stone explained. "With cultivated minds, and professing to be Christian men and women, they wish to enjoy intelligible social religious worship."[27]

Stone wondered why they should not gather together in this way.

> Living in a community of hearing persons, laboring in the same work-shops, mingling with them in social intercourse during the week, on the Sabbath they assemble by themselves for worship in the language with which they are most familiar; a language whose gracefulness, beauty, and graphic power impresses every beholder. What evils can arise from such an assembly, to which a company of French or Italian citizens, gathered for a similar purpose, would not be exposed, it is not easy to see.[28]

To Stone, deaf people lived among and worked with hearing people on a daily basis. It was only natural that they should like to gather to worship together, in a language that they could readily understand. Importantly, Stone compared the company of the deaf to "a company of French or Italian citizens," in other words, to other ethnic and linguistic minority groups. Once more, his under-standing of deafness revealed itself to be informed by a Deaf perspective.

To Howe, the existence of these separate institutions pointed to the evils of manual education. Howe would have been sensitive to Stone's analogy, for it was exactly the transformation of deafness into an ethnicity that he was trying to prevent. Manual education, by contrast, succeeded only in knitting deaf people together as a class, or even as an ethnic group. It encouraged deaf people to live a significant part of their lives apart from the life of the major-ity. The sign language was not a sign of the inherent difference of deaf people. Rather, the use of such signs made them different. The manualists' use of this language in the classroom, and the continued use of the language by the deaf themselves, transformed them into different people, people unlike hearing people. Only oralism strove to make deaf people the same.

Stone, in the end, could not quite grasp these cultural concerns. He con-tinued to believe that the question of how to educate deaf children could be answered by examining the merits of the competing systems. He believed that those who had devoted their professional lives to deaf education could best answer these questions. As for the oralist challenge, Stone defiantly asked, "And who is to decide whether these [manualist teachers] are mistaken or not? Is it a gentleman of another profession, who, however astute and distinguished he may be in his own sphere, has never given this subject his special attention, or shall it be gentlemen who have spent their lives in practical experiment?"[29] In 1866, Stone professed confidently that he knew the answer to his question. "We have no idea that under any circumstances," he predicted, "the people of New England, or of Massachusetts, will allow their deaf mutes to receive only the imperfect and unsatisfactory education that can be obtained through the medium of articulation. These are not States to go backward towards the dark ages."[30]

Massachusetts Steps In

Howe's call for a new school commanded attention and, in 1867, a Joint Special Committee of the Massachusetts State Legislature convened to hear arguments both for and against the founding of a school for the deaf in Massachusetts. Howe, the chairman of the Board of State Charities, Frank B. Sanborn, the secretary of the Board of State Charities, Thomas Talbot, a member of the Governor's Council, and Gardiner Greene Hubbard, a lawyer with a deaf daughter, argued for the establishment of a Massachusetts school for the deaf. Collins Stone, the principal of the American Asylum, William W. Turner, a former principal, and Calvin Day, one of the asylum's vice-presidents, argued in favor of continuing the practice of sending the Massachusetts deaf to the American Asylum to be educated.

Ostensibly, they gathered to debate the merits of opening a new school and of severing Massachusetts's ties with the American Asylum. But the question of methodology could not be avoided, and the issue of whether the school should be founded on the oral or the manual method was addressed again and again. Similarly the topic of deafness itself was frequently raised. Both sides presented vastly different interpretations of the nature of deafness. These images directly informed their pedagogical philosophies. The transcripts of these public debates, then, offer a window onto the methodological battlefield of nineteenth-century deaf education.

The Committee Convenes: Day One

The committee's hearings began on January 24, 1867, and the ghost of Horace Mann loomed large over the proceedings. Howe immediately cited Mann's importance to the cause of oral education.

If the gentlemen will allow me to go back to 1843, I will state that at that time I went through Germany in company with Horace Mann, then a member of the Board of Education. We went into schools there and I was astonished at the ease with which we made ourselves understood by the deaf-mute pupils, speaking to them from the lips, he [Mr. Mann] speaking German imperfectly and I but little better; and still these children, watching our lips and looking up at us, could understand us instantly, and we could make out what they said to a great extent. Mr Mann said to me, "When we get home we must give Massachusetts the benefit of this system"; and up to the day of his death he cherished this idea, and in his last letter to me he made mention of this wish. He picked out that idea as a feature of the German education that should be incorporated into our schools.[31]

By invoking Mann's spirit, Howe established a link between the events of 1843 and those of 1867. By Howe's lights, the connection could not be ignored. In 1867, Howe realized that 1843 marked the year zero for the American oralist movement.

On this opening day, Howe also took the opportunity to describe the oralist vision of deaf education. "The great law of nature in this class of unfortunates, as in all other classes," Howe argued, "demands that they should be brought, as far as possible, under the ordinary influences of society."[32] He elaborated:

> The whole object of their education is to counteract the effects growing out of their condition. How do we do this? By subjecting them to the ordinary social influences so that they shall escape the effects of their condition. And we hold that undue congregation of these persons involves the unfavorable effects growing out of their infirmity. Like all other abnormalities, there should be a division among the community, subjecting them to the ordinary healthful influences of society.[33]

"The whole object" of deaf education was not the education of the deaf child at all; rather, the object was to make the deaf child culturally hearing, "to counteract the effects growing out of their infirmity." The point of an oral education was to prevent deaf children from becoming Deaf adults.

If Howe presented the theory of oralism to the committee, Gardiner Greene Hubbard presented an example of its practical success. Hubbard had a deaf daughter, Mabel, a nine-year-old who had lost her hearing to a bout of scarlet fever at the age of five. Hubbard had sought out Howe for advice and

Mabel was educated thereafter by a tutor, Harriet Rogers, an educator self-taught in the oral method. Rogers opened a small school for deaf children in her home in Chelmsford, Massachusetts, late in 1866.

Hubbard was so impressed by the results with his own child that, he explained to the committee, he was led to draw the following conclusions about deaf education.

1. That some deaf-mutes can be taught to articulate who are congenitally deaf; that is, who have never heard.
2. That those who at an early period have lost their faculty of speech can be taught to articulate.
3. That those who preserve some portion of their hearing can also be taught to articulate.
4. That all, without great difficulty, can be taught to read from the lips.[34]

He also concluded that "as a general rule, wherever articulation is taught, the use of signs or of the manual alphabet should be entirely discarded."[35] Hubbard explained that from one-half to three-fourths of all the deaf in Massachusetts would fall into the categories that he had named; therefore oral education would suffice for most of them.[36]

Hubbard emphasized that the two methods could not be used in combination. "One must be taught to the exclusion of the other," he declared.[37] And, more importantly, if deaf children were exposed to the sign language at all, they would surely lose all interest in speaking. Drawing from his experience with his daughter, he explained to the committee that "the more that child is brought into connection with children that talk and articulate, the greater is her progress. And my belief is that if she had to be in an asylum with deaf-mutes, she would soon lose all her faculty of articulation and of reading from the lips."[38]

Hubbard's characterization of his daughter needs examination. He presented his daughter in a particular light. He stated that he feared that she would lose her speaking skills if she were "in an asylum with deaf-mutes." Mabel herself was not included in this category; Hubbard did not state that she would be at the school with *other* deaf children. Those children were "the other," not Mabel. He did not want his daughter to be with deaf-mutes; he did not even want to acknowledge his daughter as a deaf-mute. Mabel herself absorbed this self-understanding from her father. As an adult, she refused to acknowledge other deaf people in public and avoided their company zealously. And as an adult, she married Alexander Graham Bell, the fierce oralist supporter, who paid her the highest compliment one could pay an orally trained deaf person. "When I am with you, dear, and speak to you fully by word of mouth," he once remarked, "I often forget that you cannot hear."[39]

Hubbard's case for oralism had to go further than demonstrate Mabel's skills, however. The committee peppered Hubbard with questions. Would he recommend teaching all deaf children, including those born deaf, by articulation? How could it be determined which children would be most likely to thrive with the oral approach? Which criteria would he use? Hubbard's answers revealed a great deal about the prejudices of the oralist philosophy, prejudices that lingered well into the twentieth century.

Hubbard had strong opinions about who would benefit from the oral method. As he put it, "I should want to take a child of a little more than ordinary capacity, I think, or one that had more than usual opportunities of being taught [by articulation]."[40] And what would distinguish those children with the best opportunities and capacities for being taught by the oral method? "That might depend upon the circumstances of the case," Hubbard elaborated. "If the child were of poor parents, I should not attempt articulation."[41] A committee member was astounded. "Let it grow up in ignorance?" he exclaimed. "No, sir," Hubbard quickly replied. "I should send it to Hartford."[42]

This elitism would underscore oralist education well into the twentieth century. A strong class bias attached to any decision to label someone an "oral failure." An air of intellectual inferiority also attached itself to anyone deemed an "oral failure." Had the person a better upbringing and a better brain, oral training would have succeeded. Playing the class card also appealed to hearing, middle-class parents of deaf children, as it was undoubtedly meant to do. Such parents were told that they had a crucial role to play in the success of their child's oral education. They would provide the necessary home environment that would encourage the child to speak. They would not succumb to the temptation to gesture. They had the wherewithal to make their deaf child over in their image.[43] Poor parents, both financially and morally, could only be expected to produce oral failures. Their children were fit only for a manual education.

While Hubbard and Howe were building the case that it took special children and special parents to succeed with oral education, they were simultaneously trying to assert that it did not take special teachers. "It does not require any particular art or skill in the teacher to instruct deaf-mutes. That I know of my own knowledge," said Hubbard. "It requires patience and constant application."[44] He hastened to add that most of the teaching could therefore be carried on by women, who possessed the necessary patience in abundance and were cost effective besides.

The manualists at the hearing flatly contradicted this assertion. William Turner, who as principal had hired an articulation instructor to teach "semi-mutes" to speak, believed just the opposite. To teach the deaf to speak, he explained to the committee, "is an effort requiring long practice and requiring special skills on the part of the teachers."[45]

Turner's comments ended the first session. The hearing would resume on January 31.

The Committee Continues: Day Two

Perhaps unsurprisingly, the issue of teacher training was raised almost immediately as the committee reconvened. Howe tried to draw the attention of the committee to what he believed to be the cause of the impression that teaching the deaf was difficult.

> I cannot help thinking that one of the reasons why it is regarded as such a mysterious, hard and difficult matter to teach these unfortunate persons is because we have nobody in Massachusetts, except those few persons who have happened by chance to be drawn into this matter, at all familiar with it. . . . It is, as I said, regarded as a peculiar and difficult art; and yet . . . the most difficult parts of this branch of instruction can be performed by persons who are drawn to it by an intense zeal and interest in the matter, as well as by those persons to whom it has been the business of their lives, and whom we are accustomed to look upon somewhat in the light of mysterious personages—as men possessing an art which nobody else understands.[46]

The reasons for the oralist interest in this topic become clear in the light of this passage. Framing the issue in this light allowed the oralists to paint the manualists as antiquated in both method and attitude. It allowed the oralists to imply that the manualists thought of themselves as keepers of a secret knowledge. But the oralists were able to shout that the emperor was not wearing any clothes. There was no secret to teaching the deaf and there were no special skills needed in order to be a successful teacher. Manualists were not "mysterious personages" at all; they were simply teachers, and teachers wedded to a wrongheaded methodology at that.

The second session also continued to highlight the class prejudices of oralists. During this session, Howe drew Stone into a pointed conversation about practices at the American Asylum. "I have seen things . . . in their course of education which it seemed to me would be changed in a fortnight, if in Massachusetts, for the better," he announced. To prove his assertion, he addressed Stone directly.

HOWE: I would like to ask the Principal if the girls in that institution are accustomed to do much domestic work? Do they make their own beds?

STONE: Yes, sir.

HOWE: How much of the house work do they do?

STONE: They wash the dishes, sweep the rooms, and make the beds. They make their own beds, not the boys'.

HOWE: Who makes the beds of the boys?

STONE: The servants.

HOWE: That is one instance. Here are 135 beds to be made, and here are some hundred girls, most of whom, at home, are brought up to work. I would like to have them all brought up to work. To instance my own institution. Our children are blind, but we think that is a reason why they should be taught to make beds. I would ask if, at the asylum at Hartford, the boys saw the wood?

STONE: We burn coal.

HOWE: You use some wood?

STONE: Very little, sir.

HOWE: Do the boys sift the coal?

STONE: They assist in it.

HOWE: Do they do most of the work?

STONE: No, sir. They are all occupied in the shops. The boys over twelve years old are occupied in the shops in learning trades.

HOWE: That is one of the things which, I think, according to our system of managing institutions in Massachusetts, the inmates should be trained to do. They should saw and split the wood, sift the coal, and do everything of that kind that can be done. They come mostly from a class of people who are accustomed to labor; they are going back to a class of people who are accustomed to labor. . . . I speak of this as one of the things that struck me at Hartford. . . . It is a common complaint with persons in the country who have to do with deaf-mute children that they do not seem to be "handy"—do not seem to know how to do common things. They cannot do the chores about a farm, for instance. They can read and write and cipher—they have been well taught and are under good discipline in those respects—but have not been trained to do ordinary work as they ought to have been. That is one of the things which I think would be very soon rectified in Massachusetts.[47]

Here, Howe weaved a story for the committee of how manually trained students were essentially being trained beyond their class. They spent too much of their time, and evidently too successfully as well, on learning to read and write and cipher, and not enough of it on learning the useful skills and discipline of manual labor. These students "come from a class of people accustomed to labor," Howe reminded his listeners, and would—or should—return to it as well. In Massachusetts, manually trained children, properly understood to be oral failures, would be educated more in accordance with their class origins, while only their middle-class, successfully orally trained counterparts would receive the education to which they alone were rightly entitled.

Howe's class-based assumptions about deafness also grew out of his experience with blind education. He wrote in 1850, "He who prefers the body and its pleasures, the outer world, and beauty, would choose to be deaf rather than blind, but he who prefers the mind and the affections would choose to be blind rather than deaf." As literary scholary Mary Klages argues, Howe concluded that a

> wealthy man would choose to be blind . . . because he did not need the economic independence gained by manual labor, which required sight, and he could still enjoy all forms of social intercourse requiring language. A poor man . . . would choose deafness, and the sacrifice of those comforts and pleasures Howe considered luxuries, in order to be able to earn his living.[48]

Klages concludes that Howe attached middle-class values to the blind body, and working-class values to the deaf body.

Here we can see how Howe applied his class-inflected theories of the body to the example of oral deaf education. The oral deaf were also imagined as inherently middle-class. The middle-class body of the blind, in Howe's imagination, was now reconceptualized, in the context of deaf education, as a speaking body. Here the blind and the deaf could claim common ground. Both blind and deaf bodies that could speak could come to embody middle-class values. Signing deaf bodies, however, could only ever be working class.

And yet, when Stone offered the explanation that his male students were too busy learning a trade to be responsible for the daily chores of the asylum, Howe was unimpressed. In fact, he opposed teaching the boys a trade at school at all. Was this a backing away from the working-class nature of manually educated deaf bodies? Not at all, for it turns out only that Howe opposed having the boys learn a trade *at school*. He preferred instead to see the boys learn a trade in "an ordinary shop" after graduating from school.

Why? "Because everything [at school] goes on according to the deaf-mute idea," Howe answered, "and when the individual goes into an ordinary shop, he finds everything going on according to the ideas of hearing men. They are entirely different schools."[49] Shops could be run according to the deaf idea or the hearing idea but not both, and it behooved a deaf boy to learn the right idea.

By learning the hearing idea, the deaf boy would learn to comport himself as a hearing boy would; that is, he would learn to be culturally hearing, and this was to be the greatest end of deaf education. Howe reminded his listeners again that,

> say what we may about abstractions and about theories, blindness or deafness, or any infirmity of this kind, does have an unfavorable effect on the whole character. There can be no doubt about it, else God gave us these senses without object. Certain effects grow out of these infirmities which are undesirable; and the main object in the education of these children, taken as a class, should be to counteract the effect of this infirmity; to prevent it having any influence on the character; to make them just as much as possible like other children."[50]

Howe could discuss the theory and aims of oralism, while Hubbard could point to its results. He admitted that his daughter Mabel had been unwilling to speak after she lost her hearing. "If she had not been forced to speak," Hubbard admitted,

> she would have lost that power entirely. We knew no signs; we know no sign now. We did not know the manual alphabet then; and there is not a single member of our family who knows the manual alphabet now. Our little girl does not know it. She was forced therefore to resort to articulation if she would know anything.[51]

That is, Hubbard had acted to ensure that his daughter would neither sign nor fingerspell. She had been forced (as Hubbard freely conceded) by her hearing family to continue to resemble, as much as possible, other hearing children. Oral training had successfully counteracted the effects of her infirmity.

Mann's influence is seen clearly here, in both Howe's theory and Hubbard's practice. Mann had worried over the connection between thought and expression, and had raised the concern that deaf people would not think in English if they continued to be taught manually. Now Howe shared that same worry with the committee. "I would have, at whatever cost," he said," one language that should be the child's vernacular, just as I want my son, although he learns to speak French and German, to think in English, and have no other vernacular."[52] Hubbard had acted to secure that same outcome for Mabel.

Oralists believed that their actions would ensure that English would become the vernacular language of deaf people. It was not enough that they knew how to read and write English fluently; Howe admitted that deaf children from manual schools graduated with such skills. Rather, they had to think in it. Thinking in English would make deaf people culturally hearing. Speaking English would do even more; it would allow them to pass as hearing. Oral education was the best way, and in fact the only way, of guaranteeing that English would become the vernacular of deaf people. It was the method that would make English, and not sign language, the native language of the deaf.

After two days of listening to Howe's beliefs, Collins Stone revealed his impatience with the proceedings. Stone was polite but firm. "I make no imputations whatever with regard to Dr. Howe," he began.

> Of course he is sincere and conscientious in believing that he can teach deaf-mutes better than they are taught at Hartford. . . . I do not question his sincerity. . . . He has the blind and the idiotic under his care and he thinks that if he had the deaf-mute also their interests would be advanced. But we think that he is mistaken.[53]

The manualists would spend the third day of the hearing attempting to convince the committee that Howe was in error about both oralism and manualism. They would try to set the record straight.

Day Three: The Manualists Plead Their Case

When hearings resumed on February 5, 1867, the manualists monopolized the conversation. They launched their strongest assault on their oralist opponents. Stone began by asserting the unnaturalness of oral education. "All this labor to lead them to reproduce these vocal sounds does not teach them anything," Stone said. "It is simply labor on the emission of sounds and it is perfectly immense. It is only teaching these children this unnatural way of producing sound."[54]

Stone attempted to draw his listeners back to a consideration of what was natural for deaf people. He continued to stress both that the use of sign language was natural to deaf people and that it was the native language of deaf children. He asserted that the students at Harriet Rogers's school signed with one another. "Do they talk by words when by themselves?" he asked. "No, they talk by signs all the time, and they will. It is unnatural to suppose that a child who understands a natural language will ignore that for any theory you have."[55]

Here it becomes clear that manualists and oralists were still using the terms "natural" and "unnatural" quite differently. Oralists believed that sign language was unnatural, for the natural language of human beings as a species, regardless of their audiological status, was speech. As fellow human beings, deaf people were supposed to perceive the sign language as unnatural, exactly as hearing people did. As Frank Sanborn brusquely remarked, in response to Stone's comments, "All of these children . . . receive the greater part of their instruction through the sign language, which, I maintain, is no more natural to them than it is to me."[56]

The manualists understood language, regardless of modality, as being natural to human beings. Deaf people naturally used a visual/gestural language, while hearing people naturally used an oral/aural language. To suppress the natural language of a people was, to manualists like Stone, simply cruel. Stone declared that "to take away their natural mode of expression is to deprive them of a great deal of satisfaction and of pleasure. We think that these friends would deprive the deaf-mutes of a large amount of information and enjoyment, by taking away from them their natural language of signs."[57] No one had the right to take away the natural language of a distinct community. The Deaf were certainly as entitled to their natural language as hearing people were to theirs.

Indeed, Stone viewed the deaf as different from hearing people. Their native language was theirs. Yet he also regarded them as similar to the hearing in important ways—eager to learn, seeking connection, welcoming inclusion, yearning for knowledge. Stone tried to imagine his charges as deaf people in a hearing world, and to see the world of the deaf from a Deaf point of view. His was the last generation of educators of the deaf able or willing to do so. By positing that their students had the minds of hearing people trapped behind deaf ears, that the deaf students found the sign language as unnatural as they did, oralists imagined the world of the deaf exclusively from a hearing point of view. They failed to consider it from the Deaf point of view, and indeed, found it unnecessary to try. They expected deaf people to leap at the chance to enter the world as oralists imagined it, since these were deafened hearing people in need of rescuing.

The breach between both sides was therefore wider than either could ever have expected. The two groups occupied completely different mental landscapes. This was why the manualists were unable to understand Howe's contention that deaf children would become more deaf by living together. Howe feared the Deafness of the students and rightly perceived that the children became more Deaf by living together. Since he understood the end of deaf education to be the project of making these children as much as possible like other children, he had to consider their living together as a problem in need of a solution. When Howe envisioned restoring the deaf to society, he meant to hearing society, not to Deaf society.

But manualists counted Deaf society among those communities to which deaf children should be restored. Indeed, to manualists, "restored" gave the wrong impression to the listener. To be restored to society, one must have been there at some point and fallen away; but deaf people had never been in society at all. William Turner argued that hearing parents themselves, in spite of all their efforts, were never able to bring a deaf child into the society of the family by speaking. "Never has a parent established communication with such a child, even in the slightest degree, orally," Turner stated. "No perseverance of the mother—and we know how anxious mothers are that the little one shall speak—no repetition of "mamma," "pap," "good boy," "nice boy," has been able to make the deaf and dumb child produce any vocal utterance in imitation of what the mother has said, so as to establish a system of communication between them."[58]

Only by going to school was the deaf child brought into society for the first time.

> He comes to an institution where he finds for the first time in his life that there is a society that he can understand. He has enjoyed nothing like social intercourse; he has never met a community with which he could converse freely. Everywhere he goes, this motion of the lips which brings no intelligence, communicates no information to him, prevails; and now he finds himself in a community where the sign language is used; they all understand it, they are ready to catch it, and all comprehend its meaning. He looks on with perfect astonishment and perfect delight; and in a little while, mixing with this community of sign speakers, he becomes an adept and can talk signs as well as any of them.[59]

Communication restored a deaf child to society. By bringing a child into the community of sign users, one could next lead him into the community of English users. A society had to be established before one could speak of restoration. And Turner here captured quite well the meaning of this moment for a deaf child, the moment of meeting a community of signers for the first time. His understanding had clearly been informed by the perspective of his deaf students, who wrote quite powerfully of those early days of finding a community.

Understanding the meaning of deaf education in this way left Turner unable to understand the views of the oralists. "The mere fact that a deaf and dumb child is brought into a community where there are other deaf and dumb children will not make him any more deaf than he was before, for he was then as utterly deaf as he could be," Turner exclaimed. "It will not make him any more dumb than he was before, for he was absolutely dumb before he came there. How, then, can that intensify the calamity? There is some mystery about this expression; I cannot comprehend what is intended by it."[60]

Turner could not comprehend the statement perhaps because he already believed that these deaf children were meant to be Deaf children. He saw them as being exactly what they were meant to be, so he could not see that their calamity, from an oralist perspective, had been intensified. To Turner, as to Stone, it had been relieved. He did understand the real task of the oralists perfectly, however, and denied that it could be achieved. "We can never make hearing and speaking persons of these deaf mutes," he stated flatly.[61] The oralists wanted the impossible.

The Committee Concludes

The battle between the two sides raged until February 12, 1867, the last day of the public hearings. The closing hours of the debate saw the two camps as far apart as they were when the hearings began.

Samuel Gridley Howe ended as he began, by invoking the memory of Horace Mann and asking the committee to honor his legacy.[62] He acknowledged that, ideally, he "would have them, if possible, board in ordinary families and go to school as other children do." He would entirely discountenance association among deaf-mutes but "would not discountenance association between them and other persons." He "would endeavor to prevent the effects of their infirmity by bringing them into relations, as close as possible, with ordinary persons, so that their infirmity should be, so to speak, wiped out of sight."[63] Howe asked the committee to put aside the question of method and simply allow Massachusetts to charter its own school for the deaf.[64]

Gardiner Greene Hubbard renewed his attack on the natural language of signs. Everyone uses natural signs, he allowed. All people, deaf and hearing, use gestures to punctuate their speech or to clarify a thought. But at Hartford these natural signs were conventionalized. At Hartford, the natural signs, perhaps harmless in themselves, were transformed into a conventionalized language of signs. This was the Hartford school's fatal flaw, by Hubbard's lights. By providing the students with a conventionalized language of signs, the teachers ensured that the students would adopt the language of signs as their vernacular. "And . . . with the most intelligent deaf-mutes," he explained, "the sign language, to the end, is their mother tongue, their vernacular, and the English language to them is a foreign language." Hubbard continued, saying that "every one of these deaf-mutes . . . think more in signs than they do in the English language. This is an end which we wish to avoid in the teaching of deaf-mutes. We want to teach them the English language because we believe it is superior to the language of signs."[65]

Collins Stone, for his part, tried to restate that the American Asylum did not teach the sign language. "We do not instruct them in the natural language of signs," he said. "We make use of this natural language of the deaf and dumb child to teach him our language. We do not give our child instruction in the language of signs, it is their vernacular language, and we take that language to instruct them in the English language."[66] He asked the committee to recognize that oral education would not work for the majority of deaf students. Stone recommended that the state continue to send its students to Hartford to be educated.

The committee adjourned. The members subsequently visited both the American Asylum and Miss Rogers's school at Chelmsford, Massachusetts. The future of deaf education was in their hands.

Conclusion

The founding of the Clarke School in 1867 only intensified debates about Deafness and the sign language within manualist schools. More new teachers, even those who entered manual schools, reacted strongly and negatively to the use of American Sign Language. Like oralists, they demanded that English and English alone be seen as the mother tongue of Americans, hearing and deaf alike. For instance, in 1871, W. A. Cochrane recounted his arrival as a new hire at the Wisconsin School for the Deaf in the late 1860s. He accompanied the principal and watched as he taught a class. Books were opened and the principal began to sign the day's lesson. As Cochrane put it,

> I was very much surprised when I found that the signs did not follow the order of the words, but were transposed in a manner which seemed to me to be entirely useless, and to bring unnecessary confusion to the mind of the deaf-mute. . . . Immediately, there came the queries, "Why this jargon? Why this mutilation of our mother tongue? . . . Why do not the signs follow the order of the words?"[1]

John Keep quickly wrote to respond. An instructor at the American School for the Deaf, Keep was a supporter of keeping American Sign Language in the classroom. He opposed the use of signs in the order of words, the kind of signing Cochrane and others demanded. He warned his fellow teachers, "If we relinquish the use of natural signs as an instrument of instruction, we shall lose, at length, our language of signs altogether. If, for example, signs are used in the order of words in our schools, from that moment will begin a deterioration, which will work the destruction of the sign language itself."[2]

Keep's fears were well founded. Oralism, defined broadly as support of English-only deaf education, whether with speech or with methodical signs, made ever clearer that its goal was the destruction of both the sign language and the Deaf community. Attacks on the Deaf community became more pronounced in the 1870s. An anonymous contributor to the *American Annals of the Deaf* complained in 1873 that the manual system encouraged "clannishness" among the deaf. It "inspires . . . a stronger and more exclusive affinity for other deaf-mutes" and it does so "not for the passing moment merely, but for life." The proof could be found in alumni, "talking in signs, . . . attending deaf-mute conventions, reading deaf-mute papers, and marrying deaf-mutes." The author concluded, "Surely, this can only be utter perversity or original sin."[3]

The notion that deaf people were forming a dangerous clan was not an idea promoted only by oralists. Edward Miner Gallaudet, Thomas Hopkins Gallaudet's son, a man who had followed in his famous father's footsteps and was a leader in the field of deaf education in his own right, believed as much. In 1873, he likewise asserted that deaf people were becoming a "clan," and he strongly condemned this fact. He also complained of the continued existence of deaf conventions, associations, and newspapers. He criticized the deaf tendency to intermarry. He argued that anything that would "foster the idea that even after leaving school they still, though scattered in widely separated places, form a 'community,' with its leaders and rulers, its association and organs, and its channels of communication, does undoubtedly tend to make them deafer and more dumb." In short, he stood with the oralists on nearly every issue, save one. He continued to believe that sign language was necessary to educate deaf children, but even this he now termed, given its ancillary effects, "a necessary evil."[4]

There could be no greater indication that the manualists of the late nineteenth century had broken with their own past than these words from Gallaudet. As the battle between oralists and manualists wore on, the manualists looked to Edward Miner Gallaudet as the leader of the field, against the oralists, led by the late nineteenth century by Alexander Graham Bell. In fact, the two men were frequently portrayed as rivals in the period.[5]

But just like the oralists, Gallaudet stood in condemnation of the Deaf community, and he increasingly questioned the value of sign language, calling for more use of the manual alphabet with deaf students, as well as speech lessons for those who could profit from them.[6] While he continued to oppose a wholesale abandonment of the manual method, Gallaudet did believe that some oral approaches could and should be incorporated into schools for the deaf. With his support for some oralist techniques, and his assault on the supposed clannishness of the deaf, Gallaudet espoused a manualism his father would not have recognized.

This frontal assault on the Deaf community, its language, and its culture in turn fueled the growth of oralism. Without that, it is difficult to imagine that the oralists would have succeeded as they did. The reason why they were able to argue so successfully against manualism was that it was, in fact, irrefutably leading to Deafness. Even manualists could not deny that, nor did they. Like Gallaudet, some of them even warned about this transformation and condemned it as much as the oralists did. Without rallying people against Deafness, this is merely a tedious tale of narrow educational details. Why indeed should the rest of us non-Deaf care?

We care, in the end, because this is a story that teaches us about disability, culture, difference, tolerance, language, and diversity. In other words, it is a story larger than Deaf people. It tells us about ourselves. It asks us to consider how we embrace or reject difference in our midst. It forces us to wonder how well we make room for our fellow disabled citizens, even now. Do we make room for their physical difference, or do we demand that they change to accommodate themselves to the standards of the able-bodied majority? Are the able-bodied willing to let disabled people speak on their own behalf, and listen to their understanding and interpretation of disability, or do the able-bodied seek to speak for the disabled, and insist on seeing disability only from an able-bodied point of view? Do we welcome the disabled body into our public space or do we wish it would just go away? As we look to signers and to other foreign language users in our society, we must ask ourselves: do we value linguistic diversity in our nation or do we fear it? Reflecting on this history provides us with a chance to gain some historical perspective on these all-too-current political issues.

Finally, the path that the Deaf took in the nineteenth century would be followed by other disabled Americans in the twentieth century. This is also a tale of foreshadowing. How the deaf formed a Deaf community and how hearing people reacted is a precursor of later events. Even as the Deaf tried to defend their community, their definitions of deafness would be challenged by hearing outsiders. The arguments raised against the Deaf would be hurled against other disabled citizens, as the growing body of work on eugenics tells us. In looking backward here, we get a glimpse forward as well.

In many ways this story can be boiled down to the difference between Thomas Hopkins Gallaudet and Alexander Graham Bell. Both were hearing men. Both were active in deaf education, Gallaudet as a manualist, Bell as an oralist. Both married deaf women, Sophia Fowler and Mabel Hubbard, respectively. But Gallaudet became bilingual and took as his wife a woman who was both deaf and Deaf, affirming as he did so that these two different communities could nonetheless dwell comfortably together in the same household. Bell married an oral deaf woman who was fiercely opposed to

Deafness and who resented being associated with the either the deaf or the Deaf community. Her husband's highest praise for her was confirming how much like a hearing person she was. "When I am with you dear and speak to you fully by word of mouth, I often forget that you cannot hear," Bell assured her.[7] The journey from the nineteenth into the twentieth century here becomes a journey from acceptance to passing, from sign to speech, from Deafness to deafness.

Now, in the twenty-first century, it is too soon to tell where the journey goes next. The signals are mixed. The path away from Deafness is marked with increasing enrollments of deaf children in mainstream schools and the decline and, in some cases, as in Nebraska, the shuttering of residential schools for the deaf. It is also laid out by medical research into cochlear implant technology, which many assume will be the eventual death of both deafness and Deafness altogether.

But there are other signs as well. Deaf people receiving cochlear implants late in life, who had been Deaf all their adulthood, increasingly report feeling more Deaf, and not less, after getting an implant. Perversely, as one Deaf woman explained to me, now that she can hear what hearing people *really* think of deaf people, she is more motivated as a Deaf activist than ever before. It may yet be that Deaf culture finds a way to incorporate, or even co-opt, implants into its community.

And Gallaudet University, still the vibrant center of the Deaf world in many respects, seems to have learned from the 2006 campus protests that it cannot and should not be all things to all deaf people. As the protest made clear, H-Dirksen Bauman concludes, "The vision of the future is for Gallaudet to become a truly bilingual institution that explores and promotes the cognitive, cultural, and creative benefits of a bilingual education (in this case, ASL/English) to the wider world—both d/Deaf and hearing."[8]

This is a vision that takes us on the road that has been not less traveled but mostly untraveled since the nineteenth century. Yet now, as the twenty-first century opens, we find a vision that would be shockingly familiar to nineteenth-century Deaf people. This is exactly what the nineteenth-century Deaf community wanted and advocated for: bilingual education for all deaf people, bilingual institutions for and of deaf people, and the clear statement that bilingual skills would ensure the Deaf their place, as Deaf citizens, in a majority hearing world.

To implement such a vision requires renewed support for the Deaf community and its language, a support not much seen in the United States since the nineteenth century. As John Keep reminded his readers, "The first generation of teachers in the American Asylum at Hartford each paid his fifty dollars to Mr. Clerc, and received from him a regular course of lessons, and they have never been equaled in the skill and grace with which they used signs."[9] Perhaps the time is coming when their like will be seen again.

Notes

INTRODUCTION

1. There is a growing body of deaf history available. Harlan Lane's *When the Mind Hears: A History of the Deaf* (New York: Random House, 1984) offers a detailed study of the history of deaf education. Oralists, presented as the bad guys, and manualists, presented as the good guys, confront one another in this history, and quite powerfully so. However, the Deaf community they sought to educate is mostly invisible here. John Vickrey Van Cleve and Barry Crouch's *Place of Their Own: Creating the Deaf Community in America* (Washington, DC: Gallaudet University Press, 1989) is a sweeping history of the Deaf community in the United States. It foregrounds the formation of the American deaf community, treating the rise of oralism as an assault on that community's existence. Douglas C. Baynton's *Forbidden Signs: American Culture and the Campaign against Sign Language* (Chicago: University of Chicago Press, 1996) is an invaluable study of the assault on sign language and its users. Robert Buchanan's *Illusions of Equality: Deaf Americans in School and Factory, 1850-1950* (Washington, DC: Gallaudet University Press, 1999) provides a solid overview of the Deaf community, from the Deaf point of view. Most of the book focuses on the twentieth century. Susan Burch's *Signs of Resistance: American Deaf Cultural History, 1900 to 1942* explores Deaf history in the first half of the twentieth century. Hannah Joyner's *From Pity to Pride: Growing Up Deaf in the Old South* (Washington, DC: Gallaudet University Press, 2004) investigates the life of the southern Deaf community in the nineteenth century. Christopher Krentz's *Writing Deafness: The Hearing Line in Nineteenth-Century American Literature* (Chapel Hill: University of North Carolina Press, 2007) explores nineteenth-century American literature and the role and meaning of deafness in works by both deaf and hearing authors. Nora Ellen Groce's *Everyone Here Spoke Sign Language: Hereditary Deafness on Martha's Vineyard* (Cambridge, MA: Harvard University Press, 1985) is a history of the deaf and hearing community of the Vineyard.

2. See Douglas C. Baynton, *Forbidden Signs: American Culture and the Campaign against Sign Language* (Chicago: University of Chicago Press, 1996) for more on oralism's rise in the late nineteenth century and its ideas about deafness. See Susan Burch, *Signs of Resistance: American Deaf Cultural History, 1900 to 1942* (New York: New York University Press, 2002), for more on the Deaf community's resistance to oralism in the early twentieth century.

3. The secondary literature on Deaf history has not tried to distinguish the kind of signed languages, methodical or natural, that the manualists used in the nineteenth century. Douglas C. Baynton writes, "Suffice it to say for now that manualists supported the use of sign language and that oralists for a variety of reasons opposed its use" (14). He continues, "Manualist teachers in the nineteenth century at different times used both

forms of sign language and oralists opposed both" (13). See *Forbidden Signs: American Culture and the Campaign against Sign Language* (Chicago: University of Chicago Press, 1996). Timothy Reagan, in "Ideological Barriers to American Sign Language: Unpacking Linguistic Resistance," *Sign Language Studies* 11, 4 (Summer 2011), 606-36, summarizes the secondary literature on ASL education in the United States and concludes that the bifurcation of the field into oralists and manualists is "somewhat misleading in that even the 'manualists' have tended to focus disproportionately on the teaching and learning of English and for much of the past 150 years were concerned with instruction using signing rather than ASL," and writes that true bilingual/bicultural education programs emerged in great number only in the last quarter of the twentieth century.

4. For more on deaf ethnicity, see Harlan Lane, Richard C. Pillard, and Ulf Hedberg, *The People of the Eye: Deaf Ethnicity and Ancestry* (New York: Oxford University Press, 2011). For more on the rise of ethnic consciousness of the Deaf, and the 1850s as the critical decade for this transformation, see Harlan Lane, *A Deaf Artist in Early America: The Worlds of John Brewster, Jr.* (Boston: Beacon, 2004) and Christopher Krentz, ed., *A Mighty Change: An Anthology of Deaf American Writing, 1816-1864* (Washington, DC: Gallaudet University Press, 2000). For more on the emergence of the Deaf community in the nineteenth century, see Van Cleve and Crouch's *Place of Their Own* and Douglas C. Baynton, Jack R. Gannon, and Jean Lindquist Bergey, *Through Deaf Eyes: A Photographic History of an American Community* (Washington, DC: Gallaudet University Press, 2007), especially 1-59.

5. Krentz, *Writing Deafness*, 76.

6. However, this too was in the process of changing, as hearing people became more aware of themselves as hearing in the mid-nineteenth century. See Mark M. Smith, *Listening to Nineteenth-Century America* (Chapel Hill: University of North Carolina Press, 2001). For more on the history of sound, see Mark M. Smith, ed., *Hearing History: A Reader* (Athens: University of Georgia Press, 2004).

7. Krentz, *Writing Deafness*, 15.

8. Flournoy as quoted in Krentz, ed., *A Mighty Change*, 200.

9. Paddy Ladd, *Understanding Deaf Culture: In Search of Deafhood* (Toronto: Multilingual Matters, 2003), 17, 25. Ladd's book is indispensable for understanding Deaf cultural theory.

10. Krentz, *Writing Deafness*, 14.

11. All information on the controversy at the Indiana School for the Deaf from Monica Davey, "Among Twists in Budget Woes, Tensions over Teaching the Deaf," *New York Times* online edition, 26 July 2011. I have quoted from the article directly. I have also quoted readers' comments on this article, which were posted online in the hours and days following the article's initial appearance. I have referred to those authors as they signed themselves, so in some cases there are names and in others only initials.

12. See Carol LaSasso and Jana Lollis, "Survey of Residential and Day Schools for Deaf Students in the United States That Identify Themselves as Bilingual-Bicultural Programs," *Journal of Deaf Studies and Deaf Education* 8,1 (Winter 2003): 79-88. Ninety-one percent of seventy-eight day and residential schools for the deaf responded to this survey, with nineteen identifying as bilingual-bicultural (BiBi). Yet 47 percent of programs reported that no more than half their instructional staff were actually fluent in ASL, and only 21 percent reported having a formal BiBi curriculum.

13. Simi Linton, *Claiming Disability: Knowledge and Identity* (New York: New York University Press, 1998).

1. For more on the work of the Abbé de l'Epée, see Harlan Lane's *When the Mind Hears: A History of the Deaf* (New York: Random House, 1984). See also Nicholas Mirzoeff, *Silent Poetry: Deafness, Sign, and Visual Culture in Modern France* (Princeton, NJ: Princeton University Press, 1995), 31-40. For a discussion of the broader cultural implications of the emergence of the manual method in France, see Sophia Rosenfeld, *A Revolution in Signs: The Problem of Signs in Late Eighteenth-Century France* (Stanford, CA: Stanford University Press, 2001).

2. Anonymous, "College of the Deaf and Dumb," *The Literary Tablet* 3 (December 4, 1805): 22.

3. The portrait of the Braidwoods as oralists is drawn from Lane, *When the Mind Hears*, 106-11. For more on the Braidwoods, see Jan Branson and Don Miller, *Damned for Their Difference: The Cultural Construction of Deaf People as Disabled* (Washington, DC: Gallaudet University Press, 2002), 100-104, 194-96. They argue that the Braidwoods were not pure oralists, and regularly used the British two-handed manual alphabet with students. Rather, they argue, the significance of the Braidwoods lies less in their pedagogy than in their determination to see the deaf body in clinical terms and to define deafness as a pathological condition.

4. Anonymous, "Deaf and Dumb," *The Panoplist, or the Christian's Armory* vol. 1, no. 5 (October 1805), 229. For more on Francis Green, see Lane, *When the Mind Hears*, 109-11. In addition, there was an attempt to open a private school for the deaf in Virginia, in 1812. In the eighteenth century, the Bolling family, wealthy Virginia planters, had several deaf children and, as Green had done, sent them to the Braidwood Academy to be educated. The second generation of Bollings, in the early nineteenth century, desired to keep their deaf children at home. They arranged to bring the Braidwoods to them, hiring John Braidwood as a private tutor, with the hope that he would establish an oral school for the deaf in the South. The school opened on the Bolling family plantation, called Cobbs, in 1815, but the Cobbs School closed in the fall of 1816, a victim of John Braidwood's alcoholism. See John Vickrey Van Cleve and Barry Crouch, *A Place of Their Own: Creating the Deaf Community in America* (Washington, DC: Gallaudet University Press, 1989), 21-28. See also Betty Miller Unterberger, "The First Attempt to Establish an Oral School for the Deaf and Dumb in the United States," *The Journal of Southern History* 13, no. 4 (November 1947): 556-66.

5. Anonymous, "An Account of the Institution in Paris for the Education of the Deaf and Dumb," *The Monthly Anthology and Boston Review* 4 (October 1807): 525.

6. This discussion of the naturalness of the sign language draws heavily upon Douglas C. Baynton, *Forbidden Signs: American Culture and the Campaign against Sign Language* (Chicago: University of Chicago Press, 1996), 124-25.

7. Lane, *When the Mind Hears*, 182. For more on Cogswell, see also Van Cleve and Crouch's *Place of Their Own*, especially 29-46.

8. Lane, *When the Mind Hears*, 183, 184. Van Cleve and Crouch, *A Place of Their Own*, 31.

9. Van Cleve and Crouch, *A Place of Their Own,* 33.

10. This entire discussion is drawn from Edna Edith Sayers and Diana Gates's article, "Lydia Huntley Sigourney and the Beginnings of American Deaf Education in Hartford: It Takes a Village," *Sign Language Studies* 8, no. 4 (Summer 2008): 369-411.

11. Sayers and Gates, "Lydia Huntley Sigourney," 378.

12. Van Cleve and Crouch, *A Place of Their Own*, 34.

13. For more on the meeting of Sicard and Gallaudet in London, see Jill Lepore, *A Is for American: Letters and Other Characters in the Newly United States* (New York: Knopf, 2002), 98-99; Van Cleve and Crouch, *A Place of Their Own*, 34-35; Lane, *When the Mind Hears*, 158-60.

14. For more on Stewart's influence, see Phyllis Valentine, "American Asylum for the Deaf: A First Experiment in Education, 1817-1880" (Ph.D. diss., University of Connecticut, 1993), especially chapter 2.

15. Stewart as quoted in Lepore, *A Is for American*, 99. Emphasis in original.

16. The deaf teachers were George Loring (1825), Wilson Whiton (1825), Fisher Spofford (1826), John David (1831), and Edmund Booth (1832). The Yale men were Thomas Hopkins Gallaudet (1805), William Woodbridge (1811), Isaac Orr (1818), Lewis Weld (1818), William Turner (1819), Harvey Prindle Peet (1822), Charles Rockwell (1826), Elizur Washburn (1826), David Bartlett (1828), Frederick Barnard (1828), Joseph Tyler (1829), Samuel Porter (1829), Luzerne Rae (1831), Henry B. Camp (1831), Collins Stone (1832), Jared A. Ayres (1835), Ebenezer B. Adams (1835), and Lucius Woodruff (1836). My thanks to Gary Wait for his aid in tracking down these Yale graduates.

17. Edward Clarke, "An Analysis of the Schools and Instructors of the Deaf in the United States," *American Annals of the Deaf* 45 (April 1900): 235-36. The report also noted that Yale's numbers had fallen off toward the century's end. Clarke wrote, "Since 1886, there have been only four within the writer's knowledge."

18. Anonymous, "Miscellaneous: Yale Graduates," *American Annals of the Deaf* 24 (July 1879): 193-94.

19. Baynton, *Forbidden Signs*, 86, 87.

20. A Young Man Seventeen Years of Age, "A Description of a Teacher of the Deaf and Dumb," *Sixth Report of the Directors of the American Asylum at Hartford for the Education and Instruction of the Deaf and Dumb, Exhibited to the Asylum, May 11, 1822* (Hartford, CT: Hudson, 1822): 18.

21. Curriculum as described in Charles Cunningham, *Timothy Dwight, 1752-1817: A Biography* (New York: Macmillan, 1942).

22. A discussion of godly federalism may be found in John R. Fitzmier's *New England's Moral Legislator: Timothy Dwight, 1752-1817* (Bloomington: Indiana University Press, 1998). For more on New England as Dwight's model society see Christopher Grasso, *A Speaking Aristocracy: Transforming Public Discourse in Eighteenth-Century Connecticut* (Chapel Hill: University of North Carolina Press, 1999), especially chapter 7, "Reawakening the Public Mind: Timothy Dwight and the Rhetoric of New England," and Annabelle S. Wenzke, *Timothy Dwight, 1752-1817* (Lewiston, NY: Edwin Mellon Press, 1989).

23. Grasso, *A Speaking Aristocracy*, 329-30.

24. Gregory Clark, "The Oratorical Poetic of Timothy Dwight," in *Oratorical Culture in Nineteenth-Century America*, eds. Gregory Clark and S. Michael Halloran (Carbondale: Southern Illinois Press, 1993), 69.

25. Grasso, *A Speaking Aristocracy*, 330.

26. Fitzmier, *New England's Moral Legislator*, 162. For more on the antebellum reformers and their abiding faith in social progress and the power of institutions to create a better future, see Steven Mintz, *Moralists and Modernizers: America's Pre–Civil War Reformers* (Baltimore, MD: Johns Hopkins University Press, 1995).

27. Clerc as quoted in Lane, *When the Mind Hears*, 159.

28. Grasso, *A Speaking Aristocracy*, 484.

29. For more on Dwight's physical disability and its impact on his career, see Fitzmier's *New England's Moral Legislator.*

30. Kenneth Cmiel, *Democratic Eloquence: The Fight over Popular Speech in Nineteenth-Century America* (Berkeley: University of California Press, 1990), 135.

31. Grasso, *A Speaking Aristocracy*, 384.

32. Gallaudet as quoted in Lane, *When the Mind Hears*, 196.

33. There was some prejudice at work here. While lack of funds for hiring more than one instructor was cited as a reason for passing over Clerc, another was a preference for an instructor who could hear. For more on the Russian story, see Lane, *When the Mind Hears*, 155-56.

34. Laurent Clerc, "Laurent Clerc," *The Connecticut Common School Journal and Annals of Education* (March/April 1852): 105.

35. For more on Clerc's decision to accept Gallaudet's offer, see Van Cleve and Crouch, *A Place of Their Own*, 37-41, and Lane, *When the Mind Hears*, 200-205. This three-year contract struck fear in some. When Clerc returned to Paris for a visit in 1820, some worried that he would not return. A letter from Caroline Chester to Clerc in August 1820 captured the mood.

> Oh! Do not be persuaded to leave the American deaf and dumb, they need you very much and your loss to them now would be greatly felt yet I know I cannot but candidly acknowledge that the claims of your mother country are far beyond ours—we already owe you much gratitude for so long remaining in this country and for your unwearied attentions to the deaf and dumb. . . . The Asylum here has been formed so short a time that if any of its friends forsake it, it totters and may ultimately fall.

Laurent Clerc Papers, Beinecke Library, Yale University.

36. Sicard to the Bishop of Boston, 16 June 1816. Translation of letter in Laurent Clerc Papers, Number 17, Beinecke Library, Yale University.

37. Job Turner to Francois Jean Clerc, 1895 letter, and Dr. Peet to Francois Jean Clerc, 1890 letter. Both in Laurent Clerc Papers, Beinecke Library, Yale University.

38. James Denison, "The Memory of Laurent Clerc," *American Annals of the Deaf* 19, no. 4 (October 1874): 240-41. These remarks were originally delivered as a public address at the dedication of the Clerc monument at Hartford on September 16, 1874.

39. Clerc, "Laurent Clerc," 107.

40. Lane describes the trip from Paris and the subsequent fundraising effort in detail in *When the Mind Hears*; see 206-25. For a detailed account of the founding of the American School, see Van Cleve and Crouch, *A Place of Their Own*, 29-46.

41. Clerc as quoted in Krentz, ed., *A Mighty Change*, 16. This source is most accessible. The address was originally published as *An Address Written by Mr. Clerc and Read by His Request at a Public Examination of the Pupils in the Connecticut Asylum, before the Governour and Both Houses of the Legislature, 28th May, 1818* (Hartford, CT: Hudson, 1818). It was widely reprinted. See, for instance, "Deaf and Dumb Asylum at Hartford," *Christian Herald* (20 June 1818): 174.

42. As Lane notes in his discussion of the Clerc-Boardman marriage, this was a reversal of Clerc's own youthful view. When he left France, he had been unsure whether two deaf people should marry. See Lane, *When the Mind Hears*, 262-66. See also Samuel Porter, "Retirement of Mr. Clerc," *American Annals of the Deaf and Dumb* 10, no. 3 (July 1858): 181.

43. Virginia Institution, *Report of the Board of Visitors of the Deaf, Dumb, and Blind Institution for 1851* (n.p., 1852): 20.

44. For more on the Gallaudet-Fowler marriage, see Lane, *When the Mind Hears,* 267-70.

45. Van Cleve and Crouch, *A Place of Their Own,* 37.

46. D., "The Deaf and Dumb," *The Analectic Magazine* 1 (1820): 430.

47. "Laurent Clerc," *National Register, a Weekly Paper* (9 November 1816): 170. All of these institutions were meant to remake American society. As historian Steve Mintz notes, "[Reformers] viewed these asylums as models for society and instruments of liberation and emancipation" (*Moralists and Modernizers,* 81). Clerc seized the zeitgeist of the age in arguing along the same lines on behalf of deaf people.

48. "Miscellaneous Intelligence: Deaf and Dumb," *The Panoplist, and Missionary Magazine* (January 1817): 46.

49. "Miscellaneous Intelligence," 47.

50. Samuel L. Mitchill, *A Discourse Pronounced by Request of the Society for Instructing the Deaf and Dumb, at the City Hall in the City of New York, on the 24th Day of March, 1818* (New York: E. Conrad), 29.

51. "Miscellaneous Intelligence," 47.

52. "Miscellaneous Intelligence,"47. Emphasis mine.

53. For another analysis of Clerc's beliefs about writing and literacy, see Christopher Krentz, *Writing Deafness: The Hearing Line in Nineteenth-Century American Literature* (Chapel Hill: University of North Carolina Press, 2007), especially chapter 1.

54. J. M. Wainwright, "Intelligence and Remarks: Institution at Hartford for instructing the deaf and dumb: Letter from Mr. Laurent Clerc to the Rev. Mr. Wainwright," *North American Review* (May 1818): 132.

55. *Twelfth Annual Report of the Directors of the American Asylum at Hartford for the Education and Instruction of the Deaf and Dumb, as Exhibited to the Asylum, May 10, 1828* (Hartford, CT: Hudson and Skinner, 1828), 20.

56. The manual system did spread rapidly. The American School was founded in 1817. Before the emergence of oralism, these schools followed: New York School (1818), Pennsylvania School (1820), Kentucky School (1823), Central New York School (1825), Ohio School (1829), St. Joseph's School in St. Louis (1837), Virginia School (1839), Indiana School (1843), Tennessee School (1845), North Carolina School (1845), Illinois School (1846), Georgia School (1846), South Carolina School (1849), Missouri School (1851), Wisconsin School (1852), Mississippi School (1854), Michigan School (1854), Iowa School (1855), Texas School (1856), Alabama School (1858), St. Mary's School in Buffalo (1859), California School (1860), Kansas School (1861), and Minnesota School (1861).

57. J. M. Wainwright, "Intelligence and Remarks: Institution at Hartford for instructing the deaf and dumb: Mr. Gallaudet's paper," *North American Review* (May 1818): 132.

58. D., "The Deaf and Dumb," 430-31.

59. D., "The Deaf and Dumb," 430.

60. D., "The Deaf and Dumb," 430.

61. J. M. Wainwright, "Intelligence and Remarks," 127.

62. *Second Report of the Directors of the Connecticut Asylum for the Education and Instruction of Deaf and Dumb Persons, Exhibited to the Asylum, May 16, 1818* (Hartford, CT: Hudson, 1818), 5.

CHAPTER 2

1. Anonymous, "Education of the Deaf and Dumb," *North American Review* (April 1834): 316-17.

2. *Sixth Report of the Directors of the American Asylum at Hartford for the Education and Instruction of the Deaf and Dumb, Exhibited to the Asylum, May 11, 1822* (Hartford, CT: Hudson, 1822), 5.

3. *Sixth Report*, 5.

4. For another discussion of the manualist distinction between cultivated and uncultivated signs, see Douglas C. Baynton, *Forbidden Signs: American Culture and the Campaign against Sign Language* (Chicago: University of Chicago Press, 1996), 112-24.

5. Anonymous, "Education," 332.

6. Ibid., 334.

7. Ibid., 318.

8. Ibid., 332. Twentieth-century research into ASL demonstrates that the predictions of nineteenth-century teachers have come true. Nancy Frishberg's ground-breaking research into the linguistic history of ASL compared older forms of ASL signs with modern ones. She discovered that over time

> signs change away from their pantomimic or imitative origins to more arbitrary shapes. Changes occur within individual parameters to contribute toward symmetry, fluidity, locational displacement, and assimilation. These changes, on a level analogous to the phonological, are motivated by such familiar principles as ease of articulation and ease of perception. Other changes focus the lexical information in the hands (and the movement of the hands) and away from more general movements of face or body along with the hands.

See Nancy Frishberg, "Arbitrariness and Iconicity: Historical Change in American Sign Language," *Language* 51 (1975): 696-719. James Woodward has also conducted sociolinguistic research on ASL. He asserts that the creolization process owes much more to the contributions of deaf Americans, "who drastically modified (if not creolized) French Sign Language to satisfy their needs." See James Woodward, "Historical Bases of American Sign Language," in *Understanding Language through Sign Language Research*, ed. Patricia Siple (New York: Academic Press, 1978), 333-48.

9. Ibid., 334.

10. Harlan Lane, *When the Mind Hears: A History of the Deaf* (New York: Random House, 1984), 62.

11. Renate Fischer, "Language of Action," in *Looking Back: A Reader on the History of Deaf Communities and Their Signed Languages*, eds. Harlan Lane and Renate Fischer (Hamburg: Signum Press, 1993), 433-34.

12. For more on the use of methodical signs in the United States, see Baynton, *Forbidden Signs*, 118-19. See also John Tabak, *Significant Gestures: A History of American Sign Language* (Westport, CT: Praeger, 2006), 7-42.

13. Jack Gannon, *Deaf Heritage: A Narrative History of Deaf America*, ed. Jane Butler and Laura-Jean Gilbert (Silver Spring, MD: National Association of the Deaf, 1981), 22.

14. Clerc was seen as the savior of the school. As he left to return to his position in Hartford, Roberts Vaux, the principal of the Pennsylvania School, asked for Clerc's professional opinion of the remaining staff and sought his recommendations to ensure the

school's future success. Clerc viewed the most qualified teacher as Charles Dillingham, who, though hearing, had grown up with deaf siblings. Laurent Clerc Papers, Beinecke Library, Yale University.

15. *Third Report of the Directors of the Connecticut Asylum for the Education and Instruction of Deaf and Dumb Persons, Exhibited to the Asylum, May 15, 1819* (Hartford, CT: Hudson, 1819), 5-6.

16. Ibid., 6. Emphasis in original.

17. Ibid., 7.

18. Ibid., 7.

19. Ibid., 7.

20. *Sixth Report*, 4.

21. Ibid., 4.

22. Anonymous, "Education," *North American Review* (April 1834): 335.

23. Laurent Clerc to Roberts Vaux, April 1822. Laurent Clerc Papers, Beinecke Library, Yale University.

24. Anonymous, "Education," 317.

25. *Fifth Report of the Directors of the American Asylum at Hartford for the Education and Instruction of the Deaf and Dumb, Exhibited to the Asylum, May 12, 1821* (Hartford, CT: Hudson, 1821), 4.

26. *Eleventh Report of the Directors of the American Asylum at Hartford for the Education and Instruction of the Deaf and Dumb, Exhibited to the Asylum May 12, 1827* (Hartford, CT: n.p.,1827), 6-7.

27. Anonymous, "Education," 321.

28. *Sixth Report*, 4.

29. *Fourteenth Report of the Directors of the American Asylum at Hartford for the Education and Instruction of the Deaf and Dumb, Exhibited to the Asylum, May 8, 1830* (Hartford: Hudson and Skinner, 1830), 17.

30. *Twelfth Report of the Directors of the American Asylum at Hartford for the Education and Instruction of the Deaf and Dumb, Exhibited to the Asylum May 10, 1828* (Hartford: Hudson and Skinner, 1828), 20.

31. *Twelfth Annual Report of the Directors of the New York Institution for the Instruction of the Deaf and Dumb to the Legislature of the State of New York for the Year 1830* (n.p., 1831), 5, 6, 30. Burnet was hired as an assistant instructor. He had lost his hearing at the age of eight. He taught at the school from 1830 to 1831. As to Vayesse, when Laurent Clerc visited the school and met him, he remarked that Vayesse "conversed as well as if he were himself deaf and dumb." He stayed in New York from 1830 to 1834, before returning to Paris.

32. *Thirteenth Annual Report of the Directors of the New York Institution for the Instruction of the Deaf and Dumb to the Legislature of the State of New York for the Year 1831* (n.p., 1832), 9.

33. *Fourteenth Annual Report of the Directors of the New York Institution for the Instruction of the Deaf and Dumb to the Legislature of the State of New York for the Year 1832* (n.p., 1833), 10.

34. *Fifteenth Annual Report of the Directors of the New York Institution for the Instruction of the Deaf and Dumb to the Legislature of the State of New York for the Year 1833* (n.p., 1834), 27.

35. Ibid., 23.

36. All direct quotations from *Fifteenth Annual Report of the Directors of the New York Institution for the Instruction of the Deaf and Dumb for the Year 1833* (n.p., 1834), 24.

37. Ibid., 26.

38. Ibid., 26.

39. Ibid., 26.

40. Ibid., 26-27.

41. Ibid., 27.

42. Ibid., 27.

43. *Sixteenth Annual Report of the Directors of the New York Institution for the Instruction of the Deaf and Dumb for the Year 1834* (n.p., 1835), 7.

44. Ibid., 7.

45. Ibid., 7.

46. Ibid., 7-8.

47. *Sixteenth Annual Report of the Directors of the New York Institution for the Instruction of the Deaf and Dumb for the Year 1834* (n.p., 1835), 11).

48. John Burnet, *Tales of the Deaf and Dumb, with Miscellaneous Poems* (Newark: B. Olds, 1835), 86. Douglas Baynton also reports that methodical signs were increasingly abandoned beginning in the 1830s. See *Forbidden Signs*, 119.

49. F. A. P. Barnard, "Existing State of the Art of Instructing the Deaf and Dumb," *Literary and Theological Review* 2, no. 7 (September 1835): 389, 389, 391.

50. N. Southward, "American Asylum for the Deaf and Dumb," *Youth's Cabinet* 3, no. 37 (10 September 1840): 146.

51. Ibid., 145.

52. John C. Crandall, "Patriotism and Reform in Children's Literature, 1825-1860," *American Quarterly* 21 (Spring 1969): 6-7.

CHAPTER 3

1. Robert Buchanan, *Illusions of Equality: Deaf Americans in School and Factory, 1850-1950* (Washington, DC: Gallaudet University Press, 1999), 4.

2. My thanks to Gary Wait, the archivist at the American School for the Deaf, for his invaluable help with this project.

3. A Young Woman of Twenty-Seven, "A Description of My First Arrival at the Asylum," *Eighth Report of the Directors of the American Asylum at Hartford for the Education and Instruction of the Deaf and Dumb, Exhibited to the Asylum May 15, 1824* (Hartford, CT: Hudson and Skinner, 1824), 23. Given the details in the story, this was probably Maria Bailey of Norwich, Connecticut. She arrived at the school in 1817 when she was twenty years old and remained for seven years. She had a deaf sister named Harriet who also came to the American School that same year.

4. A Young Woman Twenty-Two Years of Age, "My Own Biography before I Came to the Asylum," *Eighth Report of the Directors of the American Asylum*, 32. Given the details in her story, this was most likely Nancy Dillingham, who entered the school in 1819 when she was seventeen years old and stayed for six years. She later became an assistant matron at the school, serving in that capacity from 1847 to 1874. Upon her death at age seventy-two, the American *Annals of the Deaf* recalled "her efficiency, faithfulness, and devotion of duty" (*Annals* 193 [July 1874]: 187) Her sister, Abigail, was in the first class at the American School, arriving in 1817 at age thirty-one, staying four years. Both sisters were born deaf. That first class had seven students, and three of them went on to become teachers of the

deaf, including Abigail Dillingham. She became a teacher at the Pennsylvania School in 1821. Her hearing brother, Charles, a graduate of Williams College, taught there with her.

5. H. K. [Harriet Knapp], "My Thoughts before I Was Educated," *The Thirty-First Annual Report of the Directors of the American Asylum at Hartford, for the Education and Instruction of the Deaf and Dumb. Exhibited to the Asylum, May 15, 1847* (Hartford, CT: Case, Tiffany, and Burnham, 1847), 29. Knapp was twenty-one when she wrote this and had lost her hearing at age five. She entered the school at sixteen, coming from Northfield, Vermont, in 1843. She remained for six years and married a deaf man after graduating.

6. E.A.R. [Ellen A. Richardson], "About Myself," *The Thirty-Eighth Annual Report of the American Asylum at Hartford, for the Education and Instruction of the Deaf and Dumb, Presented to the Asylum, May 13, 1854* (Hartford, CT: Case, Tiffany, 1854), 40. She was born deaf and had been at ASD for nearly four years when this was written. She came to the school in 1850 when she was ten years old from Newburyport, Massachusetts, and remained there eight years.

7. Statistic as reported in Nora Ellen Groce, *Everyone Here Spoke Sign Language: Hereditary Deafness on Martha's Vineyard* (Cambridge, MA: Harvard University Press, 1985), 3.

8. A Young Boy of Sixteen, "An Account of My Situation before and after My Instruction at the American Asylum," *Eighth Report of the Directors of the American Asylum*, 27-28. This is most likely Fisher Spofford, who entered the school in 1819, when he was eleven years old. He went deaf due to illness when he was two and a half. Spofford stayed on at the American School after completing his studies in 1826, and worked there as a teacher until 1833, making him one of the first deaf teachers of the deaf in the United States.

9. Thomas Hopkins Gallaudet, "On the Natural Language of Signs, and Its Values and Uses in the Instruction of the Deaf and Dumb," *American Annals of the Deaf* 1, no. 1 (October 1847): 58. As Gallaudet continues, these are his countrymen, for "they use his native language."

10. Rosemarie Garland Thomson, "Seeing the Disabled: Visual Rhetorics of Disability in Popular Photography," in *The New Disability History: American Perspectives*, eds. Paul K. Longmore and Lauri Umansky (New York: New York University Press, 2001), 346.

11. Thomson, "Seeing the Disabled," 347.

12. [Nancy Dillingham], "My Own Biography," *Eighth Report of the Directors of the American Asylum*, 32-33.

13. W.D.H., a Young Man Twenty-Two Years Old, "A True Story of Myself," *The Forty-Third Annual Report of the Directors of the American Asylum at Hartford, for the Education and Instruction of the Deaf and Dumb, Presented to the Asylum May 14,1859* (Hartford, CT: Case, Lockwood, 1859), 39. This was most probably William D. Hickok, who lost his hearing at age six after a bout of scarlet fever. He came to the American School in 1855. He later worked as a wool-sorter and married a hearing woman.

14. C.H.A. [Charles H. Augur], a Lad of Sixteen Years Old, Born Deaf, under Instruction Seven Years, "About Myself," *The Thirty-Seven Annual Report of the Directors of the American Asylum, at Hartford, for the Education and Instruction of the Deaf and Dumb, Presented to the Asylum, May 14, 1853* (Hartford, CT: Case, Tiffany, 1853), 39.

15. C.H.S., "About Myself," *The Thirty-Fourth Annual Report of the Directors of the American Asylum, at Hartford, for the Education and Instruction of the Deaf and Dumb, Presented to the Asylum, May 11, 1850* (Hartford, CT: Case, Tiffany, 1850), 32. This is Charles H.

Steere, from Gloucester, Rhode Island. He entered the school in 1846 at the age of fifteen, having become deaf at age six after a bout of scarlet fever. He later worked as a mechanic and married a deaf woman.

16. Thomson, "Seeing the Disabled," 347-48.

17. John T. Southwick, "Valedictory," *Twenty-Ninth Annual Report and Documents of the New York Institution for the Instruction of the Deaf and Dumb; to the Legislature of the State of New York, for the Year 1847* (New York: Egbert, Hovey and King, 1848), 67-68. A native of Albany, New York, Southwick attended the school form 1840 to 1847. He went deaf at age two from scarlet fever.

18. P. F. Confer, as quoted in Christopher Krentz, ed., *A Mighty Change: An Anthology of Deaf American Writing, 1816-1864* (Washington, DC: Gallaudet University Press, 2000), 191.

19. A Girl of Twelve Years of Age, Born Deaf, under Instruction 2½ Years, "A True Story about Myself," *The Forty-Second Annual Report of the Directors of the American Asylum at Hartford, for the Education and Instruction of the Deaf and Dumb, Presented to the Asylum, May 15, 1858* (Hartford, CT: Case, Lockwood, 1858), 24. This is most likely Paulina N. Marsh. She came to Hartford in 1855 from Roxbury, Massachusetts, and had deaf parents, as well as a deaf sister and brother, who would later follow her to the American School.

20. A Young Girl of Thirteen, "Letter of April 6, 1843," *The Twenty-Seventh Annual Report of the Directors of the American Asylum, at Hartford, for the Education and Instruction of the Deaf and Dumb, Exhibited to the Asylum, May 13, 1843* (Hartford, CT: Case, Tiffany, and Burnham, 1843), 25.

21. A Young Woman, "Letter of April 20, 1842," *The Twenty-Sixth Annual Report of the Directors of the American Asylum, at Hartford, for the Education and Instruction of the Deaf and Dumb, Exhibited to the Asylum, May 14, 1842* (Hartford, CT: Case, Tiffany, 1842), 25.

22. A Twenty-Five -Year-Old Woman, "Letter of December 7, 1842," *The Twenty-Seventh Annual Report of Directors of the American Asylum*, 25.

23. J.E.C., "My Deafness," *The Fifty-Six Annual Report of the Directors and Officers of the American Asylum, at Hartford, for the Education and Instruction of the Deaf and Dumb, Presented to the Asylum, May 4, 1872* (Hartford, CT: Wiley, Waterman, and Eaton, 1872), 44-45. This is most likely John E. Crane, from Whiting, Maine, who arrived at Hartford at the age of eighteen in 1868. He graduated from the American School in 1872 and went on to earn a B.A. from Gallaudet College in 1877. He returned to Hartford, where he taught at the American School for at least twenty years.

24. Ibid., 45.

25. George, "The Life of Myself," *The Annual Report of the Board of Directors of the Pennsylvania Institution for the Deaf and Dumb for 1849* (Philadelphia: Crissy and Markley, 1850), 30.

26. [Nancy Dillingham], "My Own Biography," *Eighth Report of the Directors of the American Asylum*, 32.

27. Groce, *Everyone Here Spoke Sign Language*, 3.

28. See ibid., 75-97, for more on deaf life on the Vineyard. All the information here is drawn largely from this chapter.

29. Ibid., 79. In fact, she reports that most Vineyard deaf took hearing spouses. Only 35 percent married other deaf people.

30. See, for instance, the following samples: By a Young Lady Twenty-Five Years of Age, under Instruction 2½ Years [probably Lovey Mayhew], "About the Indians in Chilmark,"

and By a Young Lady Twenty-One Years of Age, under Instruction 2½ Years [probably Sally Smith], "Story of a Black Man," both in *The Twelfth Report of the Directors of the American Asylum, at Hartford, for the Education and Instruction of the Deaf and Dumb, Exhibited to the Asylum, May 10, 1828* (Hartford, CT: Hudson and Skinner, 1828), 38, 39; By a Young Lady, Twenty-Seven Years Old, under Instruction 4½ Years [probably Lovey Mayhew], "An Account of My Father," and By a Young Lady, Twenty-Three Years Old, under Instruction 4½ Years [probably Sally Smith], "Martha's Vineyard and Nomansland," both in *Fourteenth Report of the Directors of the American Asylum at Hartford for the Education and Instruction of the Deaf and Dumb, Exhibited to the Asylum, May 8, 1830* (Hartford, CT: Hudson and Skinner, 1830), 25, 26; By a Young Girl Thirteen Years Old, Born Deaf, under Instruction a Year and a Half, "About My Home," *The Forty-Second Annual Report of the Directors of the American Asylum*, 21-22; R.T.W. [Rebecca T. West], a Girl of Fourteen Years Old, Born Deaf, under Instruction 2½ Years, "About My Pet Lamb," *The Forty-Third Annual Report of the Directors of the American Asylum*, 36-37.

31. Harlan Lane, Richard Pillard, and Mary French, "Origins of the American Deaf-World: Assimilating and Differentiating Societies and Their Relation to Genetic Patterning," *Sign Language Studies* 2 (Fall 2000): 38.

32. Ibid., 39.

33. See Groce, *Everyone Here Spoke Sign Language*, especially 21-35.

34. There may have been other indigenous sign languages, particularly in large cities like New York, where deaf people were more likely to live in larger numbers, but at this point there is no definite proof of such languages. See Douglas C. Baynton, Jack R. Gannon, and Jean Lindquist Bergey, *Through Deaf Eyes: A Photographic History of an American Community* (Washington, DC: Gallaudet University Press, 2007), 16.

35. For more on the history of American Sign Language, see John Tabak's *Significant Gestures: A History of American Sign Language* (Westport, CT: Praeger, 2006); see also Charlotte Baker and Carol Padden, *American Sign Language: A Look at Its History, Structure, and Community* (Silver Spring, MD: T.J. Publishers, 1978) and Edward Klima and Ursula Bellugi, *The Signs of Language* (Cambridge, MA: Harvard University Press, 1979). For more on the history of signed languages, see David F. Armstrong, *Show of Hands: A Natural History of Sign Language* (Washington, D.C.: Gallaudet University Press, 2011); William C. Stokoe, *Language in Hand: Why Sign Came Before Speech* (Washington, D.C.: Gallaudet University Press, 2001); Jerome D. Schein and David Stewart, *Language in Motion: Exploring the Nature of Sign* (Washington. D.C.: Gallaudet University Press, 1995).

36. Anonymous Woman, "Letter (3 April 1818)," *Second Report of the Directors of the Connecticut Asylum for the Education and Instruction of Deaf and Dumb Persons* (Hartford, CT: Hudson and Company, 1818), 9. My thanks to Gary Wait for identifying this writer as Abigail Dillingham.

37. Eliza Morrison, "Letter of April 17, 1820," *Fourth Report of the Directors of the American Asylum at Hartford for the Education and Instruction of the Deaf and Dumb, exhibited to the Asylum, May 13, 1820* (Hartford: Hudson, 1820), 19-20. Morrison was in the first class at the American School. She arrived in 1817 when she was sixteen years old. Morrison was born deaf in Peterborough, New Hampshire. Her two sisters, also born deaf, Polly and Sally, came to the school with her that same year. All three remained for six years. When she died in Peterborough at the age of seventy-three, her obituary in the *Silent World*

proudly noted that she was "one of the earliest pupils of the American Asylum . . . being educated under the tutorship of Thomas Gallaudet and Laurent Clerc."

38. Charlotte Conklin as quoted in the *Thirty-Second Annual Report and Documents of the New York Institution for the Instruction of the Deaf and Dumb. Made to the Legislature of the State of New York for the Year 1850* (Albany, NY: Van Benthuysen, 1851), 50. Conklin arrived at the school in 1846. She was thirteen years old, and had become deaf from measles when she was two years old.

39. W.D.H. [William D. Hickok], "A True Story of Myself," *The Forty-Third Annual Report of the Directors of the American Asylum*, 39. Hickok came to school when he was nineteen years old. He went deaf at the age of six from scarlet fever.

40. A Young Lady of Twenty-Three Years of Age, "Which Do You Consider Preferable, The Language of Speech or of Signs?" *Sixth Report of the Directors of the American Asylum at Hartford for the Education and Instruction of the Deaf and Dumb, Exhibited to the Asylum, May 11, 1822* (Hartford, CT: Hudson, 1822), 13.

41. A Young Man Fourteen and a Half Years Old, "On the Language of Signs," *Sixth Report of the Directors of the American Asylum*, 23. My thanks to Gary Wait for identifying this writer as George Loring.

42. Ben Bahan as quoted in Frank Bechter, "The Deaf Convert Culture and Its Lessons for Deaf Theory," in *Open Your Eyes: Deaf Studies Talking*, ed. H-Dirksen Bauman (Minneapolis: University of Minnesota Press, 2008), 64.

43. The integration of northern schools has not been much discussed in the secondary literature of deaf studies. Buchanan discusses African Americans in terms of their exclusion from both the educational system and the wider Deaf community (*Illusions of Equality*, 6-9). Burch asserts that "many northern and western state schools for the deaf were integrated," but does not list any of the schools by name. The rest of her discussion about race and African American deaf education focuses on segregated southern schools (Susan Burch, *Signs of Resistance: American Deaf Cultural History, 1900 to 1942* [New York: New York University Press, 2002], 35-39). Baynton largely focuses on segregated southern schools, though he acknowledges in passing that "few black children would have attended northern schools for the deaf" (Douglas C. Baynton, *Forbidden Signs: American Culture and the Campaign against Sign Language* [Chicago: University of Chicago Press, 1996], 45-48). *Through Deaf Eyes* mentions the fact that the American School for the Deaf was integrated as early as 1825, but again spends most of its time on the issue of race in the South (42-45). Ernest Hairston and Linwood Smith's *Black and Deaf in America* (Silver Spring, MD: T.J. Publishers, 1983) assumes that deaf education was segregated throughout the country during the nineteenth century (11).

44. Buchanan, *Illusions of Equality*, 17.

45. Once again, I owe a debt of gratitude to Gary Wait for his help in identifying all of these students and for tracking down Hiller. The records of the American School clearly list Charles Hiller as being of mixed race, though the records from his home of Nantucket do not mention his race. Here are the details on the other students of color from the American School, with years of attendance in parentheses: Reuben Jones, from Portland, Maine (1829-1833); Horace Way, from Stockbridge, Massachusetts (1830-1834); Cyrus Randall, from North Stonington, Connecticut (1840-1844); Henry Simons, from Southbury, Connecticut (1844-1849); the Boardwin siblings, Delia, Susan, and George, from Boston (attended together from 1845-1851); Adam Hill Metrash, from Norwalk, Connecticut

(1851-1857); Sarah Taylor, from Cambridge, Massachusetts (1860-1865); Susan Cisco, from New Haven, Connecticut (1861-1866); and Samuel Graham, from Newark, New Jersey (1866-1871).

46. As I turn to the New York School, I must thank Elizabeth G. Fuller, librarian at the Westchester County Historical Society (WCHS), for her aid in directing me to this source, "List of Pupils of the New York Institution for the Instruction of the Deaf and Dumb, including Those of the Central Asylum at Canajoharie, United with the New York Institution in 1836; Complete from May 1818 to January 1, 1854," *American Annals of the Deaf and Dumb* 6, no. 4 (July 1854): 193-241. Nearly all information about the black deaf students from the New York School comes from this list. Additional information was found in the file labeled "Afro-American Deaf Pupils" held at WCHS. The students were Crawford, a free black from New York City (1818-1824); Robinson, from Madison County, New York (1819-1822); De Grass, a resident of New York City (enrolled only for the 1821-1822 school year); Johnson, of New York City (1824-1829); Jones, described as a mulatto from New York City (1824-1829); Ryass, from Staten Island (1826-1829); Anthony, from New York City (1828-1829); Tim, from Suffolk County (1841-1843); De Hart, of New York City (1845-1852); Cuffee, of Suffolk County (1844-1848); Hill (1846-1853); Isaac Cheney, from New Orleans (1865-1870). Elizabeth Pepinger's name appears on student enrollment records for the New York School but she is not identified there as black; her racial identification comes from information found at the American School for the Deaf archives. In addition, the records of her hometown of Princeton Township, New Jersey, have her name spelled as "Pittenger" and there her race is recorded as "mulatto." My thanks to Terri Nelson, Special Collections Librarian at the Princeton Public Library, for tracking her down. Elizabeth's varying racial descriptions suggest that she may have been passing for white at school. Finally, Salina Green's case deserves more attention. Green arrived at the school in 1852 at the age of thirteen, from Greenville, Kentucky. The school later received a letter from her mother, a Mrs. S. M. Green of Madison, Wisconsin, which included a deed of manumission for her daughter, to be given to her upon her graduation from the school. Salina Green graduated in 1859.

47. For more on race and admissions at the American School, see Tabak, *Significant Gestures*, 75.

48. My thanks to Gary Wait for bring this to my attention.

49. Diana Ross McCain, *To All on Equal Terms: The Life and Legacy of Prudence Crandall* (Hartford: Connecticut Commission on Arts, Tourism, Culture, History, and Film, 2004), 18.

50. For more on this incident, see James Brewer Stewart, "The New Haven Negro College and the Meanings of Race in New England, 1776-1870," *The New England Quarterly* 76, no. 3 (September 2003): 323-55, and Hilary J. Moss, "Opportunity and Opposition: The African American Struggle for Education in New Haven, Baltimore, and Boston, 1825-1855" (Ph.D. diss., Brandeis University, 2004).

51. All information on race in Connecticut from McCain's *To All on Equal Terms*. For more on Prudence Crandall, see Susan Strane, *A Whole-Souled Woman: Prudence Crandall and the Education of Black Women* (New York: Norton, 1990) and Edmund Fuller, *Prudence Crandall: An Incident of Racism in Nineteenth-Century Connecticut* (Middletown, CT: Wesleyan University Press, 1971).

52. Hannah Joyner's *From Pity to Pride: Growing Up Deaf in the Old South* (Washington, DC: Gallaudet University Press, 2004), 124-25.

53. David attended the school from 1853 to 1862. Salina Green was there from 1852 to 1859. Ann Williams entered the school in 1851; she was still a pupil in 1854. I have not been able to figure out when she graduated. There is no indication that the rest of David's family, back in North Carolina, was aware of any of this. Joyner's is the most complete study of the Tillinghasts in the secondary literature; she draws deeply from the family's letters, and she makes no mention of it. For her coverage of the political discussions within the Tillinghast family, see Joyner, *From Pity to Pride*, 131-52. Presumably, if David had revealed this fact in a letter to his family, it would have produced a terrific response from his slaveholding relations. Nor is this mentioned in John Vickrey Van Cleve and Barry Crouch, *A Place of Their Own: Creating the Deaf Community in America* (Washington, DC: Gallaudet University Press, 1989); they too devote several pages to the Tillinghast family; see 48-59.

54. See Leslie M. Harris, *In the Shadow of Slavery: African Americans in New York City, 1626-1863* (Chicago: University of Chicago Press, 2003); Carleton Mabee, *Black Education in New York State: From Colonial to Modern Times* (Syracuse, NY: Syracuse University Press, 1979); Graham Russel Hodges, *Root and Branch: African Americans in New York and East Jersey, 1613-1863* (Chapel Hill: University of North Carolina Press, 1999); Ira Berlin and Leslie Harris, eds., *Slavery in New York* (New York: New Press, 2005).

55. Patrick Rael, "The Long Death of Slavery," in *Slavery in New York*, 143.

56. Hodges, *Root and Branch*, 227, 244.

57. Carol Padden and Tom Humphries, *Inside Deaf Culture* (Cambridge, MA: Harvard University Press, 2005), 38. For more on race in the deaf world, see especially chapter 2. Most of their discussion focuses on the late nineteenth and early twentieth centuries.

58. An Eighteen-Year-Old Boy, "On the Duty of Affording Instruction to the Deaf and Dumb," *Eleventh Report of the Directors of the American Asylum, at Hartford, for the Education and Instruction of the Deaf and Dumb, Exhibited to the Asylum, May 12, 1827* (Hartford. CT: n.p., 1827), 13.

59. E. D., a Young Lady of Twenty Years Old, "A Letter to a Deaf and Dumb Russian Girl," *Fifteenth Report of the Directors of the American Asylum, at Hartford, for the Education and Instruction of the Deaf and Dumb, Exhibited to the Asylum, May 14, 1831* (Hartford, CT: Hudson and Skinner, 1831), 23. This is most likely Elvira Derby. Born deaf, she came to the school in 1825 from Weymouth, Massachusetts, when she was fourteen. She remained at the school for five and half years, and later married a deaf man.

60. A Young Lady of Eighteen, "The Abbé De L'Epée," *The Fourteenth Annual Report of the Directors of the New York Institution for the Instruction of the Deaf and Dumb to the Legislature of the State of New York for the Year 1832* (n.p., 1833), 31.

61. Carol Padden and Tom Humphries, *Deaf in America: Voices from a Culture* (Cambridge, MA: Harvard University Press, 1988), 29.

62. Anonymous, *The Twenty-Eighth Annual Report and Documents of the New York Institution for the Instruction of the Deaf and Dumb to the Legislature of the State of New York for the Year 1846* (n.p., 1847), 64.

63. A Young Lady of Twenty-Four Years Old, "A Letter of March, 27, 1823," *Seventh Report of the Directors of the American Asylum*, 13.

64. John E. Crane, "Reminiscences of 'Old Hartford,'" *The New Era* (30 September 1915): 76.

65. A Young Man of Twenty Years Old, under Instruction Four Years, "An Account of Myself," *Fourteenth Report of the Directors of the American Asylum at Hartford for the*

Education and Instruction of the Deaf and Dumb, Exhibited to the Asylum, May 8, 1830 (Hartford, CT: Hudson and Skinner, 1830), 29.

66. A Young Man of Twenty-Three, under Instruction 3.5 Years, "About the American Asylum and Its Situation," *The Twenty-Seventh Report of the Directors of the American Asylum*, 27-28.

67. A Sixteen-Year-Old Boy Who Had Been under Instruction for Two Years and Ten Months, "A Letter Dated March 28, 1821," *The Fifth Report of the Directors of the American Asylum at Hartford for the Education and Instruction of the Deaf and Dumb, Exhibited to the Asylum, May 12, 1821* (Hartford, CT: Hudson, 1821), 26.

68. A Young Man of Seventeen Years Old, "The Mode of Instructing the Deaf and Dumb," *Tenth Report of the Directors of the American Asylum, at Hartford, for the Education and Instruction of the Deaf and Dumb, Exhibited to the Asylum, May 13, 1826* (Hartford, CT: Hudson and Skinner, 1826), 12.

69. For an early-twentieth-century recounting of the politics of oralism and the portrayal of nonspeaking Deaf people as "oral failures," see Burch, *Signs of Resistance*, 21-33.

70. A Girl of Thirteen, under Instruction for Two Years, "A Letter of April 6, 1843," *The Twenty-Seventh Report of the Directors of the American Asylum*, 25.

71. Anonymous, "Articulation," *Deaf Mute Pelican* 1 no. 24 (Saturday, November 4, 1871).

72. Ibid.

73. J.O.S., a former pupil of the American Asylum, left eight years before, after having been four years under instruction, born deaf ("Journal," *Thirty-Second Annual Report of the Directors of the American Asylum at Hartford for the Education and Instruction of the Deaf and Dumb, Presented to the Asylum, May 13, 1848* (Hartford: Case, Tiffany, and Burnham, 1848), 30. This is Joseph O. Sanger, from Westborough, Massachusetts, who entered school at age fifteen in 1836; he became a farmer after graduating and married a deaf woman.

74. William T. S., a Fifteen-Year-Old Boy, under Instruction for Three Years, Who Became Deaf at Age Six, "Subject of Deafness," *The Annual Report of the Board of Directors of the Pennsylvania Institution for the Deaf and Dumb for the Year 1870* (Philadelphia: Printed by the Order of the Contributors, 1871), 50.

75. A Young Man of Sixteen and a Half Years Old, "On the Advantage of a Deaf and Dumb Person's Being Instructed," *Eighth Report of the Directors of the American Asylum*, 20.

76. H.M.P. [Hannah M. Patten], "Letter to Mr. Benton," *Twenty-Ninth Annual Report and Documents of the New York Institution*, 80.

77. Lucinda E. Hills as quoted in the *Twenty-Ninth Annual Report and Documents of the New York Institution*, 56. Hills was born deaf, and was a pupil in the "High Class."

78. M.L. [Mary Lackie], a Young Lady Eighteen Years of Age, Who Lost Her Hearing at Seven, under Instruction Six Years, "Thoughts on Leaving School," *The Thirty-Eighth Annual Report of the Directors of the American Asylum*, 41.

79. A Young Lady Twenty-Four Years Old, "Letter to a Friend," *Seventh Report of the Directors of the American Asylum*, 13.

80. A., "Education," *Annual Report of the Board of Directors of the Pennsylvania Institution for the Deaf and Dumb, for 1851* (Philadelphia: Crissy and Markley, 1852), 27.

81. M., "Knowledge," *The Annual Report of the Board of Directors of the Pennsylvania School for the Deaf and Dumb, for 1851*, 30.

82. The term "speaking people" was used quite regularly by deaf people to refer to hearing people in the first half of the nineteenth century, and many students in the writing samples use the term often. The term is a more accurate English translation of the ASL sign for HEARING PERSON, which is made at the mouth of the signer, not at the ear. It is also a cultural signal about the appropriate ways to communicate. "Speaking people" implies that hearing people speak while Deaf people sign. Speaking becomes a hearing behavior.

83. H.K., a Young Woman Twenty-Three Years Old, Who Lost Her Hearing at Five and Has Been under Instruction Six Years, "The Place of My Education," *The Thirty-Third Annual Report of the Directors of the American Asylum, at Hartford, for the Education and Instruction of the Deaf and Dumb, Presented to the Asylum, May 12, 1849* (Hartford, CT: Case, Tiffany, 1849), 27. This was Harriet Knapp, from Northfield, Vermont, who entered the school in 1843 at age sixteen; she was deafened by scarlet fever, and later married a deaf man.

84. Anonymous, "Valedictory," *Thirty-Second Annual Report and Documents of the New York Institution*, 69.

85. Graduate of the Ohio Institution, "The Happy Educated Mute," *The American Annals of the Deaf* 2 (April 1849): 192.

86. Anonymous, "Concerning the Condition of the Deaf and Dumb," *Thirty-Second Annual Report and Documents of the New York Institution*, 57.

87. A Young Lady, under Instruction Four Years and Ten Months, "A Farewell Address to the Teachers of the American Asylum," *Twenty-Third Report of the Directors of the American Asylum at Hartford for the Education and Instruction of the Deaf and Dumb. Exhibited to the Asylum, May 11, 1839* (Hartford: Case, Tiffany, and Burnham, 1839), 25.

88. W. W. Angus, "First Anniversary of the Alumni Association of the High Class of the New York Institution for the Deaf and Dumb," *The American Annals of the Deaf* 11 (1859): 203. Walter W. Angus was one of the first graduates of the High Class at New York. He worked as a teacher at several schools for the deaf, including those in New York, Michigan, and Indiana.

89. A Nineteen-Year-Old Woman, "Educated Deaf and Dumb Persons," *Twentieth Report of the Directors of the American Asylum at Hartford for the Education and Instruction of the Deaf and Dumb, Exhibited to the Asylum, May 14, 1836* (Hartford, CT: Hudson and Skinner, 1836), 33.

90. William T.S., "Subject of Deafness," 48-50.

91. A Young Lady of Fourteen Years Old, "Writing Sample," *Ninth Report of the Directors of the American Asylum at Hartford for the Education and Instruction of the Deaf and Dumb, Exhibited to the Asylum, May 14, 1825* (Hartford, CT: Hudson and Skinner, 1825), 27.

92. Harlan Lane, *A Deaf Artist in Early America: The Worlds of John Brewster, Jr.* (Boston: Beacon 2004), 80.

93. D., "The Deaf and Dumb," *Analectic Magazine* 15 (1820): 430.

94. H.E. [Herman Erbe], "How I Lost My Hearing," *Fifty-Fourth Annual Report of the Directors and Officers of the American Asylum at Hartford for the Education and Instruction of the Deaf and Dumb, Presented to the Asylum, May 14, 1870* (Hartford, CT: Wiley, Waterman, and Eaton, 1870), 46.

95. T.L.B., a Young Man Nineteen Years of Age, Born Deaf, under Instruction Six Years, "The Eye and the Ear," *The Forty-Third Annual Report of the Directors of the American*, 42.

This is Thomas Lewis Brown (1839-1909), from Henniker, New Hampshire. He entered the school in 1851 and later became a teacher of the deaf. His father was Thomas Brown, who attended the American School from 1822 to 1827. The Browns were one of the most important Deaf families in the nineteenth century. It was at the Brown home, in 1854, that one of the first Deaf organizations in the country was officially established, the New England Gallaudet Association.

96. Mary Toles, "Which Is the Greatest Calamity, to Be Deaf and Dumb or Blind?" *Thirty-Fourth Annual Report and Documents of the New York Institution for the Instruction of the Deaf and Dumb, to the Legislature of the State of New York, for the Year 1852* (New York: James Egbert, 1853), 90.

97. Toles, "Which Is the Greatest Calamity," 90.

98. As her eulogizer indicated, Toles's life was profoundly shaped by her deafness. She was born hearing in 1836, but lost her hearing at age thirteen. As a result, Toles entered the New York School when she was fifteen, and graduated in 1853 with highest honors. In 1854, she married the vice principal of the school, Isaac Lewis Peet, and thus entered one of the celebrated teaching families of the nineteenth-century Deaf world. Isaac's father, Harvey Prindle Peet, began his career as a teacher at the American School, where he taught from 1822 to 1831. Then, he served as head of the New York School from 1831 to 1866, taking the school through the pivotal pedagogical transformation from methodical signs to colloquial signs. Isaac succeeded his father as principal in 1866. The Peets were tireless supporters of the sign language in deaf education. Isaac would visit Germany to debunk Horace Mann's assessment of the Prussian oral method in 1851. He would later serve in the American delegation to the infamous Milan Congress of 1880. The American delegation stood firmly against the conference's recommendations in favor of the oral method for all deaf children. When Toles married into the Peet family, she married into its work. She served as a substitute teacher for her husband in his classes, and she also worked as a teacher in her own right in New York from 1863 to 1867. She also married into its social prominence in the Deaf community, a role that by all accounts suited her. She died in 1901. For more on her, and the Peets, see E. A. Fay, "Mary Toles Peet," *American Annals of the Deaf* 46 (May 1901): 300-305; "Mary Toles Peet," in Guilbert C. Braddock, *Notable Deaf Persons*, ed. Florence B. Crammatte (Washington, DC: Gallaudet College Alumni Association, 1975), 12-13; John Vickery Van Cleve and Barry Crouch, *A Place of Their Own* (Washington, DC: Gallaudet University Press, 1989).

99. John Burnet, *Tales of the Deaf and Dumb* (Newark: B. Olds, 1835), 47. Emphasis in original.

100. Anonymous, "The Deaf and Dumb Boys," *Twenty-Seventh Annual Report of the New York Institution for Instruction of the Deaf and Dumb for the Year 1845* (n.p., 1846), 68-69.

101. H.E. [Herman Erbe], "How I Lost My Hearing," 46.

102. A Young Man of Fourteen and a Half Years Old, "A Description of Music," *Sixth Report of the Directors of the American Asylum*, 22.

103. In "Proceedings of the First Convention of American Instructors of the Deaf and Dumb," *American Annals of the Deaf* 3 (October 1850): 10.

104. J.E.C. [John E. Crane], "My Deafness," 44-45.

105. By a Young Lady Nearly Seventeen, "On the Public Worship of the Deaf and Dumb on Sunday," *Sixth Report of the Directors of the American Asylum*, 20.

106. H.K. [Harriet Knapp], "The Place of My Education," 27.

107. A Young Man at School Three Years, "Some Account of Myself," *Twenty-Sixth Report of the Directors of the American Asylum*, 27.

108. H.E. [Herman Erbe], "How I Lost My Hearing," 45-46.

109. Wilson Whiton, "An Original Composition," *Second Report of the Directors of the Connecticut Asylum*, 18. Whiton was a member of the first class enrolled at the American School, entering in April 1817. He became a teacher there in 1826, one of the first American deaf teachers of the deaf to work there. He remained at work there for the next forty-six years. As the *Silent World* remarked when he died in 1873, "As a teacher he was marked by a graceful and dignified sign-delivery, and distinguished for the energy with which he performed his duties. His death will be felt by those few of the first pupils of Gallaudet and Clerc who still live among us."

110. William Breg, "An Account," *Twenty-Ninth Annual Report of the New York Institution*, 56-57. In 1847, William Breg was only in his first year of schooling. When he graduated ten years later, he did so with high honors in the school's High Class. He won several academic awards for excellence in English and math. He stayed on in New York as a teacher for the 1855-1856 academic year, before accepting a teaching offer at the fledgling Michigan Institution for the Deaf. His obituary in the *Silent World* in 1876 called him "a good pioneer teacher."

111. Graduate of the Ohio Institution for the Deaf and Dumb, "The Happy Educated Mute," *American Annals of the Deaf* 2 (April 1849): 191. Emphasis in original.

112. For more on the subject of the Deaf community's relationship to assistive technology in the twentieth century, see R. A. R. Edwards, "Sound and Fury, or Much Ado about Nothing? Cochlear Implants in Historical Perspective," *The Journal of American History* 92 (December 2005): 892-920.

113. T.J.C., a Young Man of Nineteen, Lost His Hearing at Age 7½, "Valedictory," *The Thirty-Eighth Annual Report of the Directors of the American Asylum*, 47. This is most likely Thomas J. Chamberlain, from Bangor, Maine. He became deaf from scarlet fever and entered the American School in 1845 at the age of eleven.

CHAPTER 4

1. The epigraph for this chapter is from Harriet Martineau, "Letter to the Deaf," *Southern Rose Bud* 3 (April 1835): 121. The letter was dated March 16, 1834. It first appeared in the *Edinburgh Magazine*.

2. For more on American deaf organizations, see John Vickery Van Cleve and Barry Crouch, *A Place of Their Own* (Washington, DC: Gallaudet University Press, 1989), 87-97.

3. For more on Brown and Henniker, see Harlan Lane, *A Deaf Artist in Early America: The Worlds of John Brewster, Jr.* (Boston: Beacon, 2004), 69-76. For more on Henniker's place in the nineteenth-century Deaf community, see Harlan Lane, Richard Pillard, and Mary French, "Origins of the American Deaf-World: Assimilating and Differentiating Societies and Their Relation to Genetic Patterning," *Sign Language Studies* 1, no.1 (Fall 2000): 17-43.

4. William Martin Chamberlain, "Thomas Brown," *American Annals of the Deaf* 31 (July 1886): 205.

5. For more on the Smith family, see Lane, *A Deaf Artist in Early America*, 62-68.

6. All information on the genealogy of the Brown and Swett families from Lane's *Deaf Artist in Early America*. One could argue that this was another common experience of deaf

life in the nineteenth century, that is, marrying into deaf families. There is not a great deal of information about such experiences, but it is clear that there were a growing number of Deaf families during this time, particularly in New England. See Thomas W. Jones, "America's First Multi-Generation Deaf Families (A Genealogical Perspective)," in *A Deaf American Monograph* 46 (1996): 49-54. He discusses the Brown-Swett family, and from him we learn that Persis did not attend the American School; unlike her brother, she was never formally educated. Thomas Lewis Brown was educated at the American School, like his father, and he graduated from the High Class there. He went on to become a teacher at the Michigan School for the Deaf, where his salary for the 1905-1906 academic year was twelve hundred dollars, the top teacher's salary available there (Jones 50-51). Jones also briefly discusses the Harrison-Williams-Arnold family of New Jersey, the Hoagland-Blount-Reed family of Kentucky, the Holler-Christian family of Virginia, and the Lovejoy-Jellison-Berry family of Maine. See also Harlan Lane, Richard Pillard, and Ulf Hedberg, "Nancy Rowe and George Curtis: Deaf Lives in Maine 150 Years Ago," *Sign Language Studies* 7 (Winter 2007): 152-67. Lane, Pillard, and Hedberg "hypothesize that the connectedness among Deaf families in early nineteenth-century New England was a significant force in the creation of the American Deaf-World." I am inclined to agree. Lane, Pillard and Hedberg have recently expanded their argument about the importance of Deaf families, marriages, and kinship networks into a book; see their *The People of the Eye: Deaf Ethnicity and Ancestry* (New York: Oxford University Press, 2011).

7. Guilbert C. Braddock, "Thomas Brown," *Notable Deaf Persons*, ed. Florence B. Crammatte (Washington, DC: Gallaudet College Alumni Association, 1975), 6.

8. All descriptions of Thomas Brown from Chamberlain, "Thomas Brown," *Annals* 31 (July 1886): 206, 207, 208. The goals of the NEGA are taken from its constitution. See "Constitution of the New England Gallaudet Association of Deaf Mutes," *American Annals of the Deaf* 9, no. 2 (April 1857): 79.

9. Van Cleve and Crouch, *A Place of Their Own*, 90. For membership requirements, see "Constitution," 81.

10. Carol Padden and Tom Humphries, *Deaf in America: Voices from a Culture* (Cambridge, MA: Harvard University Press, 1988), 41.

11. For more on the phrase "not deaf enough," see, for instance, most of the media coverage of the so-called DPN II strike of 2006. Then Gallaudet provost Jane Fernandes was prevented by student strike from assuming the presidency of Gallaudet University. That she was seen as "not deaf enough" was one popular explanation offered for events.

12. Susan Burch, *Signs of Resistance: American Deaf Cultural History, 1900 to 1942* (New York: New York University Press, 2002), 144. They offered such praise out of sight of the hearing mainstream because the Deaf of Deaf, from a mainstream perspective, were seen not as natural leaders, but as the undesirable result of the uncontrolled breeding of defectives, in an era marked by increasing interest in and support for eugenics in the United States. Burch discusses eugenic attitudes toward the deaf community in detail in chapter 5.

13. For more on the role of the Deaf of Deaf during the DPN protest, see Katherine A. Jankowski, *Deaf Empowerment: Emergence, Struggle, and Rhetoric* (Washington, DC: Gallaudet University Press, 1997), 109-11. As Jankowski points out, all four of the student body government leaders came from Deaf families and the majority of the alumni who helped coordinate events were also Deaf of Deaf.

14. For more on Rider's career, see Elizabeth Van Schaick, "Northern New York School for the Deaf," *Franklin Historical Review* 17 (1980): 18-32. He founded a residential school himself, the Northern New York School for the Deaf, in 1884. The school closed in 1943 due to falling enrollment.

15. Rider as quoted in Van Cleve and Crouch, *A Place of Their Own*, 93. His own residential school experience undoubtedly shaped his thinking here; he attended the New York School from 1846 to 1855.

16. Alphonso Johnson, "Empire State Association of Deaf Mutes," *Deaf Mutes' Friend* 1, no. 9 (1869): 258.

17. Rider as quoted in Van Cleve and Crouch, *A Place of Their Own*, 92. Even so, there was a deaf community in northern New York. When Rider married into the Chandler family of Mexico, New York, in 1857, the Chandlers were considered "social leaders of the deaf of northern New York." See Braddock, *Notable Deaf Persons*, 13. His wife was Helen Chandler, a deaf woman, who, like her husband, was a graduate of the New York School.

18. *Deaf Mutes' Friend* 1, no. 2 (1869): 51.

19. H.C.R., "The Proposed National Convention of Deaf Mutes," *Deaf Mutes' Friend* 1, no. 6 (1869): 189.

20. Bernard Mottez, "The Deaf-Mute Banquets and the Birth of the Deaf Movement," in *Deaf History Unveiled: Interpretations from the New Scholarship*, ed. John Vickrey Van Cleve (Washington, DC: Gallaudet University Press, 1993), 29.

21. Lennard Davis, *Enforcing Normalcy: Disability, Deafness, and the Body* (New York: Verso, 1995), 77.

22. A Young Man, Twenty Years Old, under Instruction Three Years, Lost Hearing Partially at Four and Entirely at Eight, "Dialogue between a Greek Patriot and an Educated American Deaf and Dumb Man," *Fifteenth Annual Report of the Directors of the American Asylum at Hartford for the Education and Instruction of the Deaf and Dumb, exhibited to the Asylum, May 14, 1831* (Hartford, CT: Hudson and Skinner, 1831), 21-22. The author is Edmund Booth. See Harry G. Lang, *Edmund Booth: Deaf Pioneer* (Washington, DC: Gallaudet University Press, 2004), 8.

23. Davis, *Enforcing Normalcy*, 85.

24. Flournoy's characterization of the hearing as found in Christopher Krentz, ed., *A Mighty Change: An Anthology of Deaf American Writing, 1816-1864* (Washington, DC: Gallaudet University Press, 2000), 169-70.

25. Flournoy as described in Van Cleve and Crouch, *A Place of Their Own*, 61. Scholars have taken an increasing interest in Flournoy. See Hannah Joyner, *From Pity to Pride: Growing Up Deaf in the Old South* (Washington, DC: Gallaudet University Press, 2004), 107-19, for more on Flournoy's inspirations. For a reading of the deaf state that pays close attention to considerations of race and gender, see see Christopher Krentz, *Writing Deafness: The Hearing Line in Nineteenth-Century American Literature* (Chapel Hill: University of North Carolina Press, 2007), 153-64. There is a biography of Flournoy available; see E. Merton Coulter, *John Jacobus Flournoy: Champion of the Common Man in the Antebellum South* (Savannah: Georgia Historical Society, 1942).

26. An excellent published source for this conversation is found in Krentz, ed., *A Mighty Change*, 161-211. Krentz includes excerpts from all of the participants as well as a good introduction to the material.

27. Flournoy as quoted in Krentz, ed., *A Mighty Change*, 187.

28. Ibid., 166.

29. Ibid., 167.

30. Ibid., 169.

31. Harlan Lane, *The Mask of Benevolence: Disabling the Deaf Community*, 2nd ed. (San Diego: Dawn Sign Press, 1999), 43.

32. As quoted in Krentz, ed., *A Mighty Change*, 163.

33. Ibid., 168.

34. For more on Booth, see Harry G. Lang, *Edmund Booth: Deaf Pioneer* (Washington, DC: Gallaudet University Press, 2004).

35. As quoted in Krentz, ed., *A Mighty Change*, 171.

36. Ibid., 174.

37. For more on this divide within the deaf community, as reflected in this debate, see Krentz, *Writing Deafness*, 159-60.

38. As quoted in Krentz, ed., *A Mighty Change*, 179.

39. Booth's sectional argument in Krentz, ed., *A Mighty Change*, 182.

40. As quoted in Krentz, ed., *A Mighty Change*, 188-89.

41. Ibid., 189.

42. Ibid., 191.

43. Lennard Davis, *Bending Over Backwards: Disability, Dismodernism, and Other Difficult Positions* (New York: New York University Press, 2002), 156.

44. As quoted in Krentz, ed., *A Mighty Change*, 200.

45. As quoted in ibid., 211.This represented a change in Clerc's opinion over time. He had, as a younger man, argued that the American School might donate some land it owned for the sake of letting alumni set up a deaf community there. See Douglas C. Baynton, *Forbidden Signs: American Culture and the Campaign against Sign Language* (Chicago: University of Chicago Press, 1996), 30.

46. Joyner, *From Pity to Pride*, 118.

47. Krentz, *Writing Deafness*, 157.

48. John Vickrey Van Cleve, "The Academic Integration of Deaf Children: A Historical Perspective," in *The Deaf History Reader*, ed. John Vickrey Van Cleve (Washington, DC: Gallaudet University Press, 2007), 118. All information on Bartlett's school from Van Cleve 118-19; Jack Gannon, *Deaf Heritage: A Narrative History of Deaf America*, ed. Jane Butler and Laura-Jean Gilbert (Silver Spring, MD: National Association of the Deaf, 1981), 7; Edward Allen Fay, "Mr. Bartlett's Family School," *Histories of American Schools for the Deaf, 1817-1893*, vol. 3, ed. Edward Allen Fay (Washington, DC: Volta Bureau, 1893), 4.

49. There are two schools that have picked up on Bartlett's vision of the deaf and hearing going to school together. The Alburquerque Sign Language Academy in New Mexico is a public charter school that opened in 2010-2011. It offers a bilingual educational program in ASL and English. The ASL Academy serves deaf and hard-of-hearing children but also enrolls their hearing siblings, hearing children who have deaf parents, and "others who can benefit from a bilingual education." The ASL and English Lower School, and its companion school, the ASL and English Dual Language Secondary School, in New York City, offer public education to deaf and hard-of-hearing students, as well as to hearing children with deaf parents or deaf siblings and to any "non-deaf student who wants to be fluent in sign language."

50. Van Cleve, "Academic Integration," 119-20. Knapp's was open in the 1870s, Bell's in the 1880s.

51. This discussion of Gallaudet College draws from the following sources: Douglas C. Baynton, Jack R. Gannon, and Jean Lindquist Bergey, *Through Deaf Eyes: A Photographic History of an American Community* (Washington, DC: Gallaudet University Press, 2007), 51-59; Krentz, ed., *A Mighty Change*, 212-24; Van Cleve and Crouch, *A Place of Their Own*, 71-86; Gannon, *Deaf Heritage*, 38-39, 236. See also *A Fair Chance in the Race of Life: The Role of Gallaudet University in Deaf History*, eds. Brian Greenwald and John Vickrey Van Cleve (Washington, DC: Gallaudet University Press, 2008).

52. Baynton, Gannon, and Bergey, *Through Deaf Eyes*, 59.

53. Seventeen Year Old Lady, "On the Public Worship of the Deaf and Dumb on Sunday," *Sixth Report of the Directors of the American Asylum at Hartford for the Education and Instruction of the Deaf and Dumb, Exhibited to the Asylum, May 11, 1822* (Hartford, CT: Hudson, 1822), 20.

54. *The Thirty-Seventh Annual Report of the Directors of the American Asylum at Hartford for the Education and Instruction of the Deaf and Dumb, presented to the Asylum, May 14, 1853* (Hartford, CT: Case, Tiffany, 1853), 16-17.

55. All information about, and this interpretation of, St. Ann's drawn from Robert Buchanan, *Illusions of Equality: Deaf Americans in School and Factory, 1850-1950* (Washington, DC: Gallaudet University Press, 1999), 14-15 .Gallaudet's efforts also opened up another career path to deaf men—the Episcopal priesthood. He supported ordination for deaf men, and gave specific encouragement to the first deaf man to be ordained in the Episcopal tradition in 1883, Henry Syle. By 1900, there were seven deaf Episcopal priests. The willingness of the Episcopal church to open its ordained ranks to deaf men helps to account for its early popularity with deaf worshippers.

56. Gannon, *Deaf Heritage*, 186.

57. *Eighteenth Annual Report of the NYS*, 102.

58. William M. Chamberlain, "Proceedings of the Board of Managers of the New England Gallaudet Association of Deaf-Mutes, Convened at Branford, Vermont, September 6,7, 8, 1859," *American Annals of the Deaf* 11 (1859): 211.

59. Van Cleve and Crouch, *A Place of Their Own*, 91.

60. Swett (1825-1884) was the son of Persis Brown and Bela Swett. He attended the American School for the Deaf from 1839 to 1842, and married a graduate of the New York School, Margaret Harrington. He was very active in the Deaf community. He served as the first secretary of the New England Gallaudet Association and later as its president for two terms. In 1879, he founded the New England Industrial School for Deaf-Mutes in Beverly, Massachusetts. For more on his career in the mountains, see William B. Swett's "Adventures of a Deaf-Mute in the White Mountains, 1865-1868," republished by the Henniker Historical Society (Henniker, NH, 2001).

61. William M. Chamberlain, "Introductory," *Deaf Mutes' Friend* 1, no. 1 (1869): 2.

62. Jack Gannon discusses the Little Paper Family at length in *Deaf Heritage*; see 237-54. See also Beth Haller, "*The Little Papers*: Newspapers at Nineteenth-Century Schools for Deaf Persons," *Journalism History* 19, no. 2 (Summer 1993): 43-50. See Van Cleve and Crouch, *A Place of Their Own*, 98-105. My discussion draws deeply on these sources.

63. Haller, "*The Little Papers*," 44.

64. Anonymous, "Personal Department," *Silent World* 6, no. 8 (1876): 4.

65. See Van Cleve and Crouch, *A Place of Their Own*, 101-2.

66. Ibid., 100-101.

67. As quoted in ibid., 101.

68. Rider as quoted in Buchanan, *Illusions of Equality*, 13.

69. See Burch, *Signs of Resistance*, 99-128, for more on employment issues and strategies in the early twentieth century Deaf community. See also *Buchanan's Illusions of Equality*; the quoted phrase appears on page 13.

70. *Forty-Fifth Annual Report of the New York Institution for the Instruction of the Deaf and Dumb to the Legislature of the State of New York for the Year 1863* (Albany, NY: Comstock and Cassidy, 1864), 30.

71. John Carlin, "Oration: Empire State Association of Deaf Mutes," *Deaf Mutes' Friend* 1, no. 9 (1869): 265.

72. Carlin began arguing for this approach as early as 1853. For more on Carlin's ideas about fighting hearing prejudice, see Buchanan, *Illusions of Equality*, 5.

73. Carlin, "Oration," 266.

74. As Christopher Krentz points out, Carlin "epitomizes the contradictory manner in which deaf people saw themselves. . . . In his written works, Carlin displays deep ambivalence toward his deaf identity, oscillating between viewing deaf people as inferior and asserting their equal intelligence and capability" (139). For more on Carlin, see Krentz, *Writing Deafness*, 139-45.

75. William B. Swett, "A Deaf and Dumb Guide Better Than None," *Deaf Mutes' Friend* 1, no. 10 (1869): 291.

76. Swett's story as recounted in "A Deaf and Dumb Guide," 291-92.

77. Lane, *A Deaf Artist in Early America*, 102-3.

78. Anonymous, "Miscellaneous," *Deaf Mutes' Friend* 1, no. 5 (1869): 157-58.

79. *Deaf Mutes' Friend* 1, no. 10 (1869): 310. The article claims that there was once "years ago, a company of deaf-mutes who went about the country giving pantomimic entertainments," but I have found no trace of them.

80. For more on the creation of the National Theatre of the Deaf, see Stephen Baldwin, *Pictures in the Air: The Story of the National Theatre of the Deaf* (Washington, DC: Gallaudet University Press, 1995).

81. Buchanan, *Illusions of Equality*, 3.

82. For a more extensive list of schools founded by deaf people, see Gannon, *Deaf Heritage*, 19.

83. Buchanan, *Illusions of Equality*, 4.

84. Burch, *Signs of Resistance*, 21.

85. The complete list of names, as I have been able to identify them, with the schools where they taught, if known, are as follows: Ralph Atwood (Ohio, Arkansas, Beverly School), Levi Backus (Central New York), Edmund Booth (ASD), Thomas L. Brown (Michigan), Danforth Ball (Ohio), Melville Ballard (ASD, Kendall), William Bird (Virginia, ASD), John David (ASD), James Denison (Kendall), Amos Draper (Gallaudet), Josephus Edwards (private school in Georgia), James Fisher (Tennessee), John Gage, Samuel Greene (Ontario), John Hotchkiss (Gallaudet), Louis Houghton (Tennessee), George Loring (ASD), Fisher Spofford (ASD), Richard Springs, Louis Tuck (Oregon, Minnesota), Job Turner (Virginia), James Wheeler, Wilson Whiton (ASD), William Willard (Ohio, Indiana), and George Wing (Minnesota).

86. For more on Greene, see Clifton F. Carbin, *Samuel Thomas Greene: A Legend in the Nineteenth-Century Deaf Community* (Belleville, Ontario: Epic Press, 2005).

87. Information on Dillingham's teaching career from Mabs Holcomb and Sharon Wood, *Notable Deaf Women: A Parade through the Decades* (Berkeley: Dawn Sign Press, 1989), 18. Quote from Laurent Clerc from his papers, "A letter from Laurent Clerc to Robert Vaux, dated April 22, 1822," Beinecke Library, Yale University.

88. For more on Mary Rose, see Mickey Jones, "Mary Rose Totten: ISD's First Matron," *The Illinois Advance* 137, no. 3 (2003-2004): 1-2. My thanks to Gary Wait for directing me to this reference.

89. The complete list of names as I have been able to identify them, with the schools where they taught, if known, follows: Anna Barry, Mary Bierce, Catharine Brooks (ASD), Martha Cunningham (South Carolina), Elmina Clapp (ASD), Abigail Dillingham (Pennsylvania), Mary Haskell, Lizzy Lindsey, Mary Mann (ASD), Mary McKay, Olivia Record, Mary Rose (New York), Sarah Storrs (ASD), Clara Seaverns (ASD), Nancy Wing (ASD), Elizabeth Weston (ASD).

90. For more on the rise of women in oralism, see Baynton, *Forbidden Signs*, 56-82; Annemieke Van Drenth, "'Tender Sympathy and Scrupulous Fidelity': Gender and Professionalism in the History of Deaf Education in the United States," *International Journal of Disability, Development, and Education* 50, no. 4 (December 2003): 367-83; Margaret Winzer, "Talking Deaf Mutes: The Special Role of Women in the Methodological Conflict Regarding the Deaf, 1867-1900," *Atlantis* 6, no. 2 (1981): 123-33.

91. Phyllis K. Valentine, "A Nineteenth-Century Experiment in Education of the Handicapped: The American Asylum for the Deaf and Dumb," *The New England Quarterly* 64, no. 3 (September 1991): 373.

92. Van Cleve and Crouch, *A Place of Their Own*, 160. Buchanan, *Illusions of Equality*, 7.

93. Ibid., 164.

94. All information on printing in the deaf community from Van Cleve and Crouch, *A Place of Their Own*, 164-68.

95. Van Cleve and Crouch, *A Place of Their Own*, 158.

96. William Breg, "An Account," *Twenty-ninth Annual Report of the New York Institution for the Instruction of the Deaf and Dumb. Made to the Legislature of the State of New York for the Year 1847* (New York: Egbert, Hovey, and King, 1848), 56-57.

97. Information on occupations from Valentine, "A Nineteenth-Century Experiment," 358.

98. As recorded in *Record of Facts Concerning the Former Pupils of the American Asylum as from Time to Time They Come to the Knowledge of the Principals, Instructors, or Other Officers of the Institution. Commenced June 1869.* American School for the Deaf Archives and Museum, West Hartford, Connecticut.

99. List of occupations culled from "List of Pupils of the American Asylum, from the Opening of the School, April 15, 1817, to May 1, 1877," *The Sixty-First Annual Report of the Directors of the American Asylum at Hartford for the Education and Instruction of the Deaf and Dumb. Presented to the Asylum May 15, 1877* (Hartford, CT: Case, Lockwood, and Brainard, 1877).

100. Holcomb and Wood, *Deaf Women*, 18.

101. For a discussion of this portrait in particular, as well as name signs in general, see Samuel J. Supalla, *The Book of Name Signs: Naming in American Sign Language* (San Diego: Dawn Sign Press, 1992), 31-33.

102. For more on gendered aspects of eugenics, see Brad Byrom's "A Pupil and a Patient: Hospital-Schools in Progressive America," and Catherine Kudlick's "The Outlook

of *The Problem* and the Problem with the *Outlook*: Two Advocacy Journals Reinvent Blind People in Turn-of-the-Century America," both in *The New Disability History: American Perspectives*, eds. Paul K. Longmore and Lauri Umansky (New York: New York University Press, 2001). For more on how eugenics increasingly pressured deaf woman to pass as hearing in the early twentieth century, see Burch, *Signs of Resistance*, 146-49.

103. "Jubilee of the Deaf and Dumb," *Hartford Daily Courant*, Tuesday morning edition, September 14, 1850, 2.

104. "The Land of Silence," *Hartford Daily Courant*, Wednesday morning edition, August 29, 1855, 2.

105. Amos Draper, "Sophia Gallaudet," *American Annals of the Deaf* 22 (July 1877): 177.

106.   *Twenty-Third Annual Report of the Directors of the New York Institution for the Instruction of the Deaf and Dumb to the Legislature of the State of New York for the Year 1841* (New York: Mahlon Day, 1842), 46.

107. A Young Lady, Twenty-One Years Old, under Instruction 5½ Years, "The Duties of a Good Wife," *Fifteenth Report of the Directors of the American Asylum at Hartford for the Education and Instruction of the Deaf and Dumb, Exhibited to the Asylum, May 14, 1831*(Hartford, CT: Hudson and Skinner, 1831), 23-24.

108. There are few accounts of married life in the nineteenth century, as Deaf women experienced it. But for one such study of a Deaf housewife, see Jill Hendricks Porco, "Mary Ann Walworth Booth," in *The Deaf History Reader*, ed. John Vickrey Van Cleve (Washington, DC: Gallaudet University Press, 2007), 74-84.

109. Ernest Freeberg, *The Education of Laura Bridgman: First Deaf and Blind Person to Learn Language* (Cambridge, MA: Harvard University Press, 2001), 198. For more on Howe's beliefs about the blind, see Elisabeth Gitter, *The Imprisoned Guest: Samuel Howe and Laura Bridgman, the Original Deaf-Blind Girl* (New York: Farrar, Straus and Giroux, 2001) and Mary Klages, *Woeful Afflictions: Disability and Sentimentality in Victorian America* (Philadelphia: University of Pennsylvania Press, 1999).

110. Klages, *Woeful Afflictions*, 52.

111. Kudlick, "The Outlook of *The Problem* and the Problem with the *Outlook*," in *The New Disability History*, 187-213.

112. Walter Fernald, director of the Massachusetts State School for the Feeble-Minded, as quoted in Robert Osgood, *For 'Children Who Vary from the Normal Type': Special Education in Boston, 1838-1930* (Washington, DC: Gallaudet University Press, 2000), 52.

113. Steven Noll and James Trent, eds., "Introduction," *Mental Retardation in America* (New York: New York University Press, 2004), 2. This collection of essays provides a good overview of the historical treatment of the mentally retarded in American life. See also James Trent, *Inventing the Feeble Mind: A History of Mental Retardation in the United States* (Berkeley: University of California Press, 1994) and Philip Ferguson, *Abandoned to Their Fate: Social Policy and Practice toward Severely Retarded People in America, 1820-1920* (Philadelphia: Temple University Press, 1994).

114. *Deaf-Mutes' Friend* 1, no. 3 (1869).

115. "List of Pupils of the New York Institution," *American Annals of the Deaf* (July 1854): 234.

116. In 1883, Alexander Graham Bell delivered a speech to the National Academy of Sciences called "Memoir upon the Formation of a Deaf Variety of the Human Race." He was convinced that manual schools, by bringing deaf people together and teaching them

in a language that hearing people did not understand, promoted deaf-deaf intermarriage. This would produce a deaf variety of the human race if educators did not act immediately. Bell would have liked to have made such unions illegal but recognized that this would probably never happen. Instead, he recommended a switch to the oral method and day schools, so that deaf people might learn to pass as hearing and choose therefore to live in the hearing community exclusively. After "Memoir" was published, Bell became more deeply involved in the eugenics movement, serving on the Eugenics Committee of the American Breeders Association. For a transnational analysis of the Deaf community's response to Bell and other eugenic assaults on their right to marry, see Joseph J. Murray, "'True Love and Sympathy': The Deaf-Deaf Marriage Debate in Transatlantic Perspective," in *Genetics, Disability, and Deafness*, ed. John Vickrey Van Cleve (Washington, DC: Gallaudet University Press, 2004), 42-71. Brian Greenwald has argued that Bell "may actually have shielded Deaf people from negative eugenics." See his "The Real 'Toll' of A. G. Bell: Lessons about Eugenics," in *Genetics, Disability, and Deafness*, ed. John Vickrey Van Cleve (Washington, DC: Gallaudet University Press, 2004), 35-41.

117. Valentine, "A Nineteenth-Century Experiment," 356-57.

118. Geographic data from *Record of the Names of Those Present at Several Gatherings of Deaf Mutes at the American Asylum*. American School for the Deaf Museum, West Hartford, Connecticut.

119. Valentine, "A Nineteenth-Century Experiment," 358.

120. Krentz, ed., *A Mighty Change*, 141.

121. Lane, *A Deaf Artist in Early America*, 77.

122. Information on Spofford from Krentz, ed., *A Mighty Change*, 140.

123. In Gitter, *The Imprisoned Guest*, 263.

124. Additional information on Loring from Guilbert C. Braddock, *Notable Deaf Persons*, 23-25.

125. As quoted in Krentz, ed., *A Mighty Change*, 145.

126. Ibid., 147.

127. Ibid., 148.

128. Details about the artists found in Lane, *A Deaf Artist in Early America*, 75.

129. Krentz, ed., *A Mighty Change*, 154. All information on the attendees, both here and throughout this discussion, from the *Record of the Names of Those Present at Several Gatherings of Deaf Mutes at the American Asylum*

130. Lane, *A Deaf Artist in Early America*, 77-78.

131. Membership list appears in the *American Annals of the Deaf* 9, no. 2 (April 1857): 82-87. Vineyard members were Zeno Tilton, Franklin Tilton, Harriet Tilton, Sally Mayhew, Ruby Mayhew, Lovey Mayhew, Hannah Mayhew, Alfred Mayhew, and Charles Luce.

132. Krentz, ed., *A Mighty Change*, 155. All information on the Gallaudet monument found in Krentz 153-60.

133. For a report of the newspaper coverage of the Vineyard deaf, see Arthur Railton, "The Story of Martha's Vineyard: How We Got to Where We Are," *The Dukes County Intelligencer* 45, no. 4 (2004): 179-85. My thanks to the Martha's Vineyard Historical Society for directing me to this source. Negative Vineyard press also appeared in W. K. Brooks, "Can Man Be Modified by Selection?" *The Popular Science Monthly* 27 (May 1885):15-25 and S. Millington Miller, "The Ascent of Man," *The Arena* 12 (March 1895): 130-35, which would characterize the Vineyard as a "garden of affliction." For more on Bell's visit to the

Vineyard, see Nora Ellen Groce, *Everyone Here Spoke Sign Language: Hereditary Deafness on Martha's Vineyard* (Cambridge, MA: Harvard University Press, 1985), 46-48, and Robert V. Bruce, *Bell: Alexander Graham Bell and the Conquest of Solitude* (Ithaca, NY: Cornell University Press, 1973), 409-13.

134. The presence of interpreters is noted in "The Convention of the N.E. Association of the Deaf and Dumb. Second Day, Thursday, Sept. 13," *Hartford Daily Courant* (14 September 1860): 2, and "Anniversary of Deaf Mutes," *Hartford Daily Courant* (22 August 1866): 8. There were very few occasions in public life in the nineteenth century that witnessed the work of interpreters. According to the *Courant*, Rev. Thomas Gallaudet, Thomas Hopkins Gallaudet's son, most frequently interpreted at these events.

135. "The Convention of the N.E. Association of the Deaf and Dumb. Second Day, Thursday, Sept. 13," *Hartford Daily Courant* (14 September 1860): 2.

136. Ibid.

137. "Convention of Deaf Mutes," *Hartford Daily Courant* (23 August 1866): 8.

138. "The Deaf Mute Convention," *Hartford Daily Courant* (24 August 1866): 8.

139. Steven Mintz, *Moralists and Modernizers: America's Pre–Civil War Reformers* (Baltimore, MD: Johns Hopkins University Press, 1995), 106.)

140. "Convention of Deaf Mutes," 8.

141. Badger was expelled from the school in 1854. Notes from the faculty meeting minutes show that he was apparently the ringleader of a group of unruly boys who contributed to "the present disorderly and insubordinate state of the boys." It seems it was hoped that getting rid of Badger would end the problem. It would also seem that it worked. There is no further note of a disorderly state in the school the following academic year.

142. All information on the Metrashes from author's personal conversation with Metrash family descendant Dorothy Harper on May 18, 2009; from subsequent email exchanges with Charles Williams, another Metrash family descendent, who also graciously provided the 1863 letter; and from Judy Cobin, "Family's Roots in Norwalk Go Back Centuries," *The Hour*, on-line Norwalk news, article posted on February 28, 2008, accessed May 19, 2009, as well as direct email exchanges with Cobin. I owe a tremendous debt to both Mrs. Harper and Mr. Williams for so graciously sharing their family history with me. I must also thank Ms. Cobin for helping piece together the story of Adam's life in Norwalk. Finally, Adam apparently bought the oyster beds under the so-called two acre law, passed in Connecticut in 1855, which granted coastal towns the right to sell up to two acres to individuals for seeding beds, in order to encourage oystering in the state. See John M. Kochiss, *Oystering from New York to Boston* (Middletown, CT: Wesleyan University Press, 1974), 18.

143. For more on race and the NAD, see Burch, *Signs of Resistance*, 91-93.

144. For more on whiteness studies, see Noel Ignatiev, *How the Irish Became White* (New York: Routledge, 1995) and David R. Roediger, *Working toward Whiteness: How America's Immigrants Became White* (New York: Basic Books, 2005).

145. See Burch, *Signs of Resistance*, 1-6,121, 133.

146. Thomas Widd, "Conquered at Last," *Deaf Mutes' Friend* 1, no. 11 (1869): 326. Widd (1839-1906) was a remarkable figure in the Deaf world. Originally from England, he was a deaf teacher of the deaf there. He taught at his alma mater, the Yorkshire School for the Deaf, from 1859 to 1862. He then moved to Canada in 1867, where he helped to found the Mackay School for the Deaf in Montreal in 1870. Finally, he moved for health reasons to

California, where he formed the Los Angeles Association for the Deaf in 1889 and became one of the leaders of the growing Deaf community of the West Coast. See Braddock, *Notable Deaf Persons*, 91-93.

147. Anonymous, "Miscellaneous," *Deaf Mutes' Friend* 1, no.11 (1869): 342.

148. "The First Convention of American Instructors of the Deaf," *American Annals of the Deaf* 3 (October 1850): 27.

149. Comment from the *Forty-Fifth Annual Report and Documents of the New York Institution for the Instruction of the Deaf and Dumb*, 35.

150. William B. Swett, "Life and Adventures of William B. Swett," *Deaf Mutes' Friend* 1, no. 2 (1869): 35.

151. Krentz, *Writing Deafness*, 73.

152. Rosemarie Garland Thomson, "Seeing the Disabled: Visual Rhetorics of Disability in Popular Photography," in *The New Disability History: American Perspectives*, ed. Paul K. Longmore and Lauri Umansky (New York: New York University Press, 2001), 346-47.

153. William B. Swett, "How I Happened to Go to the Mountains," *Deaf Mutes' Friend* 1, no. 1 (1869): 5.

154. Christopher Krentz, "Exploring the 'Hearing Line': Deafness, Laughter, and Mark Twain," in *Disability Studies: Enabling the Humanities*, eds. Sharon Snyder, Brenda Jo Brueggemann, and Rosemarie Garland-Thomson (New York: Modern Language Association of America, 2002), 240.

155. Krentz, "Exploring the Hearing Line," 246.

CHAPTER 5

1. Van Cleve and Crouch conclude that as oralist claims of effectiveness were proven exaggerated, "Mann was ignored" (John Vickery Van Cleve and Barry Crouch, *A Place of Their Own* [Washington, DC: Gallaudet University Press, 1989], 112). Baynton argues that "Samuel Gridley Howe was a dedicated and powerful proponent of oral education, and even Horace Mann, America's pre-eminent educator, wrote in favor of oralism, yet the results of their efforts were negligible" (Douglas C. Baynton, *Forbidden Signs: American Culture and the Campaign against Sign Language* [Chicago: University of Chicago Press, 1996], 8).

2. See Mary E. Numbers, *My Words Fell on Deaf Ears: The First Hundred Years of the Clarke School for the Deaf* (Washington, DC: Alexander Graham Bell Association of the Deaf, 1947), 1-15. Numbers was associated with Clarke from 1918 to 1963. See Margret A. Winzer, *The History of Special Education: From Isolation to Integration* (Washington, DC: Gallaudet University Press, 1993), 128. She also points to the impact of Gardiner Greene Hubbard and pioneer oral teacher Harriet Rogers. These four influences, in combination, she argues, persuaded Massachusetts to act. Betty Miller Unterberger argued for the crucial influence of Horace Mann on the rise of oralism in the United States; see "The First Attempt to Establish an Oral School for the Deaf and Dumb in the United States," *Journal of Southern History* 13, no. 4 (November 1947): 565-66.

3. For this interpretation, see Harlan Lane, *When the Mind Hears: A History of the Deaf* (New York: Random House, 1984), 295.

4. See Baynton, *Forbidden Signs*, 8, and Van Cleve and Crouch, *A Place of Their Own*, 112, for more on this view of Mann and Howe.

5. Edward Miner Gallaudet, "Must the Sign-Language Go?" *American Annals of the Deaf* 44 (1899): 221-29.

6. Jonathan Messerli, *Horace Mann: A Biography* (New York: Knopf, 1972), 407.

7. For more on the honeymoon tour, see Lane, *When the Mind Hears*, 297-302.

8. Horace Mann, "Seventh Annual Report of the Secretary of the Board of Education," *Common School Journal* 6 (1 March 1844): 73.

9. For more on Mann's praise of the Prussians, and its impact on education in Massachusetts, see Michael B. Katz, *The Irony of Early School Reform: Educational Innovation in Mid-Nineteenth Century Massachusetts* (Cambridge, MA: Harvard University Press, 1968), 139-49.

10. Messerli, *Horace Mann*, 342.

11. Ibid., 445.

12. Massachusetts Board of Education, *Second Annual Report of the Board of Education together with the Second Annual Report of the Secretary of the Board* (Boston: Dutton and Wentworth, 1839), 40.

13. *Second Annual Report*, 43.

14. Massachusetts Board of Education, *Seventh Annual Report of the Board of Education together with the Seventh Annual Report of the Secretary of the Board* (Boston: Dutton and Wentworth, 1844), 33. Note that they would "participate" only passively, as observers of the conversations of hearing people, and not at all actively. Nowhere does this seem to trouble Mann.

15. *Seventh Annual Report*, 52-53.

16. Mann, "Seventh Annual Report," 75.

17. Ibid., 75.

18. *Seventh Annual Report*, 33.

19. For a more detailed discussion of the beliefs of late-nineteenth-century oralists outlined here, see Baynton, *Forbidden Signs*, 83-107, 132-48. Baynton does not trace their origins to Mann, but I believe the connections to his thought are compelling.

20. Samuel Gridley Howe, as quoted in the first hearing of the committee in the "Appendix" of the *Report of the Joint Special Committee of the Legislature of 1867 on the Education of Deaf-Mutes with an Appendix Containing the Evidence, Arguments, Letters, Etc., Submitted to the Committee* (Boston: Wright and Potter, 1867), 11.

21. Ernest Freeberg, *The Education of Laura Bridgman: First Deaf and Blind Person to Learn Language* (Cambridge, MA: Harvard University Press, 2001), 86.

22. Ibid., 13.

23. Mary Klages, *Woeful Afflictions: Disability and Sentimentality in Victorian America* (Philadelphia: University of Pennsylvania Press, 1999), 31.

24. Ibid., 30.

25. Ibid., 32-34.

26. Ibid., 36.

27. Ibid., 39-46; Freeberg, *The Education of Laura Bridgman*, 194-97.

28. As quoted in Klages, *Woeful Afflictions*, 47.

29. Ibid., 48.

30. Freeberg, *The Education of Laura Bridgman*, 107.

31. Ibid., 190.

32. Ibid., 191.

33. Ibid., 202-3.

34. See Ronald G. Walters, *American Reformers, 1815-1860*, rev. ed. (New York: Hill and Wang, 1997).

35. Freeberg, *The Education of Laura Bridgman*, 198.

36. Ibid., 208. See also Steven Mintz, *Moralists and Modernizers: America's Pre–Civil War Reformers* (Baltimore, MD: Johns Hopkins University Press, 1995), 105-6.

37. Christopher Krentz, *Writing Deafness: The Hearing Line in Nineteenth-Century American Literature* (Chapel Hill: University of North Carolina Press, 2007), 35.

38. Ibid., 47.

39. Freeberg, *The Education of Laura Bridgman*, 208.

40. "Letter of Thomas Hopkins Gallaudet to Horace Mann," *Fifty-First Annual Report of the Directors and Officers of the American Asylum at Hartford for the Education and Instruction of the Deaf and Dumb, presented to the Asylum May 11, 1867* (Hartford, CT: Case, Lockwood, 1867), 64-65. Emphasis in original. The 1844 letter was originally meant for Mann's eyes only, but, as is seen here, was later published by the American School, in 1867, as the debate over oral education was heating up.

41. Ibid., 65.

42. Ibid., 65.

43. Ibid., 65.

44. Walters, *American Reformers*, 211.

45. See Anne T. Quartararo, *Deaf Identity and Social Images in Nineteenth-Century France* (Washington, DC: Gallaudet University Press, 2008), 36-48.

46. Krentz, *Writing Deafness*, 164.

47. See ibid., 61, 131-39. Phrase on 132.

48. Krentz, *Writing Deafness*, 23.

49. Lennard Davis, *Enforcing Normalcy: Disability, Deafness, and the Body* (New York: Verso, 1995), 118

50. Davis, *Enforcing Normalcy*, 118.

51. For a discussion of Clerc's thought, see Krentz, *Writing Deafness*, especially 21-62.

52. Davis, *Enforcing Normalcy*, 48, 129.

53. For an analysis of the dynamics of deaf-hearing passing, see Krentz, *Writing Deafness*, especially 171-202.

54. It is not surprising that this argument should break out at this historical moment. As Lennard Davis reminds us, "The word 'normal' as 'constituting, conforming to, not deviating or differing from, the common type or standard . . . ' only enters the English language around 1840. (Previously the word had meant 'perpendicular'; the carpenter's square, called a 'norm,' provided the root meaning.)" See *Enforcing Normalcy*, 24.

CHAPTER 6

1. Lennard Davis, *Enforcing Normalcy: Disability, Deafness, and the Body* (New York: Verso, 1995), 24.

2. Ibid., 29.

3. Ibid., 30.

4. Mark M. Smith, *Listening to Nineteenth-Century America* (Chapel Hill: University of North Carolina Press, 2001), 6-7.

5. Mark M. Smith, "Echoes in Print: Method and Causation in Aural History," *The Journal of the Historical Society* 2, nos.3-4 (Summer/Fall 2002): 319.

6. Davis, *Enforcing Normalcy*, 4.

7. For more on the deaf use of the metaphor of silence, see Christopher Krentz, *Writing Deafness: The Hearing Line in Nineteenth-Century American Literature* (Chapel Hill: University of North Carolina Press, 2007), 139-45. There is a sense in which this adaptation of "silent" is a reclaiming, in an ironic way, of the hearing world's favorite metaphor for deafness, similar to the gay community's reclaiming of "queer" or the disabled community's use of "cripple."

8. Krentz, *Writing Deafness*, 143, 144.

9. Mark M. Smith, "Listening to the Heard Worlds of Antebellum America," *The Journal of the Historical Society* 1, no. 1 (Spring 2000): 69.

10. For more on the rise of the modern disability rights movement, see Joseph Shapiro, *No Pity: People with Disabilities Forging a New Civil Rights Movement* (New York: Times Books, 1993) and Doris Zames Fleischer and Frieda Zames, *The Disability Rights Movement: From Charity to Confrontation* (Philadelphia: Temple University Press, 2001).

11. *Twenty-Seventh Annual Report of the New York Institution for Instruction of the Deaf and Dumb for the Year 1845* (n.p., 1846), 64.

12. *Twentieth Annual Report of the New York Institution for the Instruction of the Deaf and Dumb for the Year 1838* (n.p., 1839), 19.

13. Ibid., 20.

14. *Twenty-Seventh Annual Report of the New York Institution*, 64.

15. Ibid., 64.

16. J. A. Ayres, "Home Education for the Deaf and Dumb," *The American Annals of the Deaf* 2 (April 1849): 183. School superintendent Zenas Westervelt would later deem this fingerspelling and speech approach "the manual oral method" when he adopted it for use at the Rochester School for the Deaf in the 1870s. After that, it became known simply as "the Rochester Method," a method the school used deep into the 1970s.

17. Ibid., 185.

18. Ibid., 186.

19. Ibid., 186.

20. Ibid., 185.

21. J. A. Ayres, "An Inquiry into the Extent to Which the Misfortune of Deafness May Be Alleviated," *The American Annals of the Deaf* 1 (July 1848): 222-23.

22. Charles P. Turner, "Expression," *American Annals of the Deaf* 1 (January 1848): 78.

23. Turner, "Expression," 78.

24. Lucius Woodruff, "Grace of Expression," *American Annals of the Deaf* 2 (July 1849): 193. Emphasis in original.

25. This growing discomfort with facial expressions may also be linked to the growing middle-class concern with appearances and public manners. See Karen Halttunen, *Confidence Men and Painted Women: A Study of Middle-Class Culture in America, 1830-1870* (New Haven, CT: Yale University Press, 1982).

26. Rev. John R. Keep, "Proceedings of the Fourth Annual Convention of American Teachers of the Deaf and Dumb," *American Annals of the Deaf* 9 (January 1857): 8.

27. Dunlap as quoted in Keep, "Proceedings," 8. Not all teachers present agreed with this view. Thomas MacIntire, the principal of the Indiana School for the Deaf, recom-

mended that veteran teachers offer classes in the sign language to novices, and also advised to newcomers "the study of the colloquial signs from their pupils" (9).

28. I am using "viewed" here quite deliberately, as I would posit that this clash of pedagogical opinion is also about literally seeing the disabled in a new light. Deafness is an invisible handicap, as deaf ears cannot be seen as such. Deafness is made visible by deaf behavior, most notably gesturing and signing. Participants in these nineteenth-century discussions were literally seeing that difference in a new way and reinterpreting it. For more on viewing disability, see Rosemarie Garland Thomson, *Staring: How We Look* (New York: Oxford University Press, 2009); Sander Gilman, *Seeing the Insane* (New York: Wiley, Brunner/Mazel, 1982); Erving Goffman, *Stigma: Notes on the Management of a Spoiled Identity* (Englewood Cliffs, NJ: Prentice Hall, 1963). See also Davis, *Enforcing Normalcy*, 126-57.

29. Woodruff, "Grace of Expression," 194.

30. Ibid., 196.

31. Ibid., 197.

32. Luzerne Rae, "On the Proper Use of Signs in the Instruction of the Deaf and Dumb," *American Annals of the Deaf* 5 (1852): 23-24.

33. See Douglas C. Baynton's "'Savages and Deaf-Mutes': Evolutionary Theory and the Campaign against Sign Language in the Nineteenth Century," in *Deaf History Unveiled*, ed. John Vickrey Van Cleve (Washington, DC: Gallaudet University Press, 1993) for more on the connection between Darwin's theory of evolution and oralism.

34. John Carlin, "Words Recognized as Units—Systematic Signs," *American Annals of the Deaf* 11 (1859): 16.

35. For more on Carlin's cultural politics, see Krentz, *Writing Deafness*, especially 139-45.

36. Gitter, *The Imprisoned Guest*, 116. As Gitter describes it, Bridgman's use of her voice was policed by hearing people. In the mid-1840s, her teachers labeled Laura's attempts at vocalizations "uncouth," "rude," and "unladylike" and demanded that she stop using her voice. Laura refused, arguing, "Some of my noises are not bad. Some are pretty noises."

37. Elisabeth Gitter, *The Imprisoned Guest: Samuel Howe and Laura Bridgman, the Original Deaf-Blind Girl* (New York: Farrar, Straus, and Giroux, 2001), 117.

38. J. A. Jacobs, "The Experiment Explained," *American Annals of the Deaf* 6 (April 1854): 172.

39. Ibid., 174.

40. J. A. Jacobs, "Preface to an Unpublished Work," *American Annals of the Deaf* 9 (July 1857): 137.

41. Ibid., 137. This is the earliest reference I have found suggesting that the term "methodical signs" revealed something about the style of the signing itself. The *American Journal of Education* also noted in 1857 that "methodical signs were also used at Hartford but in that school they were employed in a manner to carry with them some of the life and significance of colloquial signs. The signs used at New York were often clumsy and arbitrary as compared with those Mr. Clerc brought" ("New York Institution for the Deaf and Deaf," *American Journal of Education* 9 [June 1857]: 351).

42. Carlin, "Words Recognized as Units," 12.

43. John Carlin, "Advantages and Disadvantages of the Use of Signs," *American Annals of the Deaf* 4 (1851): 54.

44. Ibid., 54.

45. Ibid., 56.

46. Collins Stone, "Second Convention," *American Annals of the Deaf* 4 (October 1851): 27.

47. John Burnet, "The Relation of Words, Ideas, and Signs," *American Annals of the Deaf* 7 (October 1854): 5.

48. Harvey Prindle Peet, "Words Not Representatives of Signs but of Ideas," *American Annals of the Deaf* 11 (January 1859): 6.

49. Ibid., 5.

50. Ibid., 7.

51. J. A. Jacobs, "The Relation of Written Words to Signs, the Same as Their Relation to Spoken Words," *American Annals of the Deaf* 11 (April 1859): 71.

52. Ibid., 74.

53. Ibid., 68-69.

54. Harvey Prindle Peet, "Review of the Arguments of Mr. Jacobs on Methodical Signs," *American Annals of the Deaf* 11 (July 1859): 138.

55. Peet, "Review," 138-39.

56. See Douglas C. Baynton, *Forbidden Signs: American Culture and the Campaign against Sign Language* (Chicago: University of Chicago Press, 1996), for more on the rise of oralism at the end of the nineteenth century.

57. Virginia Institution, *Report of the Board of Visitors*, 19.

58. Virginia Institution, *Report of the Board of Visitors of the Deaf, Dumb and Blind Institution for 1851* (n.p., 1852), 20. The assumption that deaf children would grow into adults who would marry and have children is rather striking. Late-nineteenth-century oralists would view such things as great evils. Howe forbade contact between blind boys and girls at the Perkins Institute because he did not want to encourage the future union of "defectives." Alexander Graham Bell, the most important voice for the oralist cause at the turn of the century, wanted deaf marriages outlawed. He fretted publicly over the possible formation of a "deaf variety of the human race" if deaf people were allowed to marry and procreate.

59. Collins Stone, "Articulation as a Medium of Instruction for the Deaf and Dumb," *American Annals of the Deaf* 2 (July 1849): 239-40.

60. A New Contributor, "The Deaf and Dumb," *The Knickerbocker Magazine* 30 (June 1847): 34.

61. Ibid., 35.

CHAPTER 7

1. Lennard Davis, *Enforcing Normalcy: Disability, Deafness, and the Body* (New York: Verso, 1995), 84.

2. Samuel Gridley Howe, *Second Annual Report of the Board of State Charities; to Which Are Added the Reports of the Secretary, and the General Agent of the Board. January 1866* (Boston: Wright and Potter, 1866), 52.

3. Ibid., 52.

4. Ibid., 55.

5. Ibid., 55.

6. Ibid., 52.

7. Ibid., 52-53.

8. Ibid., 52.

9. Ibid., 53.

10. Ibid., 54.

11. Ibid., 55.

12. Ibid., 55.

13. Ibid., 55-56.

14. Ibid., 54.

15. Elisabeth Gitter, *The Imprisoned Guest: Samuel Howe and Laura Bridgman, the Original Deaf-Blind Girl* (New York: Farrar, Straus, and Giroux, 2001), 40.

16. Collins Stone, "Report of the Principal," *Fiftieth Annual Report of the Directors and Officers of the American Asylum at Hartford for the Education and Instruction of the Deaf and Dumb. Presented to the Asylum, May 12, 1866* (Hartford, CT: Case, Lockwood, 1866), 16.

17. Ibid., 16.

18. Ibid., 18.

19. Ibid., 19.

20. Ibid., 19.

21. Ibid., 20.

22. Ibid., 22.

23. Ibid., 20-21.

24. Ibid., 27.

25. Ibid., 31.

26. Ibid., 31.

27. Ibid., 33.

28. Ibid., 33.

29. Ibid., 34.

30. Ibid., 38-39.

31. Howe as quoted in the first hearing of the committee in the "Appendix" of the *Report of the Joint Special Committee of the Legislature of 1867 on the Education of Deaf-Mutes with an Appendix Containing the Evidence, Arguments, Letters, Etc., Submitted to the Committee* (Boston: Wright and Potter, 1867), 11.

32. Ibid., 4.

33. Ibid., 4.

34. Gardiner Greene Hubbard as quoted in the first hearing of the committee in ibid., 7.

35. Ibid., 7.

36. Ibid., 8.

37. Ibid., 8.

38. Ibid., 8.

39. Bell as quoted in Harlan Lane, *When the Mind Hears: A History of the Deaf* (New York: Random House, 1984), 340. For more on Mabel's life, including her distance from the deaf community, see Lilias M. Toward, *Mabel Bell: Alexander's Silent Partner* (New York: Methuen, 1984).

40. Hubbard as quoted in the first hearing of the committee in "Appendix," 9.

41. Ibid., 10.

42. Exchange between Mr. Hubbard and Mr. Bird as quoted in the first hearing of the committee in "Appendix,"10.

43. As this advice to parents becomes more explicit as the century goes on, it also becomes more gendered. It falls to the mother of a deaf child to raise her offspring in the appropriately oral way. See Emily K. Abel, "'Like Ordinary Hearing Children': Mothers Raising Offspring according to Oralist Dictates," in *Women and Deafness: Double Visions*, eds. Brenda Jo Brueggemann and Susan Burch (Washington, DC: Gallaudet University Press, 2006), 130-46.

44. Hubbard as quoted in the first hearing of the committee in "Appendix," 8.

45. William Turner as quoted in the first hearing of the committee in "Appendix," 25.

46. Howe as quoted in the second hearing of the committee in "Appendix," 30.

47. Exchange between Howe and Stone in the second hearing of the committee in "Appendix," 29-30.

48. Howe as quoted in Mary Klages, *Woeful Afflictions: Disability and Sentimentality in Victorian America* (Philadelphia: University of Pennsylvania Press, 1999), 49. Klages quote also 49.

49. Howe as quoted in the second hearing of the committee in "Appendix," 40.

50. Howe as quoted in the second hearing of the committee in "Appendix," 32.

51. Hubbard as quoted in the sixth hearing of the committee in "Appendix," 202.

52. Howe, as quoted in the second hearing of the committee in "Appendix," 50.

53. Stone as quoted in the second hearing of the committee in "Appendix," 62-63.

54. Stone as quoted in the third hearing of the committee in "Appendix," 80.

55. Ibid., 81.

56. Frank B. Sanborn as quoted in third hearing of the committee in "Appendix," 95.

57. Stone as quoted in the third hearing of the committee in "Appendix," 81.

58. Turner as quoted in the third hearing of the committee in "Appendix,"104.

59. Ibid., 101.

60. Ibid., 105.

61. Ibid., 98.

62. Howe as quoted in the sixth hearing of the committee in "Appendix,"180-81.

63. Ibid., 187.

64. Ibid., 180-82.

65. Hubbard as quoted in the sixth hearing of the committee in "Appendix," 199.

66. Stone as quoted in the sixth hearing of the committee in "Appendix," 193.

CONCLUSION

1. W. A. Cochrane, "Methodical Signs instead of Colloquial," *American Annals of the Deaf* 16, no. 1 (January 1871): 12.

2. John Keep, "Natural Signs: Shall They Be Abandoned?" *American Annals of the Deaf* 16, no. 1 (January 1871): 20.

3. An Extremist, "Perversity of Mutism," *American Annals of the Deaf* 18 (October 1873): 262-63.

4. Edward Miner Gallaudet, "'Deaf Mute' Conventions, Associations, and Newspapers," *American Annals of the Deaf* 18 (July 1873): 200-206. Direct quotations on 201. Baynton also characterized Gallaudet in this way; see Douglas C. Baynton, *Forbidden Signs: American Culture and the Campaign against Sign Language* (Chicago: University of Chicago Press, 1996), 26. Buchanan also concluded that Gallaudet "faltered in his support of sign

language," and the Deaf community as well. See Robert Buchanan, *Illusions of Equality: Deaf Americans in School and Factory, 1850-1950* (Washington, DC: Gallaudet University Press, 1999), 22-25.

5. See Winefield's *Never the Twain Shall Meet* for this Gallaudet versus Bell, manualist versus oralist, interpretation of the late nineteenth century, as well as for coverage of the two men in the press as heads of respective warring camps.

6. Buchanan, *Illusions of Equality*, 24. John Vickery Van Cleve and Barry Crouch, *A Place of Their Own* (Washington, DC: Gallaudet University Press, 1989), 113.

7. Bell as quoted in Harlan Lane, *When the Mind Hears: A History of the Deaf* (New York: Random House, 1984), 340.

8. H-Dirksen Bauman, "Postscript: Gallaudet Protest of 2006 and the Myths of In/Exclusion," in *Open Your Eyes*, ed. H-Dirksen Bauman (Minneapolis: University of Minnesota Press, 2008), 329.

9. Keep, "Natural Signs," 25.

Index

African-American Deaf: in life of Deaf community, 130–31, 134–37; at schools for the deaf, 65–69, 129, 223n43, 223n45, 224n446
All Angels' Mission to the Deaf, 109
American Annals of the Deaf, 110, 175
American School for the Deaf, 3, 30, 37, 38–39, 49, 52, 55, 56, 61, 107, 113, 118, 119, 125, 128, 130, 141, 176,188, 204, 205, 209; founding of, 3; racial integration of, 65–68, 136, 223n45
Angus, Walter W., 227n88
Anthony, John, 65, 134, 224n46
Audism, definition of, 99
Augur, Charles 55, 56, 59
Aurality, 163–64, 165
Austin, James 55
Ayres, J. A., 167, 168–69

Backus, Levi, 109, 111, 118, 126, 129
Badger, Oliver, 134, 238n141
Bahan, Ben, 65
Ballard, Melville, 117
Barnard, F. A. P., 47–48
Bartlett, David, 105, 106
Baynton, Douglas, 2, 17, 107, 211nn1, 3, 239n1
Beers, Elizabeth (Clerc), 119, 121
Bell, Alexander Graham, 105, 125, 131, 194–95, 206, 207–8, 236n116
Boardman, Eliza, 23, 120, 121, 122, 125
Boardwin family, 65, 68, 223n45; Susan, 65, 130, 134; Delia, 65, 134; George, 65, 130, 134
Booth, Edmund, 97–98, 101, 102, 103, 111

Braidwood Academy, 13, 15, 213n3
Breg, William, 87, 120, 129, 229n110
Brewster, John, Jr., 15, 115
Bridgman, Laura, 150, 152, 174
Brooks, Catharine, 118
Brown, Nahum, 89, 92
Brown, Thomas, 89–90, 92, 93, 94, 95, 126, 128, 129
Brown, Thomas L., 83, 90, 227n95, 229n6
Buchanan, Robert, 113, 116
Burch, Susan, 2, 94, 113, 117, 137, 211n1, 230n12
Burnet, John, 44, 47, 84, 175, 177, 218n31

Canajoharie Radii, 109, 111, 126
Carlin, John, 80, 107, 113–14, 126, 129, 161, 173, 174, 175, 176, 178, 180, 234n74
Chamberlain, Thomas, 88, 229n113
Chamberlain, William, 93, 102, 104, 110
Cheney, Isaac, 65–66, 224n46
Children Of Deaf Adults (CODAs), 131–32
Church services for the deaf, 107–9, 186–87, 191
Cisco, Susan, 65, 134, 223n45
Clarke School for the Deaf, 6, 77, 144, 146, 149, 182, 183, 205
Clerc, Laurent, 11, 15, 21, 22, 23, 25–27, 37, 38, 63, 72, 107, 121, 122, 126, 128, 151, 156, 157, 209, 215n35; as administrator, 38; bilingualism of, 26, 27; on Deaf state, 104, 232n45; on decision to go to the United States, 21, 22; ideas about deaf marriage, 23, 24, 27, 215n42; ideas about deaf people, 19, 23, 24–27; ideas about literacy, 19; on oralism, 27, 157; on teachers of the deaf, 41, 118, 217n14

Cochlear implants, 7, 8, 9, 88, 208
Cogswell, Alice, 14, 15, 20, 22, 23, 66, 71, 133
Cogswell, Mason Fitch, 14, 24
Confer, P. H., 58, 102–3, 104
Conklin, Charlotte, 63, 223n38
Crandall, Prudence, 67; and her school, 67, 68
Crane, John, 59, 60, 74, 85–86, 88, 221n23
Crawford, Horace, 65, 134, 224n46
Crouch, Barry, 25, 91, 98, 110
Cuffee, Aaron, 65, 224n46

Davis, Lennard, 97, 98, 103, 157, 158, 162, 163, 184
De Grass, Paul, 65, 224n46
De Hart, Joseph, 65, 224n46
De l'Epée, Abbe Charles, 12, 36–37, 97; Deaf Americans' views of, 69–73
Deaf community: employment of, 113–20; formation of, 1, 4, 11, 20, 28–29, 43, 48, 53, 62, 80–81, 88, 91–92; newspapers and periodicals of, 109–13, 127; organizations of, 89–97, 108–9, 130; political goals of, 2, 9, 27, 48, 79, 83, 96–97, 109, 112–13, 134, 157, 208; public events of 125–134, 141; and race, 134–37; transnational, 70, 71, 72, 97–98, 156
Deaf culture, emergence of, 1, 3–4, 48, 54, 91–95, 127, 156, 165, 183, 185, 190; attacks on, 6 165, 169–70, 172–74, 180, 182, 184–88, 205–7
Deaf education: attacks on bilingual/bicultural method, 170–74, 175–80, 180; bilingual/bicultural method, 3, 5, 6, 40, 43, 44–47, 48, 65, 75, 76, 105, 143, 176, 177, 178, 180, 181, 208, 232n49; bilingual/bicultural method as seen by Deaf students, 74–76, 77, 141; deaf views of, 2, 53–54, 59, 60, 63, 73–77, 77–81, 85–86, 88, 128, 157, 178; manualist conception of, 3, 28–29, 38–39, 40, 43, 46, 48, 154–55, 157; manualist views of oral education, 39, 188, 189, 200, 203; methodical sign manualism, 6, 37–40, 175, 176, 179, 180, 183; number of deaf students served in nineteenth century, 51–52, 65; oralist conception of ,

2, 5, 6, 75, 87, 88, 141, 148, 185, 187, 191, 193; oralist views of manual education, 2, 186, 187; racially integrated, 65–69
Deaf identity, 4, 9, 27, 28, 54, 62, 91–95, 104, 156, 157, 164; and Deaf of Deaf, 9, 58–59, 94–95, 141, 230nn12, 13; as ethnicity, 97–98, 127, 184, 191; and not deaf enough, 94, 230n11
Deaf marriage, 23, 24, 27, 120–25, 129, 130, 131, 132, 133, 134, 181, 206, 229n6, 236nn108, 116; interracial marriage, 134
Deaf people: and "clannishness," 153, 206; isolation of, from Deaf point of view, 53, 56, 57, 58, 59, 60, 88, 101, 102, 103, 186, 190; isolation of, from oralist point of view, 185, 186, 187, 190; and use of metaphor of silence, 135, 164, 165, 242n7; and views on Deaf art, 115–16, 234n79; and views of Deaf history, 69–73, 128, 133, 127, 128; and views on hearing prejudice, 58, 87, 98, 99, 102, 109, 112–15, 117; and views of literacy, 57, 59, 79–81; and views of manual deaf education, 53–54, 59, 73–77, 77–81, 88, 128, 157, 178; and views of oral deaf education, 2, 77; and views of physical deafness, 9, 56, 57, 61, 62, 82–88, 104; and views on the sign language, 34, 40, 52–53, 60, 63, 64; and voice, 173, 174, 189, 200
Deaf state, 97–104, 127
Deaf versus deaf, definition of, 4, 54, 91–95, 164–65
Deming, Henry, 122
Denison, James, 21, 22, 117
Derby, Elvira, 71–72, 225n59
Dillingham, Abigail, 54, 55, 60, 63, 118, 219n4, 222n36
Dillingham, Nancy, 53, 54, 55, 60, 126, 219n4
Disability: and citizenship, 9, 19, 23, 25, 48, 81, 156; historical experience of, 6, 7, 9, 30–31, 165; social construction of, 5, 54–55, 57, 84, 99–100, 103–4, 140, 157–59
Draper, Amos, 117, 123
Dwight, Timothy, 17; and godly federalism, 18–20

About the Author

R. A. R. EDWARDS is an associate professor of history at the Rochester Institute of Technology, in Rochester, New York.